Coaching and Mentoring

Third edition

Coaching and Mentoring

Practical techniques for developing
learning and performance

Eric Parsloe and Melville Leedham
Edited by Diane Newell

KoganPage

First published in Great Britain and the United States in 2000 by Kogan Page Limited
Second edition 2009
Third edition 2017

2nd Floor, 45 Gee Street	c/o Martin P Hill Consulting	4737/23 Ansari Road
London	122 W 27th St, 10th Floor	Daryaganj
EC1V 3RS	New York, NY 10001	New Delhi 110002
United Kingdom	USA	India

www.koganpage.com

© Eric Parsloe and Monika Wray, 2000
© Eric Parsloe and Melville Leedham, 2009
© Melville Leedham and The OCM, 2017

The right of Melville Leedham and The OCM to be identified as the authors of this work has been asserted by them in accordance with the Copyright, Designs and Patents Act 1988.

ISBN   978 0 7494 7762 2
E-ISBN   978 0 7494 7763 9

British Library Cataloguing-in-Publication Data

A CIP record for this book is available from the British Library.

Library of Congress Cataloging-in-Publication Control Number

2016046146

Typeset by Graphicraft Limited, Hong Kong
Print production managed by Jellyfish
Printed and bound by 4edge Limited, UK

CONTENTS

13   Implementing coaching and mentoring 243

Graham Clark

14   Roles and responsibilities in coaching and mentoring 265

Katherine Ray

15   Supervision in practice 281

Angela Hill

A PERSONAL NOTE FROM ED PARSLOE, CEO, THE OCM

The original, principal author of this book, founder of The OCM and my father, Eric Parsloe, died in November 2015. It is, then, with great poignancy that we have the opportunity to update and add to his seminal work, *Coaching and Mentoring: Practical conversations to improve learning*, in the year following his death. Eric was utterly passionate about coaching and mentoring. His principles of simplicity, rigour and pragmatism were enshrined in his situational philosophy and in the pages of this book.

At The OCM, we have taken this philosophy and applied it to organizations with the sole aim of helping to make coaching and mentoring (CAM) work for both the individual and the organization. We have added a second part to the previous edition of Eric's original book, written with Melville Leedham. Sharing our expertise and experience, we hope to create a practical guide for those charged with making coaching and mentoring work in their organization. In doing so, we hope to keep alive the legacy by enabling truly great coaching and mentoring to flourish.

PREFACE

In Part One of this book, Melville Leedham continues and updates the work Eric Parsloe and he began some eight years ago. He revisits the nature and practice of coaching and mentoring whilst maintaining that its main purpose is to help and support people to take control of and responsibility for their own learning. The purpose of this part of the book has not changed; it continues to explore the role of coaching and mentoring in developing individual and organizational learning.

As well as updating the case studies and practical examples in Part One, Melville has considerably extended and enhanced most of the chapters with new models and tools that he developed as part of his master's research. The main changes are: Chapter 2 now includes the coaching benefits scorecard pyramid model, showing how organizations can evaluate the effectiveness of business coaching in a practical way; Chapter 4 has a new section explaining the difference between transactional and transformational learning and explains the role of a transformational coach; Chapter 5 includes an examination of the recent developments in cognitive and humanistic neuroscience and the growing popularity of mindfulness as an effective approach to combating negative thoughts and feelings; Chapter 8 adds the HELP questioning tool, which is particularly useful for coaching confused or unfocused learners; Chapter 9 is completely new, devoted to all aspects of coaching supervision, including an introduction to the 'situational supervision model', which shows how different types of supervision are appropriate for different stages of a coach's development; and Chapter 10 has been expanded substantially to reflect the recent collaboration between the main professional bodies and examine the growing professionalism of the industry.

In Part Two, the practitioners and professionals of The OCM share their experience and understanding of working with coach-mentoring in organizations.

Our shared purpose and passion are the impact that coach-mentoring has for individuals, teams and organizations. Skilful coach-mentors will work authentically to maximize the benefit of their relationship with individuals and teams, but for us the true power of coach-mentoring for the organization is only released by purposeful, effective and brilliantly executed coach-mentoring strategy, plans and processes. We are fortunate to work with clients and partners who share our passion and have given us the opportunity to work and learn with them over the last decade or so. It's the outcome of that combined learning that we have sought to capture for you here.

Our intent in Part Two is to offer support to anyone working to effectively implement coach-mentoring in their organization. We want to challenge leaders of the organization, HR professionals and coach-mentors alike, to go beyond 'good enough' coaching and mentoring to investments that make a real and sustainable difference to the success of the organization and the value it creates for all of its stakeholders.

I want to thank all of The OCM team who have freely shared their ideas, expertise and time to write chapters in this book.

First, Ed Parsloe, our CEO and Eric's son. Ed has shared his deep conviction of the need for integration of strategy, from business context to all the investments that engage people in it, including coaching and mentoring (which we refer to as CAM), and helps you to think about whether an investment in CAM is right for your organization. And if it is, how to tie it in to delivering on key strategic imperatives.

Charlotte Bruce-Foulds is a very experienced coach and has a deep expertise in developing coaches, mentors and CAM in organizations. She and Graham Clark, with contributions from Katherine Ray, have partnered to create Chapter 12, where they give an overview of what coaching and mentoring are and how they are used in organizations. In this chapter, you will find an overview of coaching and mentoring culture, the forms that coaching and mentoring can take, and the topics they address.

Graham has then gone on to write Chapter 13, looking at what makes for great CAM in organizations, and how you can organize and create the right frameworks for CAM to flourish, sharing not only our experience at The OCM but his perspective from decades of consultancy and organizational development work.

Katherine has personal experience of creating and running a successful global mentoring programme at Unilever, as well as experience as part of The OCM team. In Chapter 14, she shares her views on the key roles and responsibilities of CAM in organizations, from the strategic leader to the client of coaching and mentoring. In particular, she shares her views on the role of the HR function, its leaders and the human resources business professionals (HRBP).

In Chapter 15, Angela Hill, The OCM's head of supervision, brings her wide experience, both of developing coaching and mentoring skills and of developing supervision in organizations, to explore the role of supervision in organizations for CAM – what it is and how it might be of greatest value. Supervision has a role not only in ensuring safe practice for internal coaches, but also in building coaching and mentoring capacity in organizations and in gathering organizational learning.

In Chapter 16, Jackie Elliott, an internal coach and team coach at T-Systems, as well as head of team coaching at The OCM, shares her experience and understanding of team coaching, and the role of the team coach-mentor in supporting the development of resilient high performance in teams. She takes a very practical view of the potential and possibilities for team coaching in organizations, the role of the external team coach and the role of the team leader as coach to the team.

In Chapter 17, Angela Keane, The OCM's head of culture, shares her reflections and understandings of CAM as a systemic intervention, what it means to be using coaching and mentoring in the real world of complex interrelated cultural systems, and how you need to take these into account.

In Chapter 18, I have tried to take a look ahead, to think about the changes and trends which might affect best practice for coaching and mentoring in our future organizations. My intention is to help you plan forward as you think about investments in CAM today.

Throughout Part Two, you will hear individual voices from the authors. However, we are all members of The OCM and we share its beliefs and approach, so you will see some consistency of terms, and we have tried hard to make useful links between the chapters. But what you have here are experienced practitioners and leaders of coaching and mentoring in organizations sharing their views and learning. We hope you find it useful and that it supports you in your own learning journey.

Diane Newell

PART ONE
The purpose, nature and practice of coaching and mentoring

In the mainstream?   01

When we wrote the previous edition we said you would need a very large removal van to carry all the books, journal articles, news stories and Internet references referring to coaching and mentoring. Since then the volume of publications on these topics has continued to grow, although with the increasing popularity of e-publications perhaps the physical volume is not so daunting.

Over the last decade we have all seen a tremendous amount of change in our working lives. The enormous growth of mobile and social networks has influenced our lives in many ways, not always for the better. The pace of globalization – particularly with the rapid development of the BRIC nations – has accelerated.

Against this, the economic instability of the European region and the Far East has prompted many organizations to 'batten down the hatches' and think more carefully about future investment. As a result, we are seeing organizations place much more focus on return on investment and measuring results of any training and development activities, including coaching and mentoring, so those who are doing them are doing them much more effectively.

In the world of work and the broader social community, a rich variety of examples of successful applications of coaching and mentoring abounds. It has become a mainstream focus of interest for many organizations, as well as professional institutes, management schools, corporate and community policy makers and anyone interested in people development. Coaching and mentoring, we believe, have become so integrated into work and community life that they can be described routinely as simply 'the way we do things round here'.

Despite these activities being considered as a recognized profession, it seems surprising that there is still confusion over definitions and language. Later in this chapter we will attempt to dispel some of this confusion.

Before we look at coaching and mentoring in more detail, we will first attempt to sketch the 'big picture' review of the trends, developments and influences of this explosion of activity.

The management and academic 'influencers'

Our interest in the potential for both coaching and mentoring came from our own experiences of corporate life and the management writers (who were largely from the United States) of the 1980s. It was impossible to read the new thinking on issues like 'process re-engineering', 'total quality management', 'customer service excellence', 'employee empowerment' and 'the learning organization' without recognizing that the days of the traditional management science of command and control were numbered. The notion of coaching began to enter the language of people management and development literature, either implicitly or sometimes explicitly, in accordance with one of Blanchard's situational management styles.

The 'Situational Leadership Model' was developed by Paul Hersey and Ken Blanchard in the 1970s. The model comprises four quadrants, depicting the simple concept of the four different styles of leadership that a manager may need to adopt in any given situation: see Figure 1.1. One of those quadrants is called 'Coaching'.

Figure 1.1 Blanchard and Hersey's 'Situational Leadership Model'

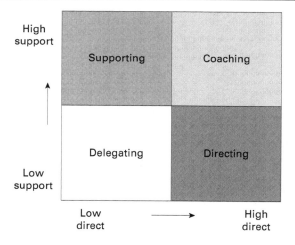

Hersey and Blanchard's use of the term 'coaching' did not have its current meaning, however: by coaching they meant a way of leading and persuading staff to adopt a manager's solution to the situation.

The US writer with the greatest early impact on the emerging profession of management coaching in Britain was most likely Tim Gallwey in his book *The Inner Game of Tennis* (1974). His simple proposition that all great tennis players needed a coach to maintain their high levels of performance was a metaphor and message that was easy to relate to the management of people's performance at work. Gallwey made this message even clearer in *The Inner Game of Work* (2000).

Gallwey's philosophy that 'Performance = Potential minus Interference' was accompanied by the message that a coach's job was primarily to release the self-knowledge and potential that everyone possesses. The key to this was to develop greater self-awareness and a sense of self-responsibility in the performer. Again, these are messages that were in tune with the emerging new thinking about management and organizational performance.

Since 2000, a number of UK universities and some in Australia have pioneered programmes leading to formal academic qualifications. Oxford Brookes University was the first to offer a master's degree in Coaching and Mentoring Practice and the first to offer a doctorate; Middlesex University offered a master's degree and a doctorate with a strong psychological emphasis and Sheffield Hallam University also built on its long involvement with mentoring research. Similar academic qualifications are becoming more widely available all the time. Anthony Grant in Australia has been widely published, advocating the need for an evidence-based approach to academic research. One positive aspect of this increasing academic involvement has been a rapid advance in respectable research-based evidence and a recognized body of literature that many consider an essential requirement for the establishment of a genuine coaching and mentoring profession. Qualifications and certification processes and requirements are explained in more detail in Chapter 10 – 'An industry or a maturing profession?'.

The sport coach 'influencers'

Not surprisingly perhaps, it has been the famous 'sports-coaches-turned-management-coaching-gurus' who were the most visible group in shaping the early thinking and approaches to applying coaching to the workplace. Among the leading exponents were John Whitmore, former champion racing driver; David Hemery, former Olympic medallist; and David Whitaker, former Olympic hockey coach. Towards the end of the 1990s, the former tennis player Myles Downey teamed up with The Industrial Society (later renamed the Work Foundation) to form a 'School of Coaching' for high-flying managers. More recently, the former Olympic swimming gold medallist Adrian Moorhouse joined up with the leading sports psychologist Professor Graham Jones and created a successful coaching company. Appropriately named Lane 4, this has helped to further consolidate the connection between sports coaching and a notion of 'best practice management'.

The medium most commonly used by this group to convey their messages is highly stimulating and memorable training courses. Here practical examples of sports coaching are used to relate to the world of work. The analogy between high achievers in sport and work has fostered the belief that it is possible to develop 'great coaches' who can help produce 'extraordinary results'. However, John Whitmore's book *Coaching for Performance* (1997, updated 2002) remains an inspiring call for a change of management philosophy. Like many pioneers before him, he has faced a growing number of other 'influencers' who challenge the sports coach approach.

The basis for some of the challenges is that the skills required to be a successful sports person are far narrower than those required to manage, for instance, a busy call centre, the intensive care ward of a large hospital or a pharmaceutical processing plant. Thus it has been claimed that the approaches and techniques are not easily transferred from one environment to the other. Indeed, to suggest that they can be easily transferred simply results in raising false hopes and expectations.

Another challenge to this school of 'influencers' relates to the difference in motivation between sport, which has a combination of personal competitiveness and pleasure, and the world of work where many, if not most, people's motivation is a mixture of reluctance, fear and resistance to change. Apart from the natural high achievers, it is claimed that the sports coaching approach often produces little real change in behaviour and performance. While we can all develop our self-awareness, most people don't aspire to be Olympic champions at work.

Despite the challenges, it remains true that this rather narrow and simplistic approach to work-based coaching continues to be a widespread basis for many training programmes, producing results that satisfy a particular segment of the market. However, John Whitmore has more recently continued his intellectual journey into the realms of the psychological and spiritual areas of transpersonal coaching, which he views as a natural evolution from his initial ideas.

The human resources professional 'influencers'

The Chartered Institute of Personnel and Development (CIPD) has more than 140,000 members in the UK and is the main professional body for those involved in the corporate world of human resources and development.

In that role it has a leading position in influencing the development of coaching and mentoring in the UK, conducting regular surveys of organizations' development activity that are accepted as authoritative. In 2015, the CIPD (2015) reported that coaching by line managers or peers along with on-the-job training and in-house development programmes remain the most commonly used and most effective development methods, in line with previous years. Interestingly, 65 per cent of the respondents said that coaching by line manager or peers is expected to grow over the next two years.

In addition:

- Just over three-quarters of all responding organizations offer coaching and mentoring to employees. This is more common in large organizations, rising to 89 per cent of the public sector.

- Nearly two-thirds of organizations use in-house coaches/trained peers and line managers. A further third use a combination of in-house and external providers. Only 4 per cent of larger and 10 per cent of smaller organizations say they rely solely on external coaches.

- 13 per cent of organizations do not currently offer coaching or mentoring but plan to in the next year.

- 9 per cent of organizations (predominantly smaller, less than 250 employees) do not offer it and have no plans to do so.

The 2015 survey also found that coaching, mentoring and buddying schemes along with in-house development schemes were among the most commonly used and most effective talent management activities. Such surveys continue to show strong evidence that coaching is not being seen as a panacea, but rather as an essential and valuable feature of a modern organization's learning and development strategy. This is indeed strong evidence that coaching and mentoring are now mainstream and no longer marginal activities.

The counselling, psychotherapy, psychology and philosophy 'influencers'

As coaching and mentoring have become more widespread, practitioners from other 'helping' disciplines have been brought into the arena, who believe that their traditional methods and approaches are highly relevant. This has certainly increased and enriched the debates and involvement of many more people in the formation of the emerging profession. We recognize the importance of this contribution and, in Chapter 5, 'Awareness of individual differences', we explore this contribution in more detail.

However, the widening of the debate has also had a somewhat negative and confusing impact. It is our opinion that too many people from the different disciplines are now trying to overcomplicate the world of coaching and mentoring. The current marketplace is swamped with a multiplicity of apparently conflicting brands and terminology: NLP, co-active, ontological, buddy, transpersonal, solutions-focused – the list goes on. Differences between the brands sometimes relate to a specific context but more often to some theoretical or academic influence that is of little relevance to the process.

The professional body 'influencers'

Inevitably, as coaching and mentoring have become so widespread, there has been pressure to form networks and associations that can lead to representative bodies bringing some coherence into an emerging profession in the UK. At the same time, existing professional bodies have recognized this need and a possible opportunity for them to extend their membership and influence.

The CIPD, representing the human resources professional, has played a leading role but it has increasingly recognized that it needs to collaborate with others. The Chartered Management Institute (CMI) is dedicated to raising the standards of management and leadership. They see coaching and mentoring as core skills for effective managers. The British Psychology Society (BPS), which has several different groups within its membership, has taken a more defensive attitude and has emphasized the case for psychologists leading the debate. The British Association of Counsellors and Psychotherapists (BACP) has adopted a position somewhere in between the other two bodies.

Far more influential in framing the debates have been the new representative bodies that we discuss in more detail in Chapter 10 – 'An industry or a maturing profession?'. The International Coach Federation (ICF), initially largely North American, now has more than 12,000 members in a range of countries around the world. They are complemented in North America by coaches mainly from the corporate sector who have formed the World Association of Business Coaches (WABC). In Europe, the European Mentoring and Coaching Council (EMCC) took a lead in developing standards and qualifications for both coaching and mentoring in the corporate world and the community. The Association for Coaching (AC) is dedicated to promoting best practice and raising the standards and ethics of coaching worldwide. In 2014 they partnered with the Association of Coaching Supervisors (AOCS). In the UK and many other European countries, national associations for coaching have been formed and energetically promote the benefits of coaching to help their largely individual membership. In the UK, a group of psychotherapist coaches formed their own association, the Association of Professional Executive Coaching and Supervision (APECS).

The existence of these various bodies with their own agendas initially added considerably to the confusion in the market. Fortunately, common sense and recognition of mutual interests have led to an increasing level of cooperation. A good example of this increased cooperation was the creation by the EMCC, the ICF and the AC in 2014 of the Global Coaching and Mentoring Alliance (GCMA), with the purpose of professionalizing the industry.

So where does that leave us?

For buyers of coaching services, it can be tempting to give up trying to navigate this swamp of theoretical models and obtuse jargon, but if one is patient, steps back and asks what all these people are doing and why, it is really pretty straightforward. If you watch coaching or mentoring in action, in most cases what you will see is simply two people having a conversation, and we all have conversations every day.

A closer analysis of these conversations would establish that they are often very focused, confidential and ideally voluntary conversations that are quite structured and follow a process that helps learning to occur, allowing performance to improve and potential to be realized. In truth, they are a very specific type of conversation and not everyone, in management for instance, is used to having the patience and skills to help people learn in this way.

It is now generally accepted that people learn in different ways and therefore it is also common sense to accept that there is no single correct theoretical approach that should be followed. Clearly, the motivation behind coaching and mentoring in education or, say, for drug users is quite different to that used for high-potential young managers in large businesses. We explore 'Helping people to learn how to learn' in Chapter 4.

The words 'coaching' and 'mentoring' have a long traditional usage and interpretation but, in the early 21st century, the activities they describe have taken on new dimensions in corporate, community and social life across the world. This has led to considerable confusion over the appropriate modern definitions. In our opinion this is mainly because of the confusion between:

- *what* they are and do;
- *why* they are used;
- *where* they have come from;
- *how* they are done.

What they are and do

Both coaching and mentoring are conversations that generically follow a simple, although slightly different, four-stage process to help and support people to take responsibility for managing their own learning and change.

Why they are used

The main purpose of both these conversations is either to improve skills or performance, or to realize individual potential and personal ambitions for the future – or any combination of these.

Where they have come from

Modern coaching and mentoring have been shaped by a range of influences and schools of thought as well as Western and Eastern cultures. As such, these conversations take from this rich tradition ideas of what it is to be human and how to help people realize their innate potential.

How they are done

These conversations take place in so many varied contexts and for so many purposes that there is no one correct way of 'how to do it'. However, successful conversations imply the building of a relationship that includes a degree of mutual trust and commitment.

There is a considerable overlap in the knowledge, competences, skills and techniques that can be used by the individual coach-mentor. However, there is also considerable flexibility to choose an appropriate style of intervention to suit the context in which the conversations take place, varying from a highly non-directive style to a highly directive style, and from theoretical or philosophic standpoints to pragmatism and common sense. Opinions vary strongly on these issues between the purists and the pragmatists who believe interventions can often be a combination of styles, even during a single conversation.

As pragmatists ourselves, we have chosen the term 'coach-mentoring' for the modern definition of these conversations. Similarly, we believe that the range of coaching and mentoring styles that can be chosen is most simply understood as related to a continuum of situations, as shown in Figure 1.2.

Figure 1.2 Situational coach-mentoring continuum

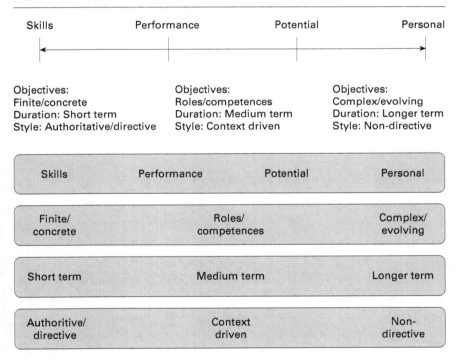

This illustrates the typical objectives and duration of the relationship for each broad purpose and the most appropriate intervention style for each situation. Professional and effective coach-mentors need the knowledge, competences, skills and techniques to be able to adjust their style seamlessly as the situation in which they are working changes, even during the same conversation.

Throughout the rest of this book we will use the term 'coach-mentor', as well as the term 'learner' (rather than coachee, mentee or client) since we believe we are all involved in the learning experience. We will also continue to keep our ideas and suggestions as simple and practical as possible, believing with Leonardo da Vinci that 'simplicity is the ultimate sophistication'.

In that spirit we will advocate a number of 'practical tips of simplicity' derived largely from our years of experience in the world of work and the community.

Simplicity Tip 1

Success comes most surely from doing simple things consistently

We have met very few people who could not become good, competent and useful coaches and mentors. The key to success is not to overcomplicate the roles or to erect unrealistic and unnecessary barriers and expectations. Our 'tips of simplicity' reflect an approach that provides the basis for successful coaching and mentoring relationships. To achieve real sophistication, however, we must also recognize that 'simple' does not mean 'easy': in fact, the opposite is probably true.

Simplicity Tip 2

First agree what you are going to talk about

Many effective coaching and mentoring conversations can happen spontaneously and informally but, if the purpose is to effect serious learning and lasting change, a series of conversations over a longer time frame is more likely to produce results. In this case, it is important to be very clear at the start of the relationship exactly what the ground rules are going to be so that you can both stay focused and disciplined. This phase of the relationship has become known as the 'contracting' phase: not in the sense of a written document but in the sense that all those likely to be affected by the conversations understand what is being aimed for. This can lead to a three- or four-way contract if managers or representatives of a sponsoring organization are involved, as they often are the paymasters.

Simplicity Tip 3

Make sure you meet

By far the most common reason that coaching and mentoring schemes fail is that the busy coach-mentor, volunteer or manager doesn't find the time to meet with his or her learners. Of course, time pressures are intense on everyone and have arguably grown significantly in recent years. Yet we all have the same amount of time available to us. So the real issue is what we choose to do with our time and what tools we can use to help us find the necessary 'extra' time. Here technology, such as the telephone, or more recently computer-based communication techniques, has a real role to play.

The tool most commonly used to help manage our time is, of course, the diary. We strongly advocate the use of some form of learning and/or planning diary in which both the coach-mentor and learner commit to each other to make contact at a specific time and on a particular day each month. The simple act of writing the commitment down increases the likelihood of it happening.

But be honest: if you don't intend to keep the commitment, don't write it down. No manager, in particular, can advocate the need for others to take personal responsibility for improving performance if he or she is not prepared to take personal responsibility for finding the time to meet. It is as simple as that.

Simplicity Tip 4

Keep it brief

Time is precious so there is no point in wasting it. Formal coaching and mentoring sessions in the workplace can be productive if they take between 30 and 75 minutes. If they are shorter you don't really have time to become focused, but if sessions take longer they run the real danger of straying into the realms of counselling or therapy sessions.

We acknowledge the need to be flexible in applying this rule. Sometimes situations are too stressful to be rushed. Sometimes learners need time to unburden themselves. Certain types of people simply don't respond easily to time-pressured situations. So the coach-mentor has to be willing to be both flexible and patient.

This is where the 'make sure you meet' tip applies. Regular meetings allow the coach-mentor to vary the length of the meetings to take account of the occasional stressful or difficult session. But after, say, three of these necessarily lengthy sessions, we would advise turning to another specialist for help. Coach-mentors cannot be expected to be able to handle every situation and they become potentially dangerous if they think they should.

Simplicity Tip 5

Stick to the basic process

At the most basic level, coaching and mentoring sessions are one-to-one meetings where the learner talks about issues he or she chooses and the coach-mentor listens and asks questions. However, the conversations need focus, structure and, especially, good time management. Sticking to a simple process that ensures this happens is therefore crucial:

- Ask the learner either to come prepared with his or her agenda or spend the first few minutes agreeing it.
- Ideally you should both write it down and then manage the time spent on each item.
- Agree that taking notes is purely optional.
- Try to make certain you both write down any action points that the learner decides he or she genuinely wants to commit to (and make sure it is the first item on the agenda for the next meeting).
- Agree the date and time for the next meeting.

The process really is as simple as that. If you adhere to it you are signifying to the learner that:

- These are *not* management, operational or performance review meetings.
- These are *not* appraisal meetings that require documentation for the personnel department.
- These are *not* disciplinary meetings.
- These *are* meetings that are controlled by the learner and focused on him or her and his or her needs and ambitions.
- In most situations the contracting phase should have ensured that they are also meetings that are completely confidential.

Simplicity Tip 6

Develop the 'ask, not tell' habit

Most managers quickly develop the habit of 'acting as managers are expected to act'. This will vary from organization to organization depending on the prevailing culture (and probably on how many different training courses managers have attended!). It will also depend on age, sex and personality type; but you can be pretty sure that there will be 'management-style' habits.

You can also be reasonably sure that many managers will be unfamiliar with acting as coaches and mentors, and not likely to fully accept the underlying philosophy that letting go of control opens the potential for higher performance. The idea that good coaching and mentoring mean moving quickly away from a 'directive' to a 'non-directive' style is one of the most difficult barriers for managers to overcome.

Developing the 'ask, not tell' habit is a vital new habit for managers and the community volunteer mentor to learn. Spelling it out as a formula of '75 per cent asking questions, 20 per cent giving answers and only 5 per cent sharing suggestions', is another way we have found to help some people adapt their style. However, it is probably the constant repetition and reminder of this tip that are the most certain way to get it established.

Even managers who can accept this philosophy intellectually have real problems with applying it. Faced with the pressures of accountability for both positive financial and customer satisfaction short-term results, many managers tend to revert to more traditional command and control styles and techniques. We appreciate that to expect otherwise is unrealistic and unsympathetic.

Simplicity Tip 7

Remember it's all about learning

Another attitude barrier that busy people have to surmount is the concept of 'self-responsibility for learning'. A deeply ingrained habit, indeed preference for some people, is to associate 'learning' with classroom or training course activities. Traditionally, organizations have taken primary responsibility for developing the skills and knowledge of their employees. They have also taken responsibility, in many cases, for planning whole careers. The role of the line manager has all too often been largely confined to conducting the annual appraisal and agreeing a 'wish list' of training courses.

Coaching and mentoring sessions on a monthly basis, discussing a personal development agenda determined by the learner, will represent a major change of behaviour for a large number of managers. In our experience only about 30 per cent of any management population will, in the short term, be open to being persuaded to try to implement this kind of change in their routines. Even then it will take three to four months before the benefits become apparent; but benefits there certainly will be and patient, persistent trust in the process will be rewarded.

One of the benefits most likely to be noticed first is the real cost-effectiveness of coaching and mentoring compared to the results of sending people on courses away from the workplace. An hour of on-the-job learning and development conversation that can be immediately related to current applications saves a great deal of time and money. Persistently reminding people that 'it's all about learning' and simply pointing out the real-life benefits help to make coaching and mentoring become the habitual 'way we do things round here'.

Simplicity Tip 8

Expect to gain yourself

Benefits from coaching and mentoring are not a one-way flow in the direction of the learner, the employing organization or the wider community. Coach-mentors almost always benefit too by learning new techniques for getting results from the people they work with. There are also the less tangible benefits of the feedback from more highly motivated and appreciative colleagues or from those who have made real breakthroughs in managing their previously difficult life situations.

Coach-mentors should not be embarrassed to acknowledge the 'self-interest' expectation. Indeed, we would positively encourage them to adopt this win–win attitude. Equally, it is worth emphasizing that our definition of the overall purpose of coaching and mentoring includes 'helping people to become the person they want to be'. This opens the possibilities of rewards from outside the immediate environment of the organizational setting.

Simplicity Tip 9

Be aware of the boundaries

Even in the community context where extreme patience is required, it is still important to keep a sense of proportion about the time spent in a programme of coaching and mentoring dealing with stressful and difficult issues. These sessions may be therapeutic but they should not become therapy.

The workplace is a robust environment and is possibly becoming even more demanding and unforgiving. We accept that counselling and therapy have an important role to play here but we believe they are jobs for specialists. Recognizing the boundaries of 'normal' stress and anxiety from those behaviours that border on clinical dysfunction is an important skill for the non-professional to develop. Making people aware of these boundaries

should be an essential element in any coach-mentor development programme. While always being prepared to listen, attempting to help beyond
the boundaries of your competence can be really dangerous.

Simplicity Tip 10

Don't try too hard

Inexperienced coach-mentors who have an idealistic and enthusiastic desire
to help people learn and change often make the mistake of expecting
immediate results and become disappointed and disheartened with their
own lack of competence or insufficient tools and techniques.

It is important to recognize that the coach-mentor is joining the learner
on a journey that has often been in progress for many years already. While
most people have the potential to change attitudes or behaviours, it usually
takes time to achieve. Coach-mentors are basically providing the time and
space for that to happen. They need to trust in the process and be content to
simply be there for their learners, bringing their own personality, values and
confidence in themselves to the situation. It is not necessary to try too hard
because it really is as simple as that.

Simplicity tips – summary

1. Success comes most surely from doing simple things consistently.
2. First agree what you are going to talk about.
3. Make sure you meet.
4. Keep it brief.
5. Stick to the basic process.
6. Develop the 'ask, not tell' habit.
7. Remember it's all about learning.
8. Expect to gain yourself.
9. Be aware of the boundaries.
10. Don't try too hard.

But please remember that simple is not easy! To remind you again of the
aphorism often attributed to da Vinci, 'Simplicity is the ultimate sophistication'.

Endnotes

CIPD (2015) Learning and Development, Annual Survey Report, CIPD, London [online] https://www.cipd.co.uk/binaries/learning-development_2015.pdf [accessed 10 October 2016]

Gallwey, W T (1974) *The Inner Game of Tennis*, Random House, New York

Gallwey, W T (2000) *The Inner Game of Work*, Random House, New York

Whitmore, J ([1997] 2002) *Coaching for Performance*, Nicholas Brealey, London

Models of coaching and mentoring

02

The purchasers of coaching and mentoring have become more discriminating since the first edition of this book. Questions they are now fond of asking potential suppliers are along the lines of: 'What is your own model of coaching?' and 'How do you measure your success?' The answers they tend to get often reflect the academic, psychological or philosophical training of the supplier. Alternatively, they may get the confident response, 'Well, mainly the GROW model'. GROW, of course, is not a model of coaching but instead a powerful mnemonic for sequencing questions in a range of situations.

Due to the potential confusion and variation of definitions and models, in this chapter we will explore a number of our preferred models of coaching and mentoring and suggest a holistic framework for evaluation.

Towards an ideal model

'Mentor' was the name of a character from Greek mythology who was a wise and trusted adviser or counsellor. Until recently, the word kept that meaning: it is a word that is regularly used by politicians, sports people, actors and other performers to describe the person whom they chose as a role model or someone who had a significant early influence on their professional careers.

'Coaching', on the other hand, only became widely used over the last two to three hundred years. It was initially used to describe the activity of helping transport a person's knowledge and skills towards a higher level, mainly by a form of teaching or tutoring. In the 20th century, however, it became most widely applied in the context of sport and performance.

We have already established that coaching and mentoring in the context of the 21st century are dynamic and expanding workplace and community activities. It is most likely that the definitions proposed by any of the recent writers on coaching and mentoring are still reasonably accurate in describing what happens in practice in many day-to-day situations.

Organizations have been moving at different speeds towards more sophisticated and effective implementation of coaching and mentoring. The most important point, however, is not that everyone has to agree on a single definition, but that everyone in a specific organization should know the definition that applies to their particular situation. In many cases, organizations are using the words interchangeably. We believe that it is much more important that the purpose and the output of the relationship are clear and agreed, rather than focusing on an exact and academic definition of the terms.

To comprehend the modern definitions, we suggest it is helpful to discuss the idea of 'ideal models' of the activities for both individual professionals and managers acting as coach-mentors. However, we recognize that all coach-mentors are likely to behave in the way that seems appropriate to them in their particular situation. Describing an ideal model, therefore, is not to suggest that it is the only way to do it, but rather that it is a benchmark to compare to your real-life practice and from which you can create your own model. Our purpose is to find some sort of common language, but any model or framework that suggests a pattern of behaviours needs to be applied with pragmatism and common sense, being driven by the needs of the learner and by his or her unique context.

Finding a way out of the confusion

With so many definitions available, it is easy to understand why so much confusion exists, but we suggest that there is a generic four-stage model that can be applied to most coaching and mentoring relationships. Like all processes, it requires each stage to be properly completed if the whole process is to work most successfully. Missing out stages or concentrating on one at the expense of the others can lead to confusion and poor results.

We are aware that our own preference for focusing on four-stage process models is not shared by some theorists and academics, who prefer to emphasize the interpersonal skills, styles, philosophical and psychological aspects of the relationship. Nonetheless, our experience, as we outlined in the previous chapter, suggests that it is more helpful to accurately understand 'what' a coach-mentor is supposed to do, before moving on to understanding 'why' and 'where' it came from and 'how' it might be done.

This chapter focuses on a model or framework tailored for the world of corporate and professional life that applies equally to the internal coach and the external coach. The following chapter will focus on adapting this model to suit the rise of community mentoring and life coaching. However, we are aware that there is also a lot of overlap and that such neat distinctions can easily become distorted. For example, many people coming for business-focused coaching may want and need to move into the more personal areas of what has traditionally been called life coaching, and vice versa. One should therefore bear in mind that such frameworks and approaches need to be blended and applied with common sense to their individual situation.

The generic coach-mentoring process

The four stages of the generic coach-mentoring process are:

1 Analysing for awareness of need, desire and self.
2 Planning for self-responsibility.
3 Implementing using styles, techniques and skills.
4 Evaluating for success and learning.

The model can be illustrated using the diagram in Figure 2.1, which helps to emphasize that this is not simply a linear process but one that is in constant motion within the whole and with considerable overlaps between the stages.

Figure 2.1 The four stages of the generic coach-mentoring process

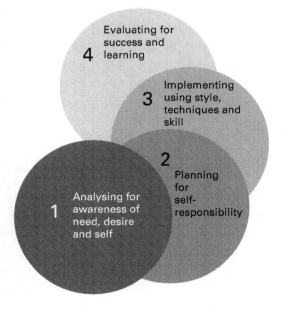

Stage 1. Analysing for awareness of need, desire and self

Coach-mentoring can only start when learners develop an awareness of the need and desire to improve their performance or change the way they have been doing things at work, as well as in life generally. Without a genuine recognition of need and desire, it is almost impossible to change behaviour. Like the old saying that you can take a horse to water but you can't make it drink, the coach-mentor needs to help the learner develop this awareness because you cannot coach-mentor someone unless he or she actually wants to be helped to change.

Learners develop awareness in a number of ways. One way is to use psychometrics or personality profiling, but it is often easier and more practical to ask questions that analyse their current performance and compare it to the level that they would like to move towards. Having clear standards or personal competences to aim for is very helpful, particularly when developing a specific skill. Using self-assessment exercises as the basis for subsequent conversations is a powerful technique for developing awareness.

At this stage it is also important to check the learning style preferences of both the learner and the coach-mentor. For the learner, this will provide insights into ways of learning about him- or herself that he or she will naturally prefer and therefore probably find easier and more enjoyable. For the coach-mentor, it is important to recognize any differences in preferences between him- or herself and the learner. This will help to guard against the natural tendency to suggest learning opportunities that may work well for him or her but which may be inappropriate for the learner. It will also help to spot situations where any obstacles to learning may be caused by the learner's choice of methods rather than an inherent difficulty with the content of the learning. This stage is sometimes described as the 'contracting stage' because it should ideally involve all stakeholders in the relationship being completely aware of the mechanics and desired outcomes.

Stage 2. Planning for self-responsibility

It has long been argued that effective learning and development only really occur when the individual takes personal responsibility for the outcome. The planning stage of the coach-mentoring process is the opportunity for the learner to begin to exercise responsibility. There is a temptation to ignore this stage, particularly if the coach-mentor or learner has an activist learning style preference and is impatient to 'get on with it'. Busy managers are also inclined to ignore this stage and often prefer the informal 'let's do it on the run' approach.

The danger of missing out on this stage is that the coach-mentoring can become ad hoc, ie unstructured and failing to focus on the real issues. If self-managed learning is the preferred approach, then planning is absolutely vital.

Coach-mentors cannot, and should not, attempt to impose learning programmes. Learners must be actively involved in the decision making, although some compromises between an ideal programme of learning and what can realistically be afforded will often be necessary. However, experience suggests that, in the work context, agreeing a Personal Learning Plan (PLP) of some kind with the learner's manager ensures that the necessary time and space in the working day will be made more readily available.

A successful PLP for any context needs to answer these key questions:

- What is to be achieved?
- How will it be done?
- Where will it be done?
- When will it start and end?
- How will it be measured?
- Who will be involved?
- Who needs to agree the plan?

In many organizations, individuals are already encouraged to have PLPs. In a minority of instances, the PLPs cover any topic that interests the learners, like a foreign language or horticulture for instance, because the organization believes that encouraging the development of the learning habit is more important than precisely what is learnt. Few organizations are likely to follow this enlightened approach, however, and most will probably insist that a PLP is clearly linked to business objectives as well as to individual aspirations.

Unlike the traditional annual appraisal Personal Development Plan (PDP) that is often, in practice, only a long wish list, to be most effective a coach-mentoring PLP should focus on only one or two specific development goals over relatively short time frames, such as the next three months. It is important, too, that any development goal in the PLP should be SMART (Specific, Measurable, Achievable, Relevant and Time framed). This simple mnemonic is often only paid lip service in practice, but it can be a very powerful technique for ensuring real focus. The PLP should be reviewed at least on a monthly basis and thus could become an integral part of the performance management process.

Stage 3. Implementing using styles, techniques and skills

Coach-mentors need to use implementation styles and techniques that are appropriate to the situation in which the learner is operating. The appropriate style and technique also need to be employed with the right balance of personal coaching skills appropriate for the particular stage of the process. Coach-mentors need to be comfortable and competent to move up and down the support challenge spectrum between directive and non-directive. They also need to provide a safe space for exploration, discovery and true learning to take place as the learners face their professional and personal challenges. The most important of these skills are generally observant listening, effective questioning and giving feedback. We will look at several coaching techniques, as well as these skills, in more detail later (see Chapters 7, 8 and 9).

Opportunities for coaching arise on many different occasions during the working day and it is important to seize them when they occur. This leads some people to argue that there is little need for formal planning and that the best coaching is informal, relying almost entirely on questioning and immediate feedback. Our experience suggests, however, that creating awareness and a sense of personal responsibility requires time for proper planning if serious change and development are to be achieved. In truth, the two approaches are in fact complementary; while formal awareness and planning are important, informal coaching can take place whenever the opportunity arises.

Our main concern about the informal approach is that once the initial enthusiasm wears off, it very often leads to no coach-mentoring at all. The most common reason for this is that people fail to find the time to do it. A more formal approach that sets aside an hour a week or month in both parties' diaries is much more likely to ensure it happens. Formalized time-tabling may sound boring, but in a hectic working environment it often produces results, especially when the manager has already signed off the PLP. Formality also often ensures regular opportunities to monitor and review progress on the PLP and to reinforce new learning.

Stage 4. Evaluating for success and learning

Many people confuse monitoring with evaluating. Monitoring is the essential activity of regularly checking that progress is being made in implementing the PLP. Evaluating is the activity of reviewing the coaching programme of which the PLPs will be only a part. It is a comprehensive activity involving the coach-mentor, the learner and other interested stakeholders such as the purchaser of external coaching. The key questions are likely to include:

- Were the measurable development goals achieved?
- Did the different components of the PLP work in the sequences they were designed to?
- What changes, if any, were made to the PLP and why?
- Have there been any clear business benefits?
- Was the coaching cost-effective and did it justify the investment?
- Were there any unexpected benefits?
- What did we learn that would lead us to do things differently next time?
- Is there a need for a new PLP to improve performance still further?

Clearly, if the answer to the final question is 'Yes', then the whole process needs to start again. This is a likely outcome, since performance needs to improve continuously.

Organizations are becoming more and more conscious of competitive pressures, and seek to maximize returns on all investment made in employee development. The increasing popularity of business coaching means it is absorbing a substantial proportion of a company's budget. *However*, there appears to be little empirical, independent research on the efficacy of business coaching. This is particularly so for the practice of coaching by external coaches.

One fundamental problem is that the business benefits derived from a coaching programme are often not realized until many months after the programme has been completed. How can a coaching programme be evaluated effectively during, or just after it is completed? How can business coaches rise to the challenge and prove their worth in measurable terms that are meaningful to businesses?

This next section proposes a framework which would enable both organizations and coaches to answer those important questions.

The coaching benefits scorecard

Having said only a small proportion of organizations formally evaluate the impact of coaching, where it is done, some specific relevant themes do appear to be commonly agreed:

1 The need to involve the customers of the coachees in any evaluation, not just the coachees themselves.

2 Some of the coaching evaluation methods are based purely on the perception of the recipient, which may be unreliable for a variety of reasons.

3 There appears to be a link between an individual's confidence and their performance, and coaching seems to improve confidence.

4 There appears to be an interrelationship or dependency between the core elements of a coaching relationship.

5 The approach companies use to measuring business coaching should integrate with other key performance indicators.

The 'Coaching Benefits Pyramid' framework model takes all these themes into account (see Figure 2.2).

Identifying coachee's benefits

This section identifies the most important benefits of business coaching from the perspective of those being coached. It is based on more than 1,100 individual feedback comments written by the coachees or learners of over 200 coach-mentors on professional development courses with The OCM. The learners had been coached for at least four sessions by what were considered to be competent coaches. Their responses were grouped into the most commonly occurring benefits:

Internal feelings:

- Increased confidence, feeling good, believe in myself, higher morale, growth (9.9 per cent).

- Received support, guidance, and encouragement, feel valued (8.3 per cent).

More tangible and visible behaviours:

- Enhanced career, and promotion prospects, helped with my future (7.8 per cent).

- Techniques and skills development (7.2 per cent).

Clarity and focus, inward and outward:

- Clarity of purpose, logical, clear goals, provided focus (6.3 per cent).

- Awareness and insights, self-analysis, strengths and weaknesses (5.9 per cent).

Time and space for thinking and reflecting:

- Helped me reflect to see the big picture, time for myself, time to concentrate (5.5 per cent).

From The OCM coachees' answers, they only listed business results as the ninth most common benefit (4.4 per cent). However, looking more closely, many other benefits were combined with business results, the most common being:

- confidence 23 per cent;
- techniques and skills 15 per cent;
- improved relationships 10 per cent;
- clarity of purpose 9 per cent.

The importance of confidence

I believe that coachees' confidence is a critically important factor often missing from the current approaches to evaluating the effectiveness of a business coaching relationship. A positive perception of a person's self-efficacy, or inner confidence, is an important factor in determining whether or not they apply the skills they have learned to the job and a good predictor of how well these skills will be maintained over time.

In the field of sports coaching these factors are more clearly recognized. Some sports psychologists believe self-confidence to be an important determinant of athletic success and recommend various coaching strategies targeted at improving it directly. From my own practice, the core of many learners' presented issues is a fundamental lack of confidence.

Build on a solid foundation

From all the research, I believe that if the coaching process has been conducted effectively, competently and professionally there is a very good expectation that the subsequent performance of the employee will improve.

If the performance of the employee improves, there should be a tangible and measurable improvement in the performance of the organization in areas directly impacted upon by the employee. This anticipated improvement in specific areas of organizational performance will in turn produce improvements in related business results.

If the above is true, one practical way of effectively evaluating business coaching would be to concentrate on the measurable factors of the coaching process, the environment in which the coaching takes place, and the various qualities of the coach. These are the foundation factors upon which the coachee can develop the feelings and behaviours necessary to improve their performance and capability. This way it would not be necessary to try to measure the impact of the coaching directly on the business results because it would be an inevitable consequence. Therefore, it would be possible to evaluate the impact that coaching has on the bottom line without spending time, money and effort trying to prove the link in directly measurable terms.

A holistic evaluation model

All of the factors identified above are itemized individually but in practice would, of course, be interconnected. There is clearly a dependent dimension in how the various aspects of an effective coaching relationship relate to each other. For any holistic evaluation model to be valid, this additional interrelationship between the various benefits needs to be accommodated.

Cross and Lynch put forward a pyramid of measures, 'The Smart Performance Pyramid' which integrated performance through the hierarchy of the organisation (Cross and Lynch, 1988). Both the hierarchical aspect and the image of a pyramid, building performance on a solid base, resonated well with the concept of building benefits from coaching. For example, confidence is the most often combined benefit with results (23 per cent) and skills development (19 per cent).

The framework in Figure 2.2 shows an adaptation of their model to fit my interpretation. I believe this model pragmatically combines the feedback from the coachees into a simple and practical evaluation framework.

Figure 2.2 Coaching Benefits Pyramid

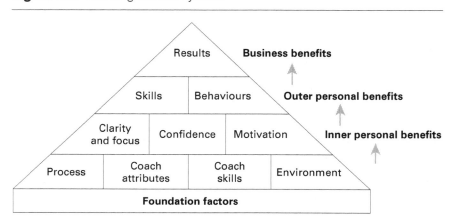

The model is based on the principle that to be fully effective, a business coaching relationship needs to be built on the firm foundation of four key factors:

1 **The skills of the coach,** such as: listening, questioning, giving clear feedback, establishing rapport, providing support.

2 **The personal attributes of the coach,** such as: knowledge, experience, qualifications, being inspirational, having belief in the learner's potential.

3 **The coaching process,** including: clear structure and discipline, being mentally challenging and stretching.

4 **The coaching environment,** providing: a safe, supportive place to discuss confidential and sensitive issues; time and space to think and reflect.

The model highlights the fact that the coaches themselves have a significant influence on the effectiveness of the coaching programme, with two separate but related facets – personal attributes and coaching skills – being seen as important.

Equally important are the often-overlooked factors of the coaching process and the environment in which the coaching takes place. The comfort and reassurance of a robust and consistent process for the individual coaching sessions and the overall programme are valued by coachees and purchasers. Purchasers described the importance of process to them in terms of whether coaches deliver what they said they would, when they said they would, to the standard they agreed they would. This applied to the actual sessions as well as the overall relationship with the client organization.

The environment in which the coaching takes place is seen to be very important and this does not mean just the physical environment. More important is the ability of the coach to create an environment in which coachees feel free to discuss confidential and sensitive issues and to provide a mental space in which they can reflect on their situation and create the time to verbalize their feelings in this safe environment.

Not enough emphasis is placed on these four foundation factors and, without these being strong, the coaching programme may not be fully effective. The presence of these four foundation factors and their effective use by the coach will enable the first level of benefits for the individual to be developed and achieved. These are the inner personal benefits:

1 **Clarity and focus** providing personal insights and exploration of themselves, their values and beliefs, providing a clear purpose and sense of direction.

2 Confidence to believe in themselves, to feel more relaxed and less stressed, to raise their morale.

3 Motivation to achieve, to improve both themselves and their organization, inspired to drive things through. Highly motivated employees will take on extra tasks in order to improve their part of the business. They will also want to excel in their work as well as seeking career progression.

The often-quoted principle in the world of business coaching, mentioned in Chapter 1, seems to be very apt in relation to these internal benefits.

$$\text{Performance} = \text{Potential} - \text{Interference}$$

The 'Interference' referred to can be due to either lack of confidence, lack of motivation or lack of clarity and focus, or perhaps a combination of all three.

The CIPD guide *Coaching and Buying Coaching Services* suggests that if the coachee is able to realize these internal benefits they are in a much better position to be able to achieve more visible output benefits of enhanced skills, knowledge and understanding and improved behaviours associated with relationships with their boss, team, peers or customers. Achieving the inner benefits is fundamental to the coachees achieving the business benefits and, therefore, must be a focus for the coach and for any evaluation process.

1 Enhanced skills, knowledge and understanding in both job-related skills and the ability to learn and develop themselves.

2 Improved behaviours with individuals and teams in all forms of relationships.

There are clear links between the human capital drivers (motivation, confidence, clarity and focus), human capital capabilities (skills and behaviours), intermediate key performance indicators (productivity, customer satisfaction), and ultimately, financial performance measures such as profit or revenue growth.

With these enhanced skills and/or improved behaviours, the coachee will be equipped and empowered to achieve the natural pinnacle of the pyramid, ie **business results** such as: improvements in performance, being more productive, enhanced career progression, and resolution of specific problems or issues.

The 'Coaching Benefits Pyramid' framework provides a valid and holistic picture of the interconnected factors of an effective business coaching relationship from the perspective of, and for the benefit of, all the stakeholders. The tendency to focus exclusively on return on investment as the only valid evaluation measure has lost sight of the importance of an effective process, the attributes of the coach and the inner feelings of the coachee.

I believe that by following the concept behind this model, organizations may be able to predict, with some confidence, that if the other categories in the model were evaluated effectively and found to be successful, relevant business results would ultimately improve.

The 'Coaching Benefits Pyramid' framework can be used throughout the life of the coaching contract to assess the suitability of the external business coach prior to the start of the relationship, to check the process at an early stage, and to quantify the personal benefits before the business benefits can be realized.

Mentoring

To understand more fully the developments in the 'models debate', let us focus for a while on mentoring. Mentoring, like coaching, can happen in many different contexts or environments:

- Business-to-business, where the main thrust is on economic regeneration and where a mentor from a large organization works with one from a small or medium-sized enterprise.

- Business-to-enterprise, where, for example, organizations like the Prince's Youth Business Trust have mentors to guide young 'starters' in business who have received grants from them.

- The UK government regularly announces programmes similar to business-to-enterprise, but where the learner may have special needs in gaining access to employment.

- Special needs and community projects, where the mentoring is more personal and designed for individual needs and where matching the mentor and learner may be critical.

- Social inclusion, where the mentoring is a nurturing relationship designed to increase the participants' social and cultural capital.

- Business-to-education, where business people volunteer to work with head teachers, teachers and students.

- Graduate or undergraduate mentoring, where more experienced graduates help to guide or counsel students through different stages of their studies.

Corporate mentoring roles are often designed to support specific groups:

- new recruits;
- graduate trainees;
- women;
- ethnic minorities;
- disabled or disadvantaged individuals;
- individuals facing a career change, redundancy or pre-retirement;
- people with a specific desire and motivation to manage their own learning and development.

It is hardly surprising that no single definition or model uniformly fits all these different contexts. They are sometimes grouped together under the title 'Diversity Mentoring'. We need to try to understand both the differences and the similarities, but we suggest that there are three broad primary types of mentor:

1 *The corporate mentor* who acts as a guide, adviser and counsellor at various stages in someone's career, from induction through formal development to a senior management position and possibly into retirement.

2 *The qualification mentor* who is required by a professional association or government-sponsored agency to be appointed to guide candidates through their programme of study, leading to a professional qualification or a National Vocational Qualification (NVQ).

3 *The community mentor* who acts as a friend, expert adviser or counsellor to individuals in a wide range of situations where the individual may be disadvantaged or in an actual or potentially distressing position.

Examples of these three types of mentor can, of course, be found in many organizations. Sometimes all three may be found simultaneously in a single large organization. In this section, we will discuss both the 'corporate' and 'qualification' mentor. The 'community' mentor is a significant development that we deal with separately in Chapter 3.

The words used to describe each stage of the corporate and qualification mentoring process are different from the generic coach-mentoring model. Here the key stages are:

1 Confirming the personal learning plan (PLP).

2 Encouraging the self-management of learning.

3 Providing support during the PLP process.

4 Assisting in the evaluation of success and learning.

The wording of the stages also reflects the different roles, responsibilities and accountabilities of a mentor separate to those of a coach or coach-mentor. Mentors in the workplace are rarely a learner's direct line manager whereas a coach very often is. The corporate and qualification mentoring process can be illustrated graphically, as in Figure 2.3.

Figure 2.3 The four stages of the corporate and qualification mentoring process

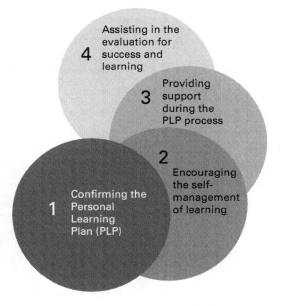

Stage 1. Confirming the personal learning plan

Final responsibility for the personal learning plan lies with the learner and his or her manager. A mentor may be involved at any stage during the preparation of the PLP, but his or her role is simply to help to confirm by providing guidance, access to information and acting as a 'sounding board'. The mentor has no direct responsibility or accountability for the learner's performance although, in the qualification context, he or she is often required to follow set guidelines.

The mentor has to prepare for the role by analysing, identifying and anticipating the likely needs that the learner will have in achieving his or her learning and development goals. The mentor will need to be sensitive to all the circumstances within which the learner is operating, including his or her personal beliefs, capabilities, aspirations and learning style preferences.

The mentor needs to encourage the development of self-awareness in the learner by showing how self-assessment and honest open questioning can help to achieve this. One of the key areas where a mentor may help is by checking that all the learning and development goals meet the SMART criteria. The mentor can also usefully draw attention to the need to set goals with short and realistic timescales. Even a long qualification programme is more successfully tackled in short manageable stages.

As with the coach-mentoring process, this stage is sometimes described as the 'contracting stage' because it should involve all stakeholders in the relationship being completely aware of the mechanics and desired outcomes.

Stage 2. Encouraging the self-management of learning

One of the characteristics of a good PLP is the extent to which it allows for self-management of the process. However, not all learners will have sufficient experience to manage the implementation of the PLP. By asking probing questions, the mentor's greater experience should allow him or her to encourage learners to think ahead and anticipate some of the administrative aspects of implementing the PLP. The mentor can also provide a useful service by giving clear explanations and reminders at the appropriate moment of the range of support options that may be available.

One of the most critical aspects of the mentoring role is to ensure that the day-to-day working relationship between the learner and the line manager is not compromised by the mentor's activities. Learners should be encouraged on all occasions to work out their own solutions to any problem they have with their line manager or other colleagues. A mentor is a 'sounding board', not a troubleshooter, and any suggestions or advice should be given as options to consider rather than instructions to act upon. Conversations need to be in confidence so that a genuine level of trust can exist. Only in the most extreme situations should a mentor intervene directly. Adopting a genuinely objective, confidential and impartial role may not always be easy in practice, but it is essential.

Stage 3. Providing support during the PLP process

As soon as the PLP starts to be implemented, the mentor needs to be available to provide support. In minimal practical terms, this means agreeing a schedule of meetings as frequently as seems necessary. It is also useful to agree methods for arranging impromptu meetings or contact to deal with any urgent and/or unforeseen difficulties.

The way in which the mentor provides guidance and information is critical. Timing, pace and level are obviously important, but imposing the mentor's natural preferences must be guarded against. Avoiding bias of all kinds and remaining objective, while at the same time fully involved, is not always an easy balance to strike.

Mentors will sometimes be asked to provide advice and make suggestions. The key here is to ensure that advice and suggestions are given only when requested and not imposed on the learner in an attempt to appear helpful. The mentor is definitely not expected to be the source of all knowledge and information, and he or she should be quite willing to direct learners to alternative and perhaps more appropriate sources.

A key role for the mentor is to help learners to deal with mistakes and setbacks which, in some line management relationships, may result in blame, guilt and feelings of inadequacy. The mentoring relationship should be non-judgemental and 'risk-free'. This allows the mentor to help the learner to treat mistakes and setbacks as real learning opportunities. Properly handled, these situations are often rich learning experiences.

At all times, the mentor should try to build self-confidence and motivation in the learner in order to develop a positive attitude and a will to complete the PLP.

Stage 4. Assisting in the evaluation of success and learning

There is a distinction between regular monitoring of progress and final evaluation at the end of the PLP. A mentor's role is to encourage the learners to arrange formal evaluations with their line managers or qualification supervisors.

Helping the learners to prepare for a formal evaluation is a useful mentoring function. Reminding them of the value of self-assessment and peer-assessment of performance standards is particularly helpful. Mentors can use reflective questions to help learners to analyse the causes of any barriers to learning that occur, as well as quantifying the benefits that were gained by themselves and the organization during the PLP process.

Formal mentoring relationships usually come to an end. Most often this occurs when a learner changes job or with the achievement of a professional or vocational qualification. Ending a relationship is often not easy. Celebrating success and recognizing the mutual benefits gained are important. The mentor should make a special effort to encourage the learner to continue to set new development and career goals. Agreeing to maintain interest and contact in the future is a positive note to end on.

To summarize the similarities and perhaps subtle differences between coaching and mentoring process models, Table 2.1 might prove helpful. It would seem that this corporate mentoring process is very close to the process that many external professional executive coaches would use to describe the services that they provide. This merely serves to underline the pragmatic use of the term 'coach-mentor'.

Table 2.1 Generic models of coaching and mentorin

	Professional and business coaching	**Corporate and qualification mentoring**
Stage 1	Analysing for awareness of need, desire and self	Confirming the Personal Learning Plan (PLP)
Stage 2	Planning for self-responsibility	Encouraging the self-management of learning
Stage 3	Implementing using style, techniques and skills	Providing support during the PLP process
Stage 4	Evaluating for success and learning	Assisting in the evaluation of success

A 'contracting' process model

A quite different process model that can be applied to all situations is the 'contracting' model or competence framework. The National Occupational Standards issued by the UK Qualification and Curriculum Authority (QCA) and the Professional Standards issued by the European Mentoring and Coaching Council (EMCC) have helped us to define a process for agreeing a 'contract' with stakeholders in the relationship. This can apply as part of a wider framework of competences for both coaches and mentors. To help understand this important process you might like to assess yourself against our model, shown in Figure 2.4.

Figure 2.4 Contracting self-assessment model

SELF-ASSESSMENT

CONTRACTING

Score yourself

1 to 10 scale, where 10 = excellent and 1 = very poor

How well do I prepare the contract with stakeholders?

- I ensure that all stakeholders understand and agree the expectations of the process before starting

- I work with, and agree with all stakeholders, the objectives and outcomes of the work

- I agree the framework for completion to include end date, number of sessions, review dates, location, pricing and terms and conditions

- I clarify the role and responsibilities of the stakeholders in the process

- I establish with the learner and stakeholders the implications of the process on their time, workload and potential changes in behaviour and attitude

- I agree the boundaries, especially of confidentiality between the learner, the stakeholders and myself

How well do I create the coaching contract with my learners?

- I determine that there is an appropriate match between my style and the needs of the learner before proceeding

- I ensure the contracts are made with full consultation with and agreement from all relevant parties including who, specifically, will be involved in the review process

- I agree with the learner a code of practice that defines the boundaries or our working relationship, including confidentiality and expectations of each other in terms of honesty and commitment to act on agreed outcomes

- I help the learner to identify and deal with the time pressures and any other potential issues that may affect the process

- We agree a schedule of sessions, where they will take place, how long they will last and the method of communication (face-to-face, telephone, e-mail, etc)

The manager or leader as a coach-mentor

Another quite different model that can prove valuable is that of the manager or leader as coach-mentor, which some people advocate should be based on a model derived from sport. For instance, coaching Olympic performers to reach even higher standards is a very sophisticated activity. The coach, who is often not at the same performance level as the performer, has to recognize that the performer has total control over performance. The Olympic coach can operate in a non-directive style and focus largely on the mental attitude of the performer rather than his or her basic skills and techniques. Coaches of top-performing teams and of stars in the performing arts also are encouraged to follow this pattern.

On the other hand, it is argued that most coaching in corporate life is undertaken by line managers rather than external professional coach-mentors. Some believe that the same non-directive approach to transferring control as in sport should always apply in the workplace too. The reality of applying that approach is illustrated in Figure 2.5.

Figure 2.5 Manager or leader as a coach-mentor model

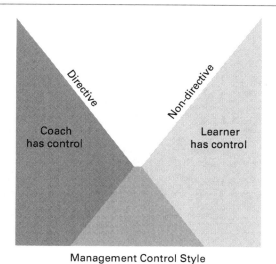

Many managers find it difficult to move quickly along the management control styles axis towards a non-directive position. Partly this is because some managers are locked into a traditional hierarchical command and control management style and are ill-suited to and personally uncomfortable with changing style.

Sometimes, too, the culture of their organization and the structure of the jobs that have to be done force them towards a directive style. For instance, in the situation of a simple, repetitive, task-oriented department with a high turnover of staff or a heavy reliance on temporary or short-contract employees, a manager-coach may be constantly forced into situations where a directive style is the only appropriate one to adopt. Similarly, in situations of great urgency, a fire alarm for instance, there is no time for a period of reflective questioning!

It is also true that where managers are held closely accountable for immediate results with severe penalties for failure, it is difficult for them to take the risk involved in letting go of control and trusting the performer to take responsibility for improving performance. This is a very real problem for many managers, and has been made worse with the increases in work-load and stress that have resulted from many experiments with re-engineering, the impact of new technology and organizational restructuring or mergers. These pressures help to explain why many coaches and learners are probably operating at around 25–30 per cent along the axis towards a non-directive style. There has been a lot of talk about sharing control and empowerment, but often there is a real and understandable reluctance to put it into practice.

Of course, there is a fundamental contradiction in this reluctance to change style. Experience shows that higher levels of performance from individuals and teams are more often achieved when people are given greater control and responsibility. So the desire and pressure for ever-higher performance standards are often, in practice, frustrated by a reluctance to risk releasing control. This frustration is likely to contribute to increased stress levels for managers.

For organizations wishing to develop the necessary 'positive coaching culture', there is no alternative but for managers to move rapidly down the coaching style axis toward the non-directive position. This implies a change in management style away from 'coaching as a manager' towards 'managing as a coach'. In persuading managers to try to adopt a new style it will be equally important to acknowledge the practical difficulties that many of them might face.

A management coaching style

'Style' is used here to describe 'the manner in which the coach-mentoring is delivered', although some writers use the term 'style' to describe different roles or types of coaching. However, these are not based solely on a psychological analysis of those involved. Coach-mentoring styles can more usefully be based on a continuum that ranges from situations where the learner is completely inexperienced to situations where the learner is highly experienced and capable, or in situations requiring very different outcomes.

When working with someone who is completely new to a situation or needs to develop a specific new skill, it may be appropriate to adopt a directive, almost instructor-like, style. When dealing with an experienced high performer, like an Olympic athlete or chief executive, it is more appropriate to adopt a non-directive style and rely mainly on questioning and feedback skills. Experience shows that the more rapidly a coach-mentor can move from a directive to a non-directive style, the faster an improvement in performance or behaviour change will be achieved. The simple explanation for this is that as you move along the axis towards a non-directive style, more control and responsibility are transferred from the coach-mentor to the learner.

A coach-mentoring competence model

To assist you further, you may care to complete the self-assessment exercise in Figure 2.6, which is based on yet another model to help you to establish your current levels of competence as a coach-mentor. Often our own perceptions are more critical than others, but we may also be unaware of some aspects of our behaviour. Self-assessment is a powerful technique for raising awareness and providing an agenda for open dialogue with your colleagues and your coach.

Figure 2.6 Coach-mentoring competence self-assessment model

SELF-ASSESSMENT
COACH-MENTORING COMPETENCE
Score yourself

1 to 10 scale, where 10 = excellent and 1 = very poor

- How well do I prepare the contract with stakeholders?
- How well do I create the coaching contract with my learners?
- How effective am I at establishing rapport?
- How effective am I at building and maintaining the relationship?
- How effectively do I manage sessions?
- How good am I at helping to clarify goals?
- How well do I help to explore options to achieve these goals?
- How good am I at ensuring the goals align with the organizational needs?
- How well do I support the development of an action plan?
- How well do I support implementation of the action plan?
- How well do I facilitate the review process and measurement of progress?
- How well do I monitor the overall coaching process?
- How well do I manage the conclusion of the relationship?
- How well do I conclude the contract with stakeholders?
- How appropriate is my approach to the learner?
- How good am I at listening?
- How good are my questioning skills?
- How well do I give and receive feedback?
- How flexible am I?
- How well do I maintain 'business focus'?

Summary

In this chapter, we have asserted that there is currently no consensus on terminology in the field of coaching and mentoring and that the current terms and definitions may continue to change as the 'revolution in thinking' continues. We have also noted that theoretical models are useful only if they are used to help us to understand new ideas or concepts; hence the benefit of designing models for ourselves that suit our own specific situations.

Although we have advocated generic four-stage models for coaching and mentoring, applications and experiences of coaching and mentoring are likely to differ in different international and cultural contexts. And, of course, we are all still learning!

Endnotes

CIPD (2004) *Coaching and Buying Coaching Services*, CIPD [online] http://www.cipd.co.uk/NR/rdonlyres/C31A728E-7411-4754-9644-46A84EC9CFEE/0/2995coachbuyingservs.pdf [accessed 10 October 2016]

Cross, K and Lynch, R (1998) The 'smart' way to define and sustain success, *Global Business and Organizational Excellence*, 8 (1), pp 23–33

Community mentors and life coaching

03

In this chapter we will explore in more depth two of the perspectives mentioned in Chapter 2: 'community mentoring' and 'life coaching'. There is a significant and growing sector of coaches and mentors whose prime focus is not on improving the business performance of their learners; instead, the focus seems to be helping people to learn how to cope with life's challenges, to be better able to change what can be changed and to accept positively what cannot be changed.

The purpose of many community mentoring programmes is to help those who, for whatever reasons, are currently excluded from or have never been in the world of work. This includes those in schools or in prisons, those with physical or mental disabilities and many other forms of social exclusion. In the health care sector, there are examples of using mentoring not only in the traditional field of developing staff but also in helping patients to cope with chronic illness. For the purposes of clarity, we have split this chapter into two perspectives: 'community mentors' and 'life coaches'.

What is life coaching?

'Life' is probably one of the most familiar prefixes to 'coaching', thanks to the media and popular coaching celebrities. A recent web search found 27 million references to life coaching. UK television programmes such as *What Not to Wear*, *How to Look Good Naked* and even *Supernanny* all have one thing in common: trying to improve a person's self-image or self-esteem. In 2005, a glossy magazine called *Psychologies* was launched in the UK, with each issue containing articles and features on life coaching. There are also regular features on therapy, mental health and lifestyle. These examples suggest that self-improvement and some aspects of mental well-being are now acceptable topics of conversation.

Exactly when the term 'life coaching' began to be used is not clear. It first became popular in the 1950s alongside the emergence of humanistic psychology, the focus on human potential and self-help. In those early days, life coaching tended to be associated with non-conformity, a challenge to conventional values, dropping out, unworldliness, etc. In some circles this is still the image conjured up when life coaching is mentioned in contrast to business coaching.

However, in recent years there appears to have been a great deal of overlap with business coaching. In both the approaches used and coaching issues addressed, both might borrow from 'inner game' principles and NLP (neuro-linguistic programming), and cover areas such as career coaching, work–life balance and confidence building. This section seeks to explore this growing area of the profession by looking at the context of life coaching and some tools and approaches.

Context

The term 'life coaching' is, for some, synonymous with 'coaching' and often used interchangeably with 'business coaching'. When searching for a definition of life coaching the ones usually quoted cover coaching in a generic sense; if the word 'life' were removed it would be difficult to identify the unique aspects of 'life coaching' from any other form of coaching.

Grant (2001) attempted to make a distinction between what he called personal or life coaching and coaching in the workplace:

> Personal or life coaching is a solution-focused, results-orientated systematic process in which the coach facilitates the enhancement of the coachee's life experience and performance in various domains (as determined by the coachee), and fosters the self-directed learning and personal growth of the coachee.
>
> Workplace coaching is a solution-focused, result-orientated systematic process in which the coach facilitates the enhancement of work performance and the self-directed learning and personal growth of the coachee.

We discussed business coaching in Chapter 2, where the focus is on addressing the development needs of the client required to achieve business outcomes rather than a focus on the personal or career goals of the person being coached. Life coaching clients tend to be individuals who are self-funding (ie not receiving external coaching via their organizational sponsor, or via an internal coach) and therefore many of the potential conflicts of interest that can exist within business coaching are removed.

For the purposes of this chapter, life coaching is taken to mean coaching that is geared totally towards achieving personal success and self-fulfilment, which goes beyond serving an organization's agenda. This allows far more scope for focusing on achieving the clients' 'ideal life' that would not often come under the remit of business or workplace coaching. However, whatever description is used, the general consensus seems to suggest that life coaching is personal coaching that is defined by the context in which it takes place, rather than the skills, tools or techniques that are employed by the coach.

The common contexts in which life coaches operate typically include:

- confidence and self-esteem;
- career transitions;
- relationships;
- dreams and aspirations;
- getting your life in order;
- health and physical wellbeing.

Confidence and self-esteem

Often people who present themselves for life coaching want to feel good about themselves; they want to be more confident in social groups and be confident to go out, meet new people and build acquaintances into friends. Generally, this will be because they have low self-esteem, high self-doubt and consequently lack confidence. Life coaching can be effective for tackling negative thoughts and lack of self-belief. Sessions might include such practical activities as making small talk and/or giving speeches and presentations.

Career transitions

Within an organization it is often difficult to discuss wanting to change careers or even saying you are dissatisfied with your current job. Someone considering a major career change or starting his or her own business might consult a life coach. Redefining or exploring core values might be part of this process. Here, people will feel freer to openly discuss issues about their job or working for the organization that they could not discuss with anyone at the same employer.

Relationships

This may focus on problems or dilemmas with their life partner or other members of their family. Business coaching can only legitimately enter these personal areas when they have a direct impact on the work performance of the individual. Life coaching can help people work through family and partner difficulties or simply help them cope with life's challenges.

Dreams and aspirations

Sometimes people who have worked hard for many years, striving for material success, try to take stock of their lives. They find themselves saying things like: 'There must be more to life than this.' They may look around at their lives and find that work no longer satisfies them or they want to 'do more with their lives'. Life coaching can be helpful for finding new direction and purpose and helping people work out the important things in their life. Looking to have more fun, enjoyment or adventure are all topics that might be difficult to discuss with a line manager or business coach.

Getting your life in order

Another aspect of people's lives where life coaching can be helpful is in creating some order and discipline. Many of us would benefit from 'de-cluttering' our homes or even our minds, using our time more effectively and generally becoming better organized. Managing our finances can also be included in this context, for example living within our budget, increasing our savings, reducing our outgoings, etc. Life coaching can be useful for those suffering from procrastination or lack of focus.

Health and physical wellbeing

Many people seem to be obsessed about their weight and/or their body shape. Recently the trend for healthier eating has become more common, with more people striving to live a generally healthier lifestyle, including giving up smoking. Life coaching can be helpful in providing the motivation to begin and encouragement to stick to a specific exercise regime, diet or quitting smoking.

An increasingly hectic and stressful life can be another reason why someone would seek a life coach. Stress can have an adverse effect on a person's health and lead to many illnesses. A report released in 2015 by the UK Health and Safety Executive showed that in 2014/15 stress accounted for 35 per cent of all work-related ill health cases and 43 per cent of all working days lost due to ill health (HSE, 2015). Half a million people a year report that stress levels are making them ill. Life coaching can be effective in helping to establish a better work–life balance. The case study opposite shows how the UK National Health Service is recognizing the potential benefits of coaching for some groups of patients.

NHS 'health coaches'

One example of what could be classed as a form of life coaching is that of 'health coach' within the UK National Health Service.

In 2005, there were 17.5 million people in the UK suffering with long-term conditions with the expectation that by 2030 this will more than double. In particular, Type 2 diabetes related to obesity is expected to grow by 54 per cent and hypertension by 28 per cent.

In February 2004, Pfizer Ltd and Haringey Primary Care Trust launched an innovative programme designed to provide individualized support and coach-mentoring for 600 patients within the London Borough of Haringey suffering from diabetes, heart failure and coronary heart disease.

The aim of this project was to investigate the benefits to patients of a telephone-based and technology-supported coach-mentoring and self-care programme using a patient-centred disease management model in England adapted from a successful disease management approach from the United States.

The programme was born out of growing recognition of the potential benefits for patients and the NHS of improving chronic disease management. As Jill Lewis (Care Manager, Development Lead, UK Pfizer Health Solutions) comments: 'Self-care is about empowering individuals to take actions to maintain their health. Support for self-care involves increasing the capacity, confidence and efficacy of the individual for self-care by providing a range of options.'

A team of dedicated care managers or 'health coaches' provide regular coaching interventions for patients based on their individual needs. The care managers, all qualified nurses, use decision support software in a systematic telephone-based coaching and coordinated care service. Each health coach is a qualified nurse, with a dedicated case load of 150–200 patients, who have been trained to provide coach-mentoring and support.

Through this regular communication and support, patients have become more successful in managing their condition and have improved their clinical outcomes and quality of life, while reducing the demands on local health services. The results of the evaluation of the programme were released in the spring of 2006.

Patient satisfaction levels included:

- 90 per cent patient satisfaction with the health coach;
- 70 per cent improved their confidence regarding health decisions;
- 61 per cent thought it enabled more useful discussion with doctor.

▶

The impacts on the individual patient included:

- improved health outcomes;
- people felt more confident to manage their condition;
- improved quality of life with greater independence;
- improved life expectancy.

Potential benefits to the NHS included:

- 40 per cent decrease in the number of primary care consultations;
- 17 per cent decrease in outpatient visits;
- 50 per cent reduction in accident and emergency department visits;
- hospital admissions and length of hospital stays halved.

Perhaps this comment from a patient on the health coach programme sums up what life coaching and community mentoring is all about: 'The programme has helped me, I am a different person since being on the programme, especially my diet and food intake. The care manager is very good and helps me to be healthy and happy.'

As you can see from the above examples, life coaching can cover any or all aspects of a person's life. Sometimes clients seek life coaching for a specific issue, such as health, relationships, finances, or career transition. On the other hand, it may be something more ambitious like creating a new life for themselves, while sometimes it's to hold on to and appreciate more what they've already got, or to regain something that seems lost. Others are drawn to coaching by a general dissatisfaction with their life or a sense that something could be better. Perhaps a more appropriate title in some of these contexts would be to call it 'lifestyle' coaching.

Approaches

Some key tools and approaches used in life coaching are familiar in other areas of coaching, such as the 'Wheel of Life' and variants of GROW, described in Chapters 6, 7 and 8. However, while the business coach borrows freely from the plethora of tools, models and psychometrics arising from the world of business, life coaches tend to fill their toolkit from much wider areas such as pop psychology, astrology, self-help and even hypnotherapy.

It is worth noting that some of the approaches used can reflect quite specific and unconventional worldviews or approaches, such as the combination of martial arts with hypnosis, or crystal healing, and would be more likely to hold appeal for like-minded clients.

Life coaching sessions tend to be shorter than business coaching, typically half an hour to an hour rather than one to two hours. Also, the frequency of sessions is often shorter: weekly for life coaching as opposed to monthly for business coaching. There appears to be a very high proportion of life coaching done over the phone and often the participants never meet the coach.

There also appears to be an emphasis on prescriptive structure and process and the benefit of programmes with a set number of steps or stages, such as:

- five top tips to make it real;
- five steps to conquer your fear;
- five ways to put the passion back;
- seven rules of success;
- change your life in seven days.

Life coaching tends to be based on the following principles:

- Define your life purpose. If your family wrote an epitaph about you today, what would they write? What would you like them to write?
- Be positive. Make sure the goals are described in positive terms and about things you want to achieve, not about things you want to stop or eliminate.
- Look to build on your personal strengths, not weaknesses. Don't allow any strength to be discounted or negated.
- Take personal responsibility for immediate challenges and problems. Don't focus on other people's problems or blame them for your situation.
- Failing to plan means you are planning to fail. Decide on a series of relevant and achievable developmental actions that will contribute towards your goals.
- Celebrate success and be proud of your achievements. List your achievements in positive terms, not as partial failures.

Community mentoring

Now let us examine community mentoring in some detail: it will soon become clear how different the context is from the world of work and qualifications as illustrated by the models in the previous chapter. The process may have many similarities, but the values and the behaviours required are quite different.

There appear to be at least four distinct forms of community mentoring emerging within the UK; they are discussed below. The distinctions are based on the nature of the objectives for the supportive relationship and the importance given to achieving those objectives, in addition to the importance attached to the social aspect of the relationship.

1. Befriending

Befriending is the term used to describe the role of volunteers who provide informal social support. The primary objective is to form a trusting relationship with the individual over time, usually to reduce isolation and to provide a relationship where none currently exists. In some cases, there may be additional stated objectives at the start of the relationship such as a growth in confidence or his or her increasing involvement in community activities. The success of the relationship is not dependent on these objectives being achieved, but they are seen as a potential benefit of befriending over time. The Mentoring and Befriending Foundation (MBF) provides guidance and support to organizations and practitioners involved in mentoring and befriending. As the UK national strategic body, MBF also works to influence policy and practice in the sector and across government.

2. Positive action

Positive action mentoring targets people in what are considered to be oppressed or minority groups. This includes young people from predominantly black or Asian ethnic communities. This form of mentoring also includes encouraging young women to enter traditionally male-dominated industries such as engineering. A key tactic here is to offer positive role models from within the targeted community where the mentor is expected to make influential introductions, open doors and remove organizational barriers.

3. Employment mentoring

Mentoring in preparing for employment is used where a school believes pupils are not achieving their potential and are capable of higher examination grades. Typically, the borderline is between grades D and C, since achieving the maximum number of grades A–C is a key measure for published school league tables in the UK. This form of mentoring is usually done by volunteers from local businesses who visit schools to increase the self-confidence of these 'borderline' pupils. The purpose is to increase the pupils' appreciation of what companies expect of future employees and to give them the confidence and knowledge to access employment opportunities.

The CIPD Steps Ahead Mentoring programme – an example of employment mentoring

In 2011, the CIPD launched the Steps Ahead Mentoring programme, which offers jobseekers (primarily 18–24-year-olds) one-to-one mentoring sessions with a CIPD member, who is an HR professional, to help them improve their employability skills, boost their confidence and find work.

Steps Ahead mentees are referred to the programme primarily by Jobcentre Plus work coaches and other selected partners. The programme is run by the CIPD (at no cost to the young people or Jobcentre Plus) with support from Nesta and the Cabinet Office via the Centre for Social Action Innovation Fund.

Steps Ahead Mentoring is currently operating across the whole of England with pilots in Scotland, Wales, and plans in place for a pilot in Ireland. CIPD also recently completed successful pilots of the programme with other groups including older workers and parent returners to work and hopes to extend Steps Ahead Mentoring support to these more widely during 2016.

The primary referral route for Steps Ahead mentees is via Jobcentre Plus work coaches. These coaches know the programme and have criteria to help judge which young jobseekers will be most suited to take part in the programme. They will then talk through the Steps Ahead Mentoring offer with the young jobseeker and provide them with details of how to sign up. The young jobseeker will then sign up voluntarily.

Steps Ahead mentors are required to be CIPD members and HR professionals to be eligible to sign up to the programme. To date, over 3,500 CIPD members have signed up to be a Steps Ahead mentor.

Once approved, Steps Ahead mentors can search via an online portal for mentees in their local area who are looking to be mentored. At this stage, only anonymized mentee details will be displayed. The mentor will

▶

then match themselves to a mentee and from there they will be able to access their contact details, get in touch and set up the first mentoring meeting.

All mentoring meetings are required to take place in a public space, for example a coffee shop, and in a location that is reasonably convenient for both mentor and mentee.

Where there is a shortage of mentors or mentees in a particular geographical location, mentors can search in other locations for mentees to support who have confirmed they are also happy to be mentored remotely. Remote mentoring can be very effective and the programme has good examples of where this form of mentoring has worked really well.

Here are three sample case studies from mentees who have participated in the Steps Ahead Mentoring programme.

Case Study 3.1 – lack of experience

Madia's story

After I finished school, I started college but wasn't able to finish my course for personal reasons. I'd been working part-time in retail until then, so I went full-time, working at the likes of Gap and Next. Pretty soon, though, I realized that it just wasn't what I wanted.

I started to look around for admin jobs, but no one wanted to employ me – I just didn't have the experience.

What did her mentor do?

Madia told her mentor that she wanted to get into financial services, insurance specifically, so they created an action plan together and Madia was asked to research her dream job and identify the steps she needed to get there.

Her mentor took her to networking events and encouraged her to speak to people about what she wanted to do.

Case Study 3.2 – self-confidence

Bathsheba's story

In spite of over five years of relevant experience, I had been really struggling to get work. My work coach said that I should apply for jobs that required the university degree I had. I did that, but I just wasn't getting any success. So I also applied for all sorts of other jobs – including factory, admin and cleaning roles – but I kept getting told that I was overqualified. My mentor saw very early that the biggest challenge to my getting a job was probably my self-confidence.

What did her mentor do?
Bathsheba's mentor started off by asking how she felt in herself, which Bathsheba said felt very human. She then looked at her CV and found that Bathsheba tended to downplay her achievements and said that those who also wanted the jobs she wanted would be doing the opposite.

Case Study 3.3 – update CV and prepare for interviews

Nathaniel's story
I left school once I'd completed my GCSEs and then went to college for a further three years. After that, I started looking around for opportunities. I found a work placement and then other temporary work. But once that ended, I was unemployed for eight months.

What did his mentor do?
His mentor had all sorts of knowledge and experience and was able to improve his CV from a one-pager to a much better two-pager. She suggested that he focus on particular experiences and how they benefited him in a way that employers would understand.

She also gave him clear insights into the sorts of things they needed to know about in an interview.

The programme is clearly a success as nearly three-quarters (73 per cent) of young people who have completed the Steps Ahead Mentoring programme have gone on to find employment or work experience.

It's not just the young jobseekers who benefit from participating in the programme. Eight in every ten of those who took part said they found the experience to be a rewarding one. Mentors state that not only does it feel good to help others and see the young people go on to find employment, but it also contributes to their own professional development by enhancing coaching and mentoring skills. Furthermore, it provides HR professionals with a far better understanding of the work challenges faced by young people. This increased understanding amongst the profession contributes to the CIPD's vision to champion better work and working lives which starts with young people being able to access the labour market.

▶

The CIPD members volunteer as mentors for a host of reasons, but a common theme is the impact of their own experience as it motivates them to help others.

Simon says:

When I graduated, I was unemployed for nine months. At the time, I had no clear advice on what to do about my situation. I would have benefited from someone giving me informal help back then, so as soon as I found out about the programme, I jumped at the chance to get involved.

Katie says:

I'd done a fair amount of mentoring in the past – although mostly within the HR profession. I felt very passionate about getting involved. With little guidance, I'd had to work very hard to gain a foothold in education and work earlier in my life – and I feel we can sometimes make it very difficult for young people to make the transition into employment. I found that helping my mentee helped me in my understanding and it's incredibly rewarding watching somebody blossom in front of you.

Barry says:

I've always had good experiences of being mentored during my career. I decided I really wanted to give something back and volunteered for Steps Ahead Mentoring after hearing Boris Johnson talk about it at a CIPD event. It's one of the few things in your working life that you do because you want to, not because you have to. Much of what we all do is part of a routine or for compliance reasons. Mentoring is different – it means helping someone establish themselves on their career and life path.

The Steps Ahead Mentoring relationship, between volunteer and young jobseeker, provides a unique opportunity for the mentee to tap into the expertise and knowledge of an HR professional. More importantly, the time and dedication our volunteers put into the process can have a huge impact on a young person's confidence, helping them to feel better equipped to take their first steps into the world of work.

Jemeela Quraishi, Development Manager,
Steps Ahead Mentoring programme

4. Social inclusion

Engagement mentoring targets those people considered to be disaffected with society or who are socially excluded. These are generally young people who have become disconnected or disengaged from the core institutions of school and work and sometimes have already been involved in the criminal justice system. The key purpose of this form of mentoring is to help these people re-enter the education system and/or the employment market.

The Fifteen Foundation – an example of engagement mentoring

Fifteen was created in London by Jamie Oliver in 2002. Millions watched the UK Channel 4 programme that followed Jamie's ups and downs as he got to grips with the challenges of handling 15 tough young people who thought they might want to be chefs. Fifteen London continues to be a very successful restaurant and recruits 20 youngsters each year. There are now Fifteen establishments in Cornwall, Amsterdam and Melbourne and the Fifteen Foundation has a goal to grow Fifteen into a global brand.

The director of the Fifteen Foundation, Liam Black, said:

Fifteen exists to reach out to young people who are often disregarded in society – the focus all too often is on what's wrong with them. Fifteen focuses on what's right with them, providing opportunities and support through which they can find and develop the best in themselves. This involves a unique encounter with food and Jamie Oliver's inspiring approach to cooking and service. But Fifteen is so much more than a chef training project. Food and cooking are the means to the end. The purpose is personal transformation for each young person. After graduation, our young people move on a lot more confident, having made some lifelong friends and with a great chance of making a career at the top of the restaurant business.

We work with young people who often come from troubled families, who have 'failed' at school and who have experienced homelessness, drug and drink problems, have been ensnared in the criminal justice system, and consequently have low self-esteem, self-defeating patterns of behaviour, and social networks that serve to keep them locked in to poverty and underachievement. We are under no illusions that we can 'fix' them. We cannot sort out family problems, undo a criminal record

▶

or compel them to give up smoking weed. What we can do is provide them with more choices, open doors to new networks and opportunities and invite them to step through, helping them develop new skills to deal with their old problems.

The chefs and senior managers have clearly been carrying out an informal but very effective mentoring role with these young people. In 2006, they decided that they needed to build an even stronger culture of mentoring and coaching throughout the business. They took six members of staff through a six-month course to become qualified mentors and others to become qualified to teach mentoring to the franchise partners around the world. The programme has had a positive impact among the staff, increasing active listening and other supportive behaviours.

'I am really enjoying it and actually get as much out of the sessions with my three mentees as I hope they do,' said Liam.

It is clear that mentoring is growing in popularity and that there is a real resurgence in organizations using mentoring to develop their employees. We often think about mentoring as something that only happens within organizations; typically, the organization wanting to develop a more junior employee by pairing them with an internal more senior mentor. Whilst external mentoring exists it is less known than internal mentoring, as individuals who have an external mentor tend to arrange the mentoring themselves through their network or through a recommendation. However, it is clear from these examples that mentoring has a greater reach and benefit than just being an internal organizational development tool.

What is starting to happen is organizations taking mentoring and applying it to address real-life challenges outside their organization. They have successfully demonstrated that mentoring can be used in many different contexts but still using the traditional approach whereby someone who has more experience provides advice, guidance and support to someone with less experience.

External mentoring seems to be on the increase – there are more and more mentoring organizations being set up: The Cherie Blair Foundation is using mentoring to help women entrepreneurs in developing and emerging countries; The Aspire Foundation is using mentoring to support women in charities and social enterprises that are impacting women and girls; Mentore, founded by Baroness Karren Brady, is a premium business mentoring service where high-potential employees can be matched with a senior external mentor; and Mentorsme provides mentoring for small- to medium-sized enterprises. This rise in external mentoring over the past few years seems set to grow even more over the coming years as people realize the potential that mentoring can bring by connecting the right people together to address a clear purpose.

There is an additional form of community mentoring we need to include in this chapter: 'learning mentors'. These differ from the previous examples as they are in paid employment specifically as mentors rather than undertaking a voluntary role alongside their proper jobs.

The learning mentor

We have already mentioned the voluntary role of 'preparation for employment mentor', which first started in the UK with the Business-Education Partnerships in 1993. Although this voluntary scheme still continues, in 1999 the UK government announced the creation of a new full-time post in the state education system – the learning mentor as one of the three main strands of its 'Excellence in Cities' policy. This was a package of measures designed to improve inner-city education in the UK. Over the years, this initiative was widened to cover what became known as 'excellence clusters'. This development was possibly the most significant endorsement of the power of mentoring as a new approach to learning and as such, the creation of these full-time professionals justifies the exploration of this role in more detail.

The original target was 1,000 learning mentors in place. Since then, the learning mentors concept has spread rapidly and by 2010 there were estimated to be around 12,500 working across the primary and secondary education sectors. However, the total number is believed to be significantly higher since there are many directly funded posts not included in this estimate.

Learning mentors were also established as part of the Children's Workforce, supported through the Children's Workforce Development Council (CWDC). The CWDC was established following the UK government's commitment to workforce reform in the green paper *Every Child Matters*, and was responsible for the implementation and support of the government's Children's Workforce Strategy. From April 2012 the leadership of the CWDC's programmes of work was taken over by either the Department for Education (DfE), the Teaching Agency or the Children's Improvement Board (CIB).

The establishment of this important new occupational group has been formally recognized in the UK through the National Occupational Standards for Learning, Development and Support Services (NOS LDSS) issued by the Qualification and Curriculum Authority (QCA).

These learning mentors are generally salaried staff who work with school and college students to help them address barriers to learning. With the objective of providing a bridge across academic and pastoral support roles, these mentors aim to ensure that individual students engage more effectively in learning and so achieve appropriately. They are now seen as a key ingredient in many schools and colleges to improve the achievement levels of students.

The official description of the work is to provide 'support and guidance to children, young people and those engaged with them, by removing barriers to learning in order to promote effective participation, enhance individual learning, raise aspirations and achieve full potential'. The work of the learning mentors falls into these broad areas:

- Providing a complementary service to existing teachers and pastoral staff in school and to others providing services to children and their families outside school (such as Social and Youth Services, the Education Welfare Service, the Probation and Careers Service and business, community and voluntary workers) so enhancing existing provision in order to support learning, participation and the encouragement of social inclusion.

- Developing and maintaining effective and supportive mentoring relationships with children, young people and those engaged with them, targeting help to those who need it most in deprived areas, especially those experiencing multiple disadvantages.

- Raising standards and reducing truancy and exclusion in the target areas, and helping local education authorities and schools to make accelerated progress in their achievement of truancy, exclusion and other relevant targets.

- Working within an extended range of networks and partnerships to broker support and learning opportunities, and improve the quality of services to children and young people.

There is clear evidence that such schemes are proving effective, as the following quotations confirm:

> Learning mentors are making a significant effect on the attendance, behaviour, self-esteem and progress of the pupils they support... the most successful and highly valued strand of the EiC programme... In 95 per cent of the survey

schools, inspectors judged that the mentoring programme made a positive contribution to the mainstream provision of the school as a whole, and had a beneficial effect on the behaviour of individual pupils and on their ability to learn and make progress. (Ofsted, 2003: 46)

Pupils receiving support from learning mentors were one and a half times more likely to achieve five or more examination results at grade A* to C than young people with similar prior attainment who had not been mentored. (Morris *et al*, 2004)

Learning mentors are very skilled at helping students work through and overcome problems, often from outside school, that are preventing them from learning. Through a combination of individual counselling and support sessions, group work, residential trips and after-school activities, they are helping students to achieve significantly higher grades than originally predicted. They are providing support for those students considered the most vulnerable. (Hanson School, Bradford, September 2005)

Over the last year the mentoring project has worked with 80 students on a 1:1 or group work basis. Attendance has improved by 71 per cent; punctuality has improved by 73 per cent; behaviour has improved by 76 per cent; academic progress has improved by 69 per cent; and personal organization and involvement in school activities has improved in almost all cases. (Morecambe High School, 2007)

Young adults who face an opportunity gap but have a mentor are 55 per cent more likely to be enrolled in college than those who did not have a mentor. (Bruce and Bridgeland, 2014)

In addition to better school attendance and a better chance of going on to higher education, mentored youth maintain better attitudes toward school. (Herrera *et al*, 2013)

Examples from the 'personal specification' used by individual schools in recruiting the learning mentors highlight the differences in the way this type of mentoring is expected to be delivered. The specification states that the key skills and competences for learning mentors would include:

- The ability to engage constructively with, and relate to, a wide range of young people and families/carers with different ethnic and social backgrounds.
- The ability to work effectively with, and command the confidence of, teaching staff and senior management within the school.

- Working with others, the ability to assess and review young people and family circumstances and plan appropriate responses, drawing on in-school and external advice and expertise where necessary.
- A proven track record of working with young people, and an ability to see a child's needs in the round.
- A desire to do something worthwhile for young people, to understand their needs and to gain insights into how they think.
- Knowledge of, and ability to work effectively and network with, a wide range of supporting services in both the public and private sectors; ability to draw on a wider range of support, information, opportunities and guidance.
- Ability to identify potential barriers to learning and jointly engage in strategies to overcome these barriers.
- Ability to see the mentoring role as a long-term activity designed to achieve the goals in the learning action plan and not a quick-fix/trouble-shooting role.
- Ability to engage in joint goal setting with the individual child as part of the learning action planning process.
- Having time and energy to put into the relationship.
- Being up to date with current 'know-how'.
- Possessing competences in the skills of networking, counselling, facilitating and developing others.
- A willingness and ability to learn and see potential benefits.

This ambitious specification also required the creation of an infrastructure of contact and communication, not only among learning mentors, but with others working in the public and private sectors.

Unfortunately, there is a real debate about the domination by the so-called 'social worker/therapist lobby' of the discussions on the nature of the necessary skills development and professional standards required. But as Helen Fisher, Head of Staff Health Care at Birmingham City Council, suggests:

Personally, I agree wholeheartedly that in terms of community and learning mentors, there is no room for turf wars between the therapy/social work lobby. In fact, the schemes have appeal by virtue of their distance from the professions, as for some individuals it must feel as if the authorities have dominated their lives.

Community/learning mentors reinforce potential, not pathology or marginalization. Obviously the coach-mentor needs to be appropriately trained (in the broadest sense) in basic counselling/coaching skills, and having a keen awareness of ethics, standards and particularly boundaries is vital. In the context of the relationship, contingency plans need to be agreed in advance for providing support to mentors who have to deal with distressing life stories and events with ongoing support and development from supervision, which models the relationship they are themselves trying to create.

Mentoring forms compared

We believe there are many key elements to any successful community mentoring programme. But it is important to understand the challenges, similarities and differences between 'corporate', 'qualification' and 'community' mentoring with greater clarity. Undoubtedly, the basic four-stage process model of analyse–plan–implement–evaluate applies here, as in the corporate coach-mentor and the qualification mentor roles. For community mentoring, however, the differences in the language and behaviours required are perhaps best captured in a model on the following lines:

Stage 1. Gaining understanding and awareness.

Stage 2. Motivating for action.

Stage 3. Supporting the plan.

Stage 4. Reviewing and maintaining momentum.

The model is shown in Figure 3.1.

Figure 3.1 The four stages of the community coach-mentoring process

Stage 1. Gaining understanding and acceptance

Unlike the world of work where time needs to be tightly managed, the community mentor has to be prepared to spend as long as it takes to build a close rapport and gain a sense of trust and confidence in the learner, who is likely to be extremely uncertain. Projecting the right balance between empathy and firmness is not easy. The mentor also has to be able to provide access to a range of information and support agencies; establishing the boundaries between the mentor's role and that of other professionals is key. The issue of building trust needs to be handled in a way that demonstrates that the mentor is impartial: he or she has no hidden agenda and really believes that there is no right way of doing the things that the 'establishment' and those in authority are 'pushing'.

Helping the learners to develop a self-awareness and acceptance of their existing strengths and weaknesses is a similar requirement to other types of mentoring. The style and tone of voice require greater sensitivity than is perhaps acceptable in the more robust environment of the workplace. The credibility of the mentor 'having been there, done that and lived to tell the tale' can be very powerful in this instance. For example, a young teenage mother struggling to manage normal but unruly children may not respond well to someone who, although well-meaning, comes across as yet another 'expert' giving her instructions. However, someone who has been through a similar experience is more likely to encourage a positive response.

Stage 2. Motivating for action

Community learners often have a sense of personal inadequacy or feel they have already been labelled as 'failures'. Overcoming this negative self-perception and motivating them to construct an action plan to help to change their circumstances is no easy task, and the volunteer mentor can have a particularly valuable role here. Training for both mentors and their learners and other support is required. The most effective method is for the mentor to role-model the usefulness of keeping records, setting goals, reflecting on progress and making use of other support, supervision and training opportunities.

The key is a combination of firmness and encouragement with patience and empathy: undoubtedly, a difficult cocktail of skills to be mastered. Setting goals, for instance, often needs to be taken in very small steps and in a way that recognizes the huge difficulties some people have in mastering this discipline. Lack of patience and unrealistic expectations of the speed of progress are two of the main reasons for drop-out and failure. In this respect, the contrast with corporate mentoring is probably most vivid.

Stage 3. Supporting the plan

Having encouraged the learner to decide a plan of action that involves a gradual step-by-step route to a goal, the community mentor – unlike the other types of mentor – cannot simply sit back for a while and expect the learner to become a self-starter overnight.

A hand-holding role may sound patronizing, but being prepared to accompany learners on their first visit to an after-school activity, the library or a government agency may be just what is required. Providing support during a plan often means just 'being there to talk' on a regular basis. The most common obstacles to achieving the goals arise from life circumstances outside a formal programme, and the personalized mentoring relationship can be used to work through personal and domestic issues. The danger for mentors who are too enthusiastic or too keen to be 'helpful' is that they may create a situation where the learner becomes too dependent on them. Striking the correct balance is not easy, and the availability of a mentor to the mentor (sometimes called a supervisor) can be invaluable in helping to manage this type of situation.

Stage 4. Reviewing and maintaining momentum

All programmes need to be monitored to review progress during the plan and to evaluate the outcomes at the end. Monitoring and reviewing are a constant process, but evaluation really takes place at the end of a programme or the completion of a plan.

In a corporate or qualification context, this may mean completing a skills development programme or being awarded a professional qualification. In a community context, the achievements may seem more modest, but are equally valuable. For instance, being able to open a bank account and to write your name on the cheques may be a huge success for someone who is severely dyslexic and who may feel he or she has been unfairly labelled as a failure by the education system. The need to celebrate these successes and at the same time to build motivation to set new goals is the same in all contexts.

A structure for a final evaluation session that has been found to work well is to ask the following sequence of questions:

- What did you actually do?
- What had you hoped to achieve?

- What did you actually achieve?
- Were there any unexpected learning points?
- How would you describe the personal benefits?
- What do you think you could do next to build on your achievements?

If the relationship has been successful, the chances of continuing progress, even without the formal involvement of the mentor, will usually be high.

The emergence of the coach-mentor

The challenge for both community mentoring and life coaching is to create appropriate and relevant development programmes and take a broader approach to setting national standards and qualifications that effectively meet the variety of needs of the emerging profession. One aspect of these developments will be gaining agreement on the language and theoretical models on which the new standards are to be based. These need to be seen alongside other government initiatives: the aim of 3,000 business-to-headteacher mentors and the 1,000 volunteer business-to-business mentors, for instance. In our opinion, these legitimize the role of 'community mentor'. The claim for the recognition of 'community mentors' alongside the 'corporate' and 'qualification mentors' as a profession is clearly strong.

Also, the enormous growth in life and lifestyle coaches seen in recent years and the blurring of the distinction between business coaching and life coaching, and indeed with the professional executive coach and executive mentor, must be acknowledged. This blurring of distinctions strengthens our view that the new professionals can realistically call themselves professional 'coach-mentors' and acknowledge this spectrum of support roles and the overlap of skills, attributes and qualities needed by everyone involved.

In Chapter 2, we introduced a model to help us to understand the similarities and differences between 'professional and business coach-mentoring' and 'corporate and qualification mentoring'. In this chapter we add the extra context of 'community mentoring' to provide a full picture; see Table 3.1.

You will note that we have added another four labels to each stage of the summary process (see Figure 3.2), which gives an even simpler generic model that encapsulates our thinking.

To help complete this chapter, you may care to do the 'Mentoring volunteers health check' in Figure 3.3. (Bear in mind that corporate and qualification

Table 3.1 Expanded summary model of coaching and mentoring

	Professional and business coaching	Corporate and qualification mentoring	Community mentoring
Stage 1 (Awareness)	Analysing for awareness	Confirming the Personal Learning Plan (PLP)	Gaining understanding and acceptance
Stage 2 (Responsibility)	Planning for self-responsibility	Encouraging the self-management of learning	Motivating for action
Stage 3 (Action)	Implementing using style, techniques and skills	Providing support during the PLP process	Supporting the plan
Stage 4 (Reflection)	Evaluating for success and learning	Assisting in the evaluation of success	Reviewing and maintaining momentum

Figure 3.2 The four stages of the coach-mentoring process

Figure 3.3 Mentoring volunteers health check

SELF-ASSESSMENT

MENTORING VOLUNTEERS HEALTH CHECK

Tick the box as appropriate, where A = Definitely, B = Partially, C = Not at all

	A	B	C
• Do you understand how mentoring differs from other roles you are asked to play in your organization?			
• Do you really want to take on the role and are you willing to make the necessary time available?			
• Are you comfortable in being asked to assess your own strengths and weaknesses and relate them to the learners' development needs so that you can guide them to other sources of help where it is appropriate?			
• Are you sure that you can invest time early on in the relationship to establish rapport and a regular schedule for discussions?			
• Do you know how to enable the learners to produce a realistic development plan, and ensure that it is 'signed off' by all the relevant people?			
• Will you be able to keep the relationship on a professional level, particularly where there are differences in gender (sensitivity to potential misinterpretation in language and behaviour will be important in these situations)?			
• Do you understand the distinction between counselling and advising, and whenever possible, will you encourage the learners to work out their own solutions with you acting only as a sounding board?			
• Are you aware that you will be a role model, and that how you are seen to manage yourself in day-to-day situations will affect the relationship you have with the learners?			
• Are you sure that the feedback you give will be clear, honest and constructive, and designed to build confidence and ongoing commitment in the learners?			
• Will you be able to recognize when the time has come to end the relationship, and aim to end on a positive and supportive note by sharing the value you have both gained from the experience?			

mentors often volunteer for the role in addition to their existing jobs, while to a large extent community mentors usually volunteer for their role in their non-work time.

Endnotes

Bruce, M and Bridgeland, J (2014) *The Mentoring Effect: Young people's perspectives on the outcomes and availability of mentoring*, MENTOR: The National Mentoring Partnership [online] http://www.mentoring.org/images/uploads/Report_TheMentoringEffect.pdf

Grant, A M (2001) *Towards a Psychology of Coaching: The impact of coaching on metacognition, mental health and goal attainment* [online] https://www.researchgate.net/publication/228598134_Towards_a_psychology_of_coaching [accessed 30 August 2016]

Herrera, C, DuBois, D and Grossman, J (2013) *The Role of Risk: Mentoring experiences and outcomes for youth with varying risk profiles*, MDRC [online] http://www.mdrc.org/sites/default/files/Role%20of%20Risk_Final-web%20PDF.pdf [accessed 30 August 2016]

HSE (2015) Work-related stress, anxiety and depression statistics in Great Britain 2014/15 [online] http://www.hse.gov.uk/statistics/causdis/stress/ [accessed 30 August 2016]

Morris, M, Rutt, S and Eggers, M (2004) *Pupil Outcomes: The impact of EIC*, National Foundation for Educational Research, Slough

Ofsted (2003) *Excellence in Cities and Education Action Zones: Management and impact*, Ref: HMI1399, Ofsted Publications Centre, London

Helping people to learn how to learn   04

We have asserted that the main purpose of coaching and mentoring is to help and support people to take control and responsibility for their own learning. It is important to explore this issue in some detail. It is a sobering thought to realize that up until the mid-1980s it was quite possible to be very successful in managing a business or community organization without even mentioning the word 'learning'. Certainly, that was our own experience.

For a growing number of people in the public, private and independent sectors, the concept of the 'learning organization' is now seen as an accurate blueprint of the way organizations need to be structured and to behave in the 21st century. The blueprint may be visionary, but each organization – small, medium or large – will, it is argued, be required to build its own version if it is to be successful. Coaching and mentoring, we believe, will need to be essential parts of this blueprint as organizational learning involves all the individuals in the organization.

The broad argument for the learning organization is that:

- we are now in a world of global information and technology-driven organizations;
- success will depend on the speed with which new information or intelligence is communicated and applied to current operations, problems and opportunities;
- storage, transfer and retrieval of this new information is essentially technology-driven, but application of that information is people-driven and will be heavily dependent on the strength of conversations, relationships and personal, social and professional networks;
- applying the new information effectively means that people – and organizations – will need to learn to do things differently and quickly;
- since new information is becoming continuously available, learning will need to be continuous both for individuals and for organizations.

It therefore follows that only individuals and organizations that actively manage their learning processes will be successful – or, indeed, survive and thrive!

What is a learning organization?

In *The Power of Learning*, Mayo and Lank (1994) offered the following definition: 'A learning organization harnesses the full brain power, knowledge and experience available to it, in order to evolve continually for the benefit of all its stakeholders.'

This challenge of how to harness the maximum capability from their people is still fundamental to organizational development, for as Reg Revans (in Pedler, 2008) explained: 'Development depends on learning agility and learning needing to be equal to or greater than the rate of change.' A more in-depth perspective was offered by Senge (1992), who noted:

> Most of us, at one time or another, have been part of a great 'team', or group of people who functioned together in an extraordinary way – who trusted each other, who complemented each other's strengths and weaknesses and compensated for each other's limitations, who had common goals that were larger than individual goals and who produced extraordinary results. I have met many people who have experienced this sort of profound teamwork – in sports or in the performing arts or in business. Many say they have spent much of their life looking for that experience again. What they experienced was a learning organization.

Senge, author of *The Fifth Discipline*, and the follow-up, *The Fifth Discipline Fieldbook*, provided practical ways to initiate new ways of thinking in organizations. He is credited as one of the main architects of the concept of the learning organization. He points out that the unit of the small team or small business may be the best way to recognize how the learning organization works in practice. Recent stories of organizational failures, in local authorities, police, government departments, financial institutions, etc, appear to confirm that the larger the organization, the more difficult it is to learn. These cases seem to be due, in the main, to lack of effective communications and accountability. How many times do we hear the phrase 'Lessons need to be learnt', or 'Lessons have been learnt'? Does that mean they are not learning organizations? Successful large organizations may, of course, comprise a large number of small teams working coherently together towards a shared vision and common goals.

Senge's focus on the team in the world of sport and the performing arts also helps to highlight the potential role of the coach and mentor within a learning organization. As we have already mentioned, successful sporting and performing arts teams have long been associated with the high profile given to their coaches and mentors. Now businesses are recognizing the key role of coach-mentors in facilitating organizational change.

Constraints and contradictions

However, there are other powerful forces that are changing both the way organizations are structured and the way that they will increasingly behave. In most organizations there is constant pressure to reduce costs and maximize profits, or give greater value for money for the services they provide. This has led to a widespread short-term focus on immediate results and constant efforts to reduce costs and consequently the numbers of people employed in organizations.

Flatter management structures, process re-engineering and excellent customer service initiatives result in greatly increased pressures on people. It has also meant an end to the idea that people will have a job for life or a single career that is actively managed and developed for them by the organization for which they work. People have become more responsible for managing their own careers and for continuous learning of new knowledge and skills if they are to remain 'employable'.

There is clearly a potential conflict between the need for organizations to actively structure and manage the learning potential of their people and the pressures to change the nature of employment contracts towards a short-term 'only as we need you' basis. New attitudes and new techniques have been developed to reconcile these conflicts. As Handy comments in *The Age of Unreason* (2002) this is changing people's psychological contract with their employers and the need for individuals to both create and manage their portfolio career.

This 'Psychological Contract' concept was first identified by Schein in the 1960s and has since been simply defined by Armstrong (2006):

> ... the employment relationship consists of a unique combination of beliefs held by an individual and his or her employer about what they expect of one another.

Globalization and the growth of digital technology shifted everything we knew about organized work onto an entirely different level – especially in terms of complexity, rate of change, connectivity and the mobility of people and activities.

This has resulted in significant changes in perceptions and attitudes to traditional corporations, markets and governance. Examples of extremely potent 'community'-driven enterprises are becoming common. Social connectivity and technological empowerment pose a real threat to the old-style corporate models. Younger generations have seen the free market model and traditional capitalism fail, and fail young people particularly. Certain industries no longer need a massive hierarchical corporation to connect supply and demand.

Employees are increasingly mobile, flexible and adaptable – they no longer expect to stay working for the same employer for their entire career. They can more easily find alternative employment than 20 years ago. They are not limited to working in their local town, region, or even in the same country. In fact, with modern technology, geographical location is for many workers irrelevant, and will become more so. The significance and complexity of a Psychological Contract have grown in response to all of these effects, and clearly the world of work will continue to change, so the significance and complexity of such a contract will grow even more.

Also consider the connectivity of workers today. In past times, trade unions were the vehicle for people power. Instead, increasingly today the vehicle is the Internet and modern social networking, which enable awareness and mobilization of groups of people on an awesome level of sophistication and scale, the effects of which we are only beginning to witness.

The proliferation of digital technology, which the younger generations understand and exploit infinitely better than older people, is a major liberation for employees. Employees no longer rely on employers for access to technology. Now there are many examples where employers depend more and more on employees for technological optimization and exploitation.

These fundamental changes to the world of work are reflected in the development of more empowered and self-sufficient employees, and their own development within a learning organization. We are moving from the information age defined by the knowledge workers into a 'conceptual age' in which workers rely not just on deep technical capability but also on skills of pattern recognition, tacit knowledge and wisdom born of experience.

Jay Cross (2012) said:

> … work converging with learning into the new conceptual workplace. Conceptual work involves gaining experience, developing new thoughts and new ideas and developing new lines of business. In this new era of work, the potential value that an employee can create is many times greater than it was because they no longer have physical limits.

If this is indeed the conceptual age, it is clear that people will need more self-awareness, an understanding of how they impact on others, how they make better and quicker decisions, how they influence and network with others, as well as how to innovate. Some of these behaviours are cognitively driven, but some are emotional/affective and to understand them will require insights from behavioural sciences and neuroscience, which will be explored more fully in the next chapter.

Training and development were previously seen as predominantly under the control of the employer. Employees used to depend on their employer to advance their learning and skills, and thereby their value in the employment market. This is clearly no longer the case. Employees are progressively able to take control of their own learning and development, again predominantly through greater access to, and availability of, technology.

It seems that any reasonably well informed person can search or socially network almost anything they need relevant to their career and or development. With information so widely and easily available there is a need to critique, make sense of and relate it to their world context. Employees in almost every company are enabled to transform their own lives by acquiring the knowledge and skill to take control of their careers, to see how their own work is part of, and contributes to, the larger work of their companies and to society as a whole. This approach is often described as 'transformational or transformative learning'.

Transformational learning

Learning to think differently and learning how to learn requires a transformation in a person's thinking. As distinct from transactional learning which is learning how to do things better or differently. Transformative learning challenges and changes a person's concepts and values and results in a mind shift to a new paradigm or 'world view'.

For an organization to transform in this sense requires a personal transformation from the influencers within the organization. This is primarily because employees take their lead from their leaders, therefore their visible transformation is critical. Organizational change is significantly enhanced by the leaders role-modelling the new desired behaviours. The success of such an organizational change is proportional to the observed change in the key influencers. The result of such authentic transformation increases the potential for continuous learning for both the leader and the employees.

Levels of learning

Traditional learning consists of acquiring new information, facts, ideas, skills and techniques, which conform to our existing views and beliefs. This will produce small improvements in our performance and enable us to do more of what we currently do slightly better. This is known as 'single loop' learning.

The next level of learning is known as 'double loop' learning. This helps people change their mental models and frame of reference and consequently reshape their thinking and behaviours to enable them to do something different. This level of learning equips people with the ability to see a problem or situation from a different perspective and so be able to come up with alternative and new options for action.

To achieve transformational learning requires the third level, called 'triple-loop' learning. This learning comes from a deep and challenging self-reflection which is described in more detail at the end of this chapter. This level of learning is seen by many as challenging because it changes the way a person sees the world in which they live and changes how they view themselves. This can have a profound effect on how a person chooses to live their future life, considering that their old ways are now redundant or inappropriate for their new expanded world view.

This can seem very scary, to let go of long-held and familiar concepts and old habits. For a person to fully realize their potential they need to be willing to let go, face challenges and step into the unknown.

This transformational learning can lead to fundamental changes to a person's working practices and even their lifestyle. It can also lead to a person feeling much more fulfilled, stable and content with their situation. This self-actualization will equip people better to face future challenges in a stronger and healthier position.

Transformational coaching

The support of a coach-mentor can be very helpful in many ways for anyone experiencing transformational learning.

- **A guide who knows the way.** Transformational learning requires a person to step into, what is for them, the unknown. It can be very helpful to be accompanied by someone who has been there themselves or is familiar with what to expect.

- **A supporter.** It is very important to work with someone who is fully present and able to create a safe space for the individual to explore and express who they really are.

- **A critical friend.** Challenging a person's assumptions and preconceived ideas encourages deeper and more meaningful self-reflection. This helps the individual re-evaluate their view of the world and their perspective on perceived challenges and constraints.

- **A rear-view mirror.** It is often helpful to encourage someone to look back at past successes and transformations to reflect on what they did to make them successful. Recalling past success can often boost confidence to go forward to the next transformation.

Towards a learning organization model

Psychologist and author Graham Guest has written extensively in various publications on this subject and advocates the importance of understanding how mental models can help us to understand complex new ideas and to bring alive the concept of the learning organization. Discussing Senge's ideas, he writes (Guest, 1999):

- Mental models are deeply ingrained assumptions by which we make sense of the world. In a learning organization these models will always be challenged to discover whether they are the best representations of exactly what is happening at any one time.

- Personal mastery is the discipline of continually clarifying and deepening personal vision; it represents the learning organization's spiritual foundation.

- Team learning starts with dialogue, which in turn involves learning how to recognize the patterns of interaction in teams.

- Building shared vision involves adopting shared pictures of the future that foster genuine commitment rather than merely compliance.

- Systems thinking, Senge's fifth discipline, sees beyond isolated events into deeper patterns and connections; while event thinking is linear, systems thinking is cyclical, relying on constant feedback.

To these five disciplines, Guest suggests adding the three complementary processes of:

1 coaching;

2 mentoring; and

3 effective benchmarking.

A learning organization could therefore be represented as in Figure 4.1.

Figure 4.1 A model of 'the learning organization'

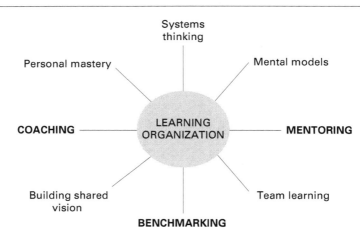

The new agenda for the learning organization

The concept of the learning organization produces an agenda for all types of organizations that includes:

- an increased focus on learning and development as the critical means of ensuring organizational effectiveness and sustainable competitive advantage;
- encouraging as many people as possible, and certainly all managers, to become coaches to ensure learning occurs in the workplace and elsewhere;
- establishing mentoring programmes to help to support learning (sometimes these will involve specially trained coach-mentors);
- identifying the key personal skills necessary for individuals to operate successfully in a learning organization as well as their life in general.

In a learning organization, people will be regularly encouraged to accept the continual need to move from their current standards of performance to higher levels and to see that continuous learning is the key to continuous improvements in performance. It is an essential role of the coach-mentor to help to maintain the focus on learning opportunities and benefits.

Therefore, it will come as no surprise that we offer the following definition of the overall aim of coaching and mentoring within the learning organization:

> The aim is to help and support people to manage their own learning in order that they may develop their skills, improve their performance, maximize their potential, and enable them to become the person they want to be.

This is supported by Caplin (2003) who says: 'Learning is the only unique resource which we have.'

Choosing how best to learn

Only a few lucky people find learning easy. One of the main reasons is that most of us are used to being taught in much the same way. Yet we know that, given the chance, we prefer to choose to work in ways that suit us best. Learning is highly personal and individualistic. So, to make learning 'easier', why not help people choose to learn in ways that suit them best? To do this, the coach-mentor needs to appreciate at least the basics of what we now understand about the way that people learn. They might well start by examining their own approaches and preferences.

From a range of publications, we are aware that there is some fascinating research being done on the power and potential of the brain's design for human learning, development and growth – how we think through all of our nerve nets: with our brain and our heads; with our emotions and feelings; and with our spirits to make sense and meaning of our experiences. There is also a developing appreciation of how the brain has a huge untapped capacity to grow and develop new neural pathways throughout our lives, which develops our intelligences, enables us to learn, unlearn and relearn, and which consequently enables us to change our perceptions, perspectives and behaviours. As Lucas (2001) says: 'The brain loves to explore and make sense of the world; likes to make connections; thrives on patterns; loves to imitate and does not perform well under too much stress.'

There is a great deal of research available on how adults learn best. It is often suggested that there are three key questions you need to be able to answer before beginning to understand what approach might suit you:

1 How do you perceive information most easily: do you learn best by seeing, hearing, moving or touching?

2 How do you organize and process the information you receive: are you predominantly left brain, right brain, analytical or global?

3 What conditions are necessary to help you to take in and store the information you are learning: are they emotional, social, physical and environmental factors?

It is now widely accepted that, for deep learning to take place, it is preferable for people to use several intelligences working together and supporting each other. Intelligence is now often considered in three main areas:

1 IQ (intelligence quotient) – focuses on the linear, logical and rational.

2 EQ (emotional intelligence) – focuses on our self-awareness and management of self in relation to others and the environment.

3 SQ (spiritual intelligence) – focuses on our search for meaning, integration and authenticity.

Other writers, such as Gardner (2006), emphasize that in fact there are multiple intelligences and people apply their 'learning intelligences' in many different ways, such as their ability to:

- speak and write well;
- reason, calculate and handle logical thinking;
- paint, take great photographs or create sculpture;
- use their hands or body;
- compose songs, sing or play musical instruments;
- relate to others;
- access their inner feelings.

Emotional intelligence

An emotional content to learning is inevitable, because learning begins in that part of the brain. (Colin Rose)

As we have discovered more about the way the brain works, the more it has become clear that there is an important connection between learning and our emotions. As Maddern (1994) explains in *Accelerated Learning*: 'Emotional intelligence, it is claimed, is a far more accurate indicator of future success than the historical attachment to measuring IQ and classroom-based learning success.' The theory of EQ has been credited to the US academics John D Mayer and Peter Salovey, who define emotional intelligence as: 'The ability to perceive, to integrate, to understand and reflectively manage one's own and other people's feelings' (Salovey *et al*, 2004).

Science journalist Daniel Goleman is currently the best-known writer on the subject. Goleman's contribution to the EQ arena has been to translate the wealth of academic research on the subject into language that the non-academic can understand. He has therefore given credibility to the case for new and more sophisticated learning methodologies that practitioners have long understood but have, until recently, failed to convince the policy makers to accept.

The insights gained from emotional intelligence, it is claimed, help to explain why the traditional predominance of classroom-based education and training has so often failed so many people. Put simply, it is now possible to show scientifically why learning knowledge about facts, learning technical skills and learning personal skills each involves different parts of the brain and thus requires different approaches and especially different time dimensions.

Our spiritual intelligence

In recent years there has been increasing interest in spiritual intelligence (SQ), or what some people are calling the 'ultimate intelligence'.

Zohar and Marshall (2001) have written well and extensively on this. They say SQ is the intelligence with which we balance meaning and value and use to place our lives in a wider context. They go on to suggest that SQ is the ultimate intelligence in that it integrates all our intelligences, for without it both EQ and IQ cannot function and will crumble away.

Advances in science have given us permission to pay attention to, value and process information and learning that we are absorbing not only from our minds, but from also our hearts, gut and body. It is beginning to be recognized that we learn through our body's systems: with our brain and with our heads, with our emotions and our feelings, and with our spirits to derive meaning from our experiences. As Rogers (in Lucas, 2001) explains: 'Significant learning combines the logical and intuitive, the intellect and the feelings, the concept and the experience, the idea and the meaning.'

Our learning preferences

Clearly, there are a number of variables to consider when you begin to think about how you might learn more easily. Considering learning as a process offers some valuable practical insights.

Learning can be described as the process of acquiring new knowledge, understanding, skills and/or wisdom. It is also believed to be a continuous cycle, and Figure 4.2 illustrates how people learn from experience. As we have all found, the process does not have a beginning, middle or an end. Depending upon the learning situation, people – and indeed organizations – can enter the cycle at any time. The most effective learning, however, will take place when you take the opportunity to complete all the stages in the cycle.

Figure 4.2 The learning process (based on Kolb's cycle)

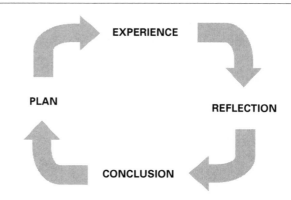

Experience This is the actual learning experience. It may be:
- Reactive – something that happens to you; or
- Proactive – an experience that you deliberately seek out.

Reflection A non-judgemental look back at what happened in the learning experience. This vital stage can be achieved quite quickly without seriously disrupting the work activity.

Conclusion Drawing conclusions from the thoughts and notes made at the reflection stage to identify the lessons learnt.

Plan Planning and testing the lessons learnt from the conclusions, so that they can be related and applied to similar situations in the future.

The Mellander Learning Cycle (Lucas, 2001) further develops the Kolb Learning Cycle and argues that learning is built up from an iteration of:

- Motivation: being mentally prepared and receptive.
- Information: having facts and data changed into information.
- Processing: having information converted into experience and insight.
- Conclusion: having the moment of discovery as experience and insight are converted into knowledge and wisdom.
- Application: having knowledge converted into skills and attitudes.
- Feedback: experiencing further reflection and refinement.

Everyone will find some stages in this learning cycle easier than others. Your preference for a particular stage in the continuous learning cycle reflects your preferred learning style. Recognizing your own style, or combination of styles, will help you to select learning opportunities that best suit you. Equally important, learning style analysis suggests what you may have to do to adjust your preferences to make the most of the learning opportunities that are actually available. Life does not always present us with the options to do exactly what we choose.

Peter Honey and Alan Mumford are acknowledged as UK experts and influential thinkers on the topic of learning styles, although other writers have questioned some of their ideas. In their book, *Using Your Learning Styles* (1986) they identified four styles which link with the learning cycle discussed above. They have characterized the styles as follows.

Activists (experience)

- Activists are open-minded rather than sceptical. This tends to make them enthusiastic about everything new.
- Their philosophy is 'I'll try anything once' – they tend to act first and consider the consequences later.
- They fill their days with activity and tackle problems by brainstorming.

People who feel that they fit this description are likely to learn best from activities where:

- it's appropriate to 'have a go';
- they can get involved in short activities such as role-plays, and where they are in the limelight;
- they are thrown in at the deep end;
- there is a lot of excitement and a range of changing tasks to tackle, usually involving people.

Reflectors (reflection)

- Reflectors like to stand back and consider experiences, observing them from many different perspectives and listening to others before making their own comment.
- The thorough collection and analysis of data about experiences and events is what counts, so they tend to postpone reaching definitive conclusions for as long as possible.
- When they act, it is as part of a larger picture that includes the past as well as the present and others' observations as well as their own.

People who fit this description are likely to learn best from situations where:

- they can stand back from events and listen and observe;
- they can carry out research or analysis;

- they can decide in their own time, and have the chance to think before acting;
- they have the opportunity to review what they have learnt.

Theorists (conclusion)

- Theorists adapt and integrate observations into complex but logically sound theories, thinking through problems in a step-by-step way.
- They tend to be perfectionists who are uncomfortable unless things are tidy and fit into a rational scheme.
- They are keen on basic assumptions, principles, theories, models and systems thinking.

People who feel they are theorists are likely to learn best when:

- they are intellectually stretched, eg through being allowed to question assumptions or logic;
- the situation has a structure and clear purpose;
- they can deal with logical, rational argument, which they have time to explore;
- they are offered interesting concepts, although they might not be immediately relevant.

Pragmatists (plan)

- Pragmatists are keen on trying out theories, ideas and techniques to see if they work in practice.
- They positively search out new ideas and take the first opportunity to experiment.
- They like to get on with things and act quickly and confidently on ideas, being impatient with extensive discussion.

As a pragmatist, you are likely to learn best from situations where you can:

- use techniques with obvious practical benefits;
- implement what you have learnt immediately;
- try out and practise techniques;
- see an obvious link between the subject matter and a real problem or opportunity at work.

Many people have found Honey and Mumford's learning preference types both helpful and easy to apply (perhaps because they tend to simplify a much more complex set of explanations).

We are not suggesting that people cannot learn from situations that do not suit their preferences. However, the learning experience is enhanced if there is a blended approach between the activist, reflector, pragmatist and theorist learning experiences and where learning opportunities are taken, transferred and cross-referenced from work and home, past and present. Our experience has shown that people learn more effectively if they can:

- choose learning opportunities that suit their preferred learning style(s);
- harness their multiple intelligences;
- go through the whole of the learning cycle.

This makes it important for individuals to develop each of their learning styles so that they can successfully adapt their style of learning to take advantage of each stage in the cycle. Knowledge of these learning styles will help you to:

- recognize your preferred learning styles and those of your colleagues;
- design or seek out learning opportunities that will suit your preferred learning style;
- focus on developing your least preferred styles so that you can make the most of the learning cycle.

Learning reflects personal style and preferences. The key to optimizing learning lies in understanding your own and your learners' learning style and preferences both in the perception and the processing of information.

Many people have found that recognizing their own style is one of the most revealing and powerful pieces of information they can obtain. It often helps to explain many earlier problems with learning and gaining qualifications and, of course, it helps to highlight the differences between colleagues and friends, both in terms of learning and also in how they prefer to work.

Learning with our head and our heart

As we have discovered more about the way the brain works, the more it has become clear that there is an important connection between learning and our emotions. It is also clear that our IQ (intellectual intelligence), EQ (emotional intelligence) and SQ (spiritual intelligence) support each other, cooperating across thinking systems to link together the logical, serial and deterministic with our creative and contextualizing intelligences. To maximize their learning, people need to hold together thinking and doing with processes of feeling and being. In other words, to think with their heads and their hearts, which might seem to cut across much of traditional Western religious, education and business models.

Taking responsibility for your own learning means learning at the levels of both the head and the heart. Knowing what you think about an issue is only half of the story and, therefore, you have only learnt half of what there is to learn. Understanding how you feel about an issue is the second, and perhaps more difficult, half.

Getting into the habit of treating yourself as a whole person will enhance your learning. Regularly asking yourself, 'How do I feel about this issue?' and, more important, 'Why do I feel this way?' is a good discipline to get you started down the route of self-awareness and understanding. This is a basic building block for someone serious about learning. Making this link between thoughts, feelings and behaviour is the key to developing new insights and self-awareness which, in turn, can facilitate self-management.

The language of learning

When you are trying to understand new ideas, apply new techniques or develop new attitudes at work, it can be very confusing indeed if key terms are defined in ways that can be interpreted differently by different people. This is certainly true with terms like 'learning', 'training', 'development', 'coaching' and 'mentoring'. While it is quite reasonable for organizations to choose their own definitions to suit their own situations, the reality is often that this clarity is not provided.

Tute (1995) highlighted some of these issues:

> Training, education and development are close relations. Yet, in vital respects, training is the polar opposite of education and development. Consider first who owns the learning agenda, because that determines the effect the outcome has on the business's future.
>
> Take training: in its pure form, the learning agenda is someone else's. The direction is outside-in. Authority is top-down. Source material is an external view of best practice, whether set by national standards, a profession or trainer. The values are conformity and compliance.
>
> Compare this with education and development. The agenda is that of the learner. The direction is inside-out. Authority is bottom-up. Source material is the learner's untapped potential and the variety of values found in humankind. The values are challenge and change.

Pilots learn to fly aircraft through the process of training. MBA students learn to manage the future through the process of education. The effect of training is convergence. The effect of education and development is divergence. Values, opinions, behaviour and culture are all affected. If we train MBA students and educate pilots, we are headed for a nosedive.

Julie Starr provides a definition of the role of coach-mentoring for learning in her book *The Coaching Manual* (2016): 'Coaching is about enabling people to create change through learning. It is also about being more, doing more, achieving more, and above all contributing more.'

Learning or development?

The learning 'process' shows that people learn from experiences, whether they happen accidentally or are actively sought, for example by attending a series of lectures, or using an open learning module. As a result of these learning experiences, people reflect on them – consciously or unconsciously – and therefore draw conclusions that lead them to plan to act differently next time. This, in turn, leads to a new experience and thus the cycle begins again. Indeed, it is likely to be a continuous process. For learning to be optimized and sustained, the cycle must be completed.

Development, on the other hand, is the 'process' of moving from one level of performance to a new and different level. Development can be said to have occurred when a learner can demonstrate that he or she can perform consistently at the new level of performance. Development therefore implies the need for clear standards of performance and for methods of measurement or assessment against those standards.

The development process is also related to the state of mind or attitude of the performer. It is sometimes illustrated graphically, as a development cycle. The development cycle can be best described as moving from unconscious incompetence through to unconscious competence: from 'I don't know what I don't know', through 'I do know what I don't know', 'I can do it if I think about it', to 'I can do it naturally without thinking'. If we do not constantly strive to develop and start a new and higher cycle of development, there is the danger of moving into bad habits or apathy. It is then possible to become unconsciously incompetent again while we think we are still competent, because the skills have changed or we have not kept up to date. Figure 4.3 provides an illustration of this cycle.

Figure 4.3 The development cycle

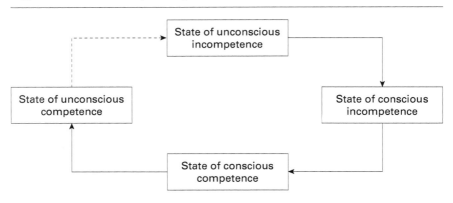

A popular example of this model is driving a car:

- Unconscious of the need for competence – at an early age, an individual may be completely unaware of the needs or techniques for driving a car.

- Conscious of incompetence – as they enter their teens, people become aware of the need to pass a driving test with its clear standards of both knowledge and skill.

- Conscious competence – after driving lessons and passing the test, people tend to drive in a very deliberate way, observing the rules and techniques they have been taught.

- Unconscious competence – after several years' experience of driving, people tend to do it automatically to the standards required.

However, how many of us can say we would pass the driving test now if we had to retake it? Have we kept up to date with the Highway Code? Do we know and always obey all the current regulations? Or have we become unconsciously incompetent again?

Development can clearly be seen to be a progression from one stage to another, but what drives the development process is the learning of new knowledge, understanding, skills and behaviours. This can be illustrated as in Figure 4.4

Seen in this way, it is clear that different learning needs exist and different learning techniques are required at different stages of the development process to drive individual performance to higher levels. It also illustrates the very real change that can occur when someone reaches a prescribed level of performance and operates with unconscious competence. Apathy and complacency can set in; this is often described as the 'comfort zone'. The

Figure 4.4 The development cycle progression

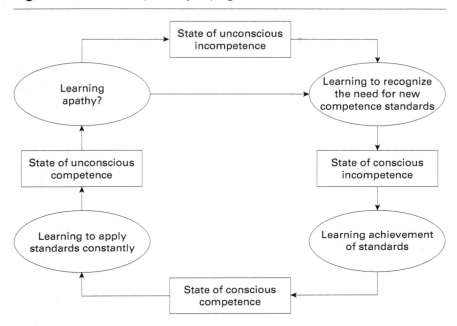

task for the coach-mentor is to be able to recognize all the stages of the development process and their related learning needs and, in particular, the importance of avoiding the learning apathy or unconscious incompetence stage.

Self-managed learning

These examples show that one of the key purposes of coach-mentoring is to empower the learner to take charge of his or her own learning: to become what might be called a 'self-managed learner'. The emphasis on many development programmes is to encourage learners to do the work themselves and to reflect back so the coach-mentor acts as a mirror. The discipline of the self-managed learning approach puts the onus on learners to use their coach-mentor as a sounding board but to solve their own problems. The coach-mentor's role is to ensure it is the learner's agenda that is discussed.

We believe that encouraging self-managed learning has many benefits:

- It encourages people to reflect on the wide range of learning opportunities available to attain goals. Getting people to think more flexibly about the opportunities that are out there, about learning, about developing themselves and about the pros and cons of where they are at the moment can be very advantageous and contribute significantly to morale.

- It can also improve the capacity for individuals to deal with change. When there are potential organizational changes being announced, many people find it inherently threatening. Coach-mentoring can contribute to people's comfort about change and give a greater sense of self-determination. It can also help as part of a cultural shift.

- It can help to address communication deficits. The process can expose a few gaps in comprehension, for example where line managers are not making it clear to staff what is expected of them. Following such a process can help to identify where some of the basics have been neglected.

Learning inefficiencies

In his book *Effective Learning* (1999), Mumford highlights the main reasons for learning inefficiencies. We perceive these as a continuum ranging from failures of perception to failures of implementation. Our interpretation is shown in Figure 4.5.

Figure 4.5 A five-point scale of learning inefficiencies

PERCEPTION

The individual does not recognize an activity as learning – he or she simply sees it as 'doing a piece of work'.

The learning opportunity is not perceived as relevant to the needs of, and the benefits sought by, the learner.

The learner partially recognizes something as involving learning, but fails to use the opportunity fully.

An off-the-job learning experience is badly designed and/or implemented.

The opportunity for learning is provided in a way that fits poorly with the way in which an individual likes to learn.

IMPLEMENTATION

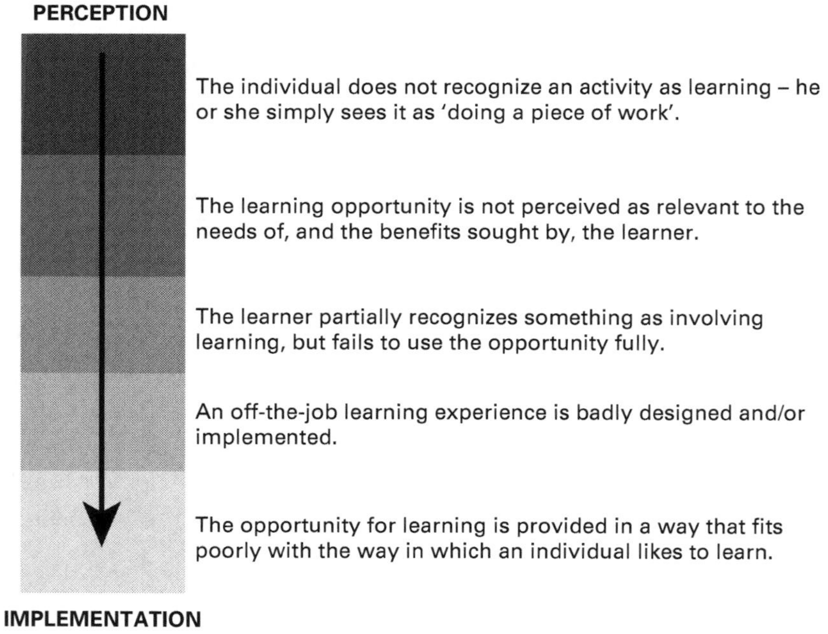

A successful coach-mentor, therefore, needs to understand the range of factors that influence a learner's perception of learning opportunities as well as the factors that influence the effective implementation of those opportunities. Motivational factors are also critical. We'll consider each of these in turn.

Perception of opportunities

The first step in developing an accurate perception of learning opportunities is to establish that a real need to learn exists. Some people may be genuinely unaware that they need to learn anything new at all. Once a need has been recognized, however, it is likely that previous experiences of learning will significantly affect perceptions or paradigms. People who equate learning only with the classroom or training course will have a limited vision of learning and will need to be made aware of the many opportunities for learning that exist in the workplace. Past experiences of learning – particularly if they were negative – will also have a powerful influence.

As Hay (1995) explains: 'I understand paradigm shift to mean that we change to such a different model for perceiving the world that we realize that we have shifted to a different level of awareness.' It is probably true to say that most people are only vaguely aware of the learning process and are therefore quite likely to miss opportunities.

This is particularly true when it comes to recognizing the valuable opportunities to learn from mistakes. All too often, mistakes are associated with blame and denial and are quickly passed over and forgotten. The culture of the organization is important in this respect. If the prevailing culture is one of blame and fear, then the perception of learning needs and opportunities is likely to be correspondingly low. Similarly, if the structure and nature of a job are restrictive, repetitive and boring, it is more difficult to stimulate enthusiasm for on-the-job learning. Creating a genuine and active learning culture around a learner's current job is a key task of the modern coach-mentor.

Implementation of learning opportunities

Assuming a reasonably high level of awareness and perception of learning opportunities, learning effectiveness can be significantly influenced by the possibility or reality of the way the opportunities are implemented.

For instance:

- A learner may imagine that a range of opportunities exists for him or her, but in reality these may not actually be easily available or affordable.

- The impact of the line manager and colleagues may also influence the implementation of opportunities. The line manager who only pays lip service to the need for learning will often find reasons to deny access or adequate time.

- Operational pressures from colleagues and direct reports may also lessen a learner's willingness and ability to seize relevant opportunities.

- The quality of the coach, mentor, trainer or facilitator will have a powerful influence on the quality of the learning experience.

- Learners themselves may have blockages to learning of which they may be unaware. This is particularly true of what are called 'defensive barriers' when, for reasons of status, prestige or pride, a learner unconsciously fails to take maximum advantage of a learning opportunity.

- Blockages to learning may come from the learning methods employed. The learning design or technology used may simply be inappropriate to the content.

- The learning institution itself may be inappropriate – a college environment might be unsuitable for a programme for high-flying marketing executives, or an Outward Bound course inappropriate for learning basic financial management techniques.

- The method of assessing and evaluating performance, progress and results can also be critical. An obsession with passing a test to gain a qualification can be a block to developing a wider understanding of a subject or skill.

An awareness of these 'implementation factors' is crucial if the coach and mentor are to help to avoid learning inefficiencies.

The learner's motivation

An individual's desire to make the most of learning opportunities is often influenced by his or her perception of the rewards and punishment involved. 'The more you learn, the more you'll earn', for example, has become a recognized phrase. A person's social and career successes to date, as well as his or her future aspirations and vision, are also important motivational influences. These perceptions will clearly be different for individual people at various stages of their careers.

Our own research evidence suggests, however, that learners are motivated most effectively by the interest, enjoyment, satisfaction and challenge of the learning process itself rather than simply by the rewards and punishments related to learning. The former factors are termed 'intrinsic' motivators, the latter 'extrinsic' motivators. As we have already seen, individual learning style preferences and learning capabilities each have a bearing on a learner's motivation. Faced with opportunities that do not appeal or which seem too difficult, a learner's motivation is likely to be low.

Finally, an individual's self-confidence and general personality have to be taken into account. Building self-confidence, self-awareness and self-esteem is a critical part of the modern coach-mentor's role. The higher the levels of confidence, awareness and esteem, the higher the learner's motivation to seize learning opportunities and to take responsibility for improving his or her levels of performance will be.

The challenge for the modern coach and mentor is first to recognize the interrelated influences in the 'learning matrix' and then to identify techniques, tactics and skills to handle them. Figure 4.6 illustrates the range of influences that have to be managed by the successful coach or mentor.

Figure 4.6 The learning efficiency matrix

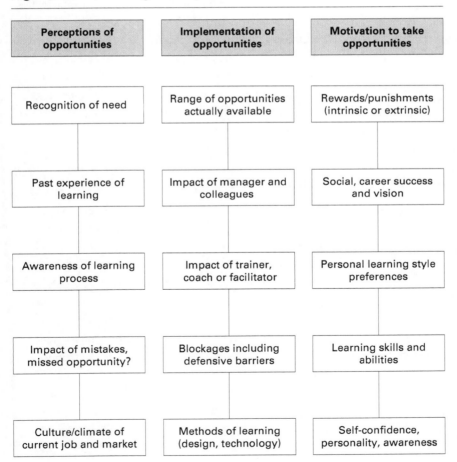

Perceptions of opportunities	Implementation of opportunities	Motivation to take opportunities
Recognition of need	Range of opportunities actually available	Rewards/punishments (intrinsic or extrinsic)
Past experience of learning	Impact of manager and colleagues	Social, career success and vision
Awareness of learning process	Impact of trainer, coach or facilitator	Personal learning style preferences
Impact of mistakes, missed opportunity?	Blockages including defensive barriers	Learning skills and abilities
Culture/climate of current job and market	Methods of learning (design, technology)	Self-confidence, personality, awareness

Training inefficiencies

Coaching and mentoring have now become one of the most frequently used approaches in the UK corporate learning armoury, after on-the-job training and the traditional training course. Viewing them as just another weapon in the learning mix may suit some organizations. For others, they may provide what some people describe as the 'essential glue that makes training courses stick'. What they are referring to is that coaching and mentoring programmes can provide an ongoing and one-to-one opportunity to reinforce and apply the learning that occurs in a typical classroom-based training course. As with Goleman's popularizing of emotional intelligence, so coaching and mentoring may now be the 'popular' answer to deficiencies that have long been known to exist with traditional training methodologies.

In the last century, research by the German psychologist Ebbinghaus (1850–1909) produced results (since validated by scores of other research) which showed that 90 per cent of what was learnt in a class was forgotten within 30 days and 60 per cent was forgotten after one hour. Similarly, Roy Harrison, policy adviser for the Institute of Personnel and Development, reported US research which showed that on average only 10–20 per cent of learning through training transfers into people's work (Harrison, 1998). Other surveys have shown that more than half of those attending training courses felt that 'they already knew most or quite a lot of the content', a third felt that 'the training made no difference at all to their performance' and only 2 per cent felt that 'the training had broken new ground'.

With our current level of understanding about how people learn, the main explanation for these types of deficiencies is most probably the application of the outdated approaches of delivering learning (Goleman, 1996):

> People have not made a clear distinction in training methodologies between kinds of abilities, technical skills and the domain of personal abilities, that I call emotional intelligence. But the brain does... Emotional intelligence, unlike the cognitive and technical skills, entails a more primitive part of the brain – the limbic centres or the emotional brain. The emotional brain learns differently from the neo-cortex, where technical skills and cognitive abilities reside. The neo-cortex learns fine in the classroom model, or from a book or from a CD-ROM. In other words, it learns quickly, it can learn in a single trial, its mode is associational. It ties new knowledge to an existing network and that happens very quickly in the brain.
>
> The emotional brain learns in a completely different mode, through repetition, through practice, through models. In other words, it learns through a model which is that of habit change. That being the case, people need a certain set of elements in a training approach if it is going to be effective.

Goleman bases his criticisms of these traditional methods on what he sees as the widespread failure to appreciate the implications of emotional intelligence theories. He claims: 'It should come as no surprise then that we advocate that, for certain topics (like personal skills), coaching and mentoring could be most sensibly seen as "preferred options" in helping people to learn.'

Structured reflection

Helping people to learn how to learn is the main aim of the coach-mentor. It is clear that new approaches to learning are essential. It is also clear to us that the definition of learning merely as a process does not really suit its overall importance in our emerging society. We therefore offer the following definition: 'Learning is both a process and a continuous state of mind, which transcends all traditional organizational boundaries and structures, and has become a central feature of the way we live.'

So how does an individual increase his or her ability to learn? Lucas (2001) believes it is through studying the 5Rs: 'So, think not of the 3Rs, but of the exciting new 5Rs – Resourcefulness, Remembering, Resilience, Reflectiveness, and Responsiveness. These skills are at the heart of what makes a competent lifelong learner.'

Whitmore (1997) believes these qualities are at the core of coaching: 'Building awareness, responsibility and self-belief is the goal of a coach... our potential is realized by optimizing our own individuality and uniqueness, never by moulding them to another's opinion of what constitutes best practice.'

We believe Whitmore's goal for coaches is best achieved by concentrating on the most important of Lucas's 5Rs: reflectiveness or 'structured reflection'. As Warren Bennis wrote (in Lucas, 2001):

> Reflecting on experience is a means of having a Socratic dialogue with yourself, asking the right questions at the right time, in order to discover the truth of yourself and your life. What really happened? Why did it happen? What did it do to me? What did it mean to me? In this way, one locates and appropriates the knowledge one needs or, more precisely, recovers what one had forgotten, and becomes, in Goethe's phrase, the hammer rather than the anvil.

Reflection can be considered as essentially a mental process. It provides a way of thinking about relatively complex experiences or unstructured and disparate thoughts, behaviours and feelings for which there is no obvious pattern or theme, with the purpose of extracting learning and meaning.

The OCM use a powerful tool called the 'Reflection note', which forces learners to take a structured and disciplined approach to reflecting on their experiences and on the links between thoughts, feelings and behaviour. Reflective writing provides an opportunity for coach-mentors to gain further and deeper insights from their practice through deeper reflection on their experiences, and through further consideration of other perspectives from people and theory.

When reflecting on an experience in order to learn, we would encourage you to explore the model illustrated in Figure 4.2. This corresponds to the four learning style preferences described earlier:

1 What has happened and why did it happen that way? (Activist)

2 How did you think, feel and behave? (Reflector)

3 What have you learnt from, what sense can you make from, the experience? (Theorist)

4 What are you going to do in the future as a result of this experience? (Pragmatist)

Reflection note

- Exactly what happened and what do you believe caused it to happen that way?
- How did you think, feel and behave during the experience?
- What were the main learning points for you from this experience?
- What might you do differently in the future, if anything, following this learning experience?

Reflective learning

Elaine Patterson had been a senior manager and director in the NHS and Civil Service for over 20 years when maternity leave forced a re-evaluation of her priorities, interests and commitments. Elaine had always been interested in people and people development and came to the Oxford School's coaching and mentoring qualification programmes because of the content and blended learning approach. Below are extracts from her final assessment to the school. We have included what Elaine wrote about her learning experience to illustrate the profound and transformational effects of deep learning.

The blended learning programme was completely new to me but gave me a useful range of complementary challenges and support, while also freeing me to experiment. The process felt iterative, dynamic and unfolding rather than linear.

I found the focus on holistic learning, reflection and the production of evidence of learning new but, once I broke through my initial hesitation, refreshing. I also regularly reviewed my progress against my self-assessment scores.

I enjoyed the challenge of separating out my observations of what was happening from how I behaved, thought or felt about the situation and from which I could surface my main learning and resulting action points.

As I worked through the programme and pulled from past and current work and life experiences I felt that I was continually asking myself:

- What am I learning about myself?
- What am I learning about myself as a coach-mentor?
- What am I learning about my learners?
- What am I learning about coach-mentoring in the context of my organization and work?

My learning curve felt initially very faltering and steep but then rapidly accelerated as I was able to put the parts of the jigsaw together – and it felt very reminiscent of learning to ski! I felt unsure, excited but willing to discover and explore. I felt like a tanker starting to leave the dock but gradually with practice and commitment felt myself start to feel in the flow; to start to relax and open up; to trust myself to find the 'knight's move' question; to rewire based on a dialogue with experience and learning; a moving from 'doing' to 'being'...

From this I have learnt to appreciate and accept strengths without focusing only on my gaps and areas for development. I now actively welcome and encourage feedback as well as being comfortable with providing constructive feedback. I have also learnt to ditch a misplaced and handicapping sentimentality, to be more direct in expressing myself and my needs appropriately, and to be more pragmatic.

Building 'ballast'

It was in my reading about spiritual intelligence that I had become aware that while I had a strong values system I needed to create an explicit belief system or 'ballast' to support my practice as a coach-mentor. That I needed to develop a strong calm and peaceful centre within myself and that the seeds of my exploration had been germinating for a long time triggered by changing family circumstances.

▶

I felt that I needed some framework which would provide meaning and which would help me to organize my understanding of life's apparent paradoxes or dichotomies. I learnt from Gibran's *The Prophet* that the seeds of one also contain the seeds of the other, ie love and loss; life and death; happiness and sadness; similarity and difference; togetherness and solitude; giving and receiving; trust and betrayal; and how a person's response to these inherent fractures determines an individual's capacity and capability for joy and happiness, reconciliation and forgiveness, and empathy and understanding.

Reflecting in action

I have learnt that the quality of the relationship is happening in the conversation. I have moved into reflecting in action, which is about both being in the moment and having a helicopter view of what is happening at that moment. A major learning for me is to forget about the skills and techniques and focus on the process. When I do this I have found that a greater relaxation and the release of ego paradoxically enable me to make a better social and emotional connection with the learner. Also, I have learnt to be more aware of the range of possible blocks or obstacles which can dilute focused concentration; and to acknowledge where barriers occur and for these to be honestly addressed either with the learner, as part of my own reflective practice and/or with my supervisor.

I have also learnt how to observe objectively without judgement – feeling almost like a state of 'nothingness', 'of letting go' – and where instead judgement is replaced by an all-encompassing spirit of curiosity about what is being said and what the individual is experiencing. I now try to spot what is missing or hidden and to communicate with the conscious mind through thoughts, feelings, imagery and sounds. To relax and trust that in focusing intention, thoughts and feelings follow; to experience the other person for who they are as well as what they are saying and to spot where this is going wrong. I realize that it is possible through processes of insight, self-awareness, intentional effort, practice and emotional commitment to reconfigure the brain and change behaviours.

Changing paradigms or triple-loop learning

Standing back, I am now aware that I have been through a process of triple-loop learning which surpassed my expectations, providing me with the opportunity to achieve a number of paradigm shifts.

Looking back, I can see that the themes underlying my work with all of my learners ultimately revolved to some extent around their search for identity; a reframing; a challenging of assumptions about themselves and their contexts; a reconnection with their values; and a search for authenticity to some degree or another. Triple-loop learning has helped me to 'listen' to how I feel and has enabled me to make a significant move to a different plane of self-awareness, self-management and responsibility. Triple-loop learning greatly deepened my personal development during the programme – and beyond – and helped me translate this into my signature presence as a coach-mentor with my learners.

Awareness of self

My developing self-awareness grew out of the task set for me to move from my current reality at the start of the programme to the achievement of my SMART goals. For me this has hinged on the development of my emotional intelligence – ie in how I manage myself and my relationships with others – together with my spiritual intelligence – ie my creative, integrative, meaning-giving and transformative centre. This with reflective practice has enabled me to move into self-coaching.

I realize that a new perception of self has emerged where my journey has taken me from director to coach-mentor; from being office-based to working from home; to working on a process rather than a content agenda; from employee to freelancer; from a DINKY (double income no kids) to a networked mum with a range of work and leisure activities including voluntary, community and school work; from doing to being. I am now building my life in line with my values, beliefs and way that I want to live.

'In the moment'

The work on myself has enabled me move from textbook to 'in the moment' coaching. My improved self-awareness and management of myself have enabled me to manage my own reactivity when I enter the 'coaching bubble' in order to better focus totally on the learner's needs, to instinctively build empathy and rapport, to listen attentively, to ask the incisive question, to give constructive feedback, to demonstrate integrity, and to create openness and trust with positive intention.

Principles of adult learning

Summing up the key principles from this chapter, we believe the main purpose of coaching and mentoring is to help the learner to learn. This is best achieved by the following.

Learning as dependent on an emotional readiness

Learning starts with an emotional readiness, a 'get ready, go and steady', and is the relationship between the learner's interior and exterior world. Learning requires the creation of a supportive learning environment and a learner's determination and motivation to act.

Learning cannot take place without a secure base and working with the right blend of competence, support and challenge tailored for each individual learner. Fear, threat, and anxiety physically and chemically shut down the brain's capacity to learn, reducing awareness, inhibiting calculated risk-taking and forcing fight or flight.

Where coach-mentoring is taking learners on an intellectual and emotional journey from current reality to their goal, the key to success lies in providing a psychological safety, a sense of time and space without fear of failure blended with challenges that do not scare but build self-esteem and self-belief. Learning has to be fun and enjoyable with a focus on what excites, enthuses, draws and inspires.

Learning starts with developing the learner's self-awareness

Learning starts with the learner's developing awareness, both in knowing what is happening and knowing what is being experienced. Awareness is built with focused attention, clarity and concentration – and is dependent on good-quality feedback. It is what we are not aware of that controls us. Therefore, the skill of the coach-mentor is to raise and sustain the level of awareness to the appropriate level within the goals and context of each learner.

Learning with purpose

To be effective, learning has to have a clear purpose. People need to know why they need to learn something and need to be involved in the planning and evaluation of their learning. In coaching and mentoring, the purpose of learning is almost always to achieve some kind of change. This may be to embrace a positive change or to cope appropriately with a negative change. It is the process that drives the development of increased knowledge, increased self-awareness, increased emotional and spiritual intelligence as well as increased skills and abilities.

Learning comes from experience

Adults need to learn experientially and will draw upon their reservoir of experience (including mistakes) for learning. Structured reflection helps the individual to focus and so extract the maximum effective learning from his or her experiences. The role of the coach-mentor is to suggest a motivation and a structure to improve the learner's reflection skills.

Learning as a lifelong journey

Learning has no end point and is never finished – moving instead to different levels of performance, understanding and awareness. Coach-mentors should strive to make their clients independent, self-aware and self-developing learners. Coach-mentors need to be careful not to build any dependence into the coach-mentoring relationship.

Endnotes

Armstrong, M (2006) *Armstrong's Handbook of Human Resource Management Practice*, 10th edn, Kogan Page, London

Caplin, J (2003) *Coaching for the Future: How smart companies use coaching and mentoring* CIPD, London

Cross, J (2012) New architecture v. learning, *HR Examiner* [online] http://www.hrexaminer.com/new-architecture-v-learning-by-jay-cross/ [accessed 30 August 2016]

Gardner, H, (2006) *Multiple Intelligences: New horizons in theory and practice*, 2nd edn, Basic Books, New York

Goleman, D (1996) *Emotional Intelligence*, Bloomsbury Publishing, London

Guest, G (1999) *Building Learning Organisations*, paper to the European Consortium of Learning Organisations Conference, Glasgow

Handy, C (2002) *The Age of Unreason: New thinking for a new world*, Random House, New York

Harrison, R ([1991] 1998) *People Management*, CIPD, London

Hay, J (1995) *Transformational Mentoring: Creating developmental alliances for changing organisational cultures*, Sherwood Publishing, Watford

Honey, P and Mumford, A (1986) *Using Your Learning Styles*, Peter Honey Publications, Maidenhead

Kolb, D A (1984) *Experiential Learning: Experience as the source of learning development*, Prentice-Hall, Englewood, NJ

Lucas, B (2001) *Power Up Your Mind: Learn faster, work smarter*, Nicholas Brealey, London

Maddern, J (1994) *Accelerated Learning*, Accelerated Learning Centre, Bristol

Mayo, A and Lank, E (1994) *The Power of Learning: A guide to gaining competitive advantage*, CIPD, London

Mumford, A (1999) *Effective Learning*, CIPD, London

Pedler, M (2008) *Action Learning for Managers*, 2nd edn, Gower, Aldershot

Salovay, P, Brackett, M and Mayer, J (2004) *Emotional Intelligence: Key readings on the Mayer and Salovey model*, National Professional Resources Inc, New York

Senge, P (1992) *The Fifth Discipline*, Random House, New York

Starr, J (2003) *The Coaching Manual*, Pearson Education, Oxford

Tute, W (1995) *People Management*, CIPD, London

Whitmore, J ([1997] 2002) *Coaching for Performance*, Nicholas Brealey, London

Zohar, D and Marshall, I (2001) *Spiritual Intelligence: The ultimate intelligence*, Bloomsbury, London

Awareness of individual differences

05

New sections have been added to this chapter in recognition of the continued growth in interest across the coaching and mentoring profession in philosophy, psychology and human nature. One of the key functions of coaching and mentoring is to enhance self-awareness. It is our contention that if coach-mentors are unaware of their own make-up (of who they are, of their own motivations), then they are unlikely to be capable of fully understanding and helping the person they are coaching.

Each learner and each coach-mentor is different and these many differences make each of us unique. It follows then that each coach-mentoring relationship is also unique. When we think of individual differences, we typically refer to personality traits, values, beliefs, interests, intelligence, ability, personal motivation, learning styles and self-concept, race, religion and gender, to name just a few. Therefore, the best coach-mentoring interventions should be designed to identify and accommodate these personal differences and individual needs. As such, it is important that coach-mentors understand more clearly how and why people behave as they do. This brings us into the realms of psychology, psychotherapy and philosophy. These are well-established disciplines with a wide variety of theories and often strongly held differences of interpretation and opinions.

It is our view that it is not necessary to be fully qualified in these disciplines to be an effective coach-mentor but it is important to have a reasonable grounding in some of the more widely agreed aspects of these disciplines. Also it is not uncommon for sophisticated purchasers of coaching and mentoring services to ask providers to explain their particular approach. These client requirements may challenge some coach-mentors to articulate their theories about personal development, psychological models and approaches. In this chapter then, we discuss those aspects that we believe are of importance to a coach-mentor as an introduction for those who may wish to probe more deeply.

Beliefs and values

If you believe you can or you believe you can't you are probably right.
(Henry Ford)

Beliefs are those things that a person holds to be absolutely true. An individual may have thousands of beliefs, many of them adopted at early stages of his or her life from other people who were significant at that time. Even though a person's beliefs are driven by his or her values, they are important in their own right because they help shape behaviour and how events are interpreted. Some beliefs are empowering and useful to have, but there are also those that are limiting. Most people have a belief or point of view about human potential, from, 'I can do anything' through to the other end of the spectrum: 'I am the way I am and cannot change.'

The coach-mentor comes into the relationship with his or her own thoughts, opinions and judgments of the learner. A part of managing oneself while coaching is to be able to identify one's own stuff and deal with it appropriately. Coach-mentors need to understand themselves as a coach before they can hope to understand what might be going on with the learners. So if the coach-mentor can establish the learners' values, it may help them to make fulfilling choices, take appropriate decisions, formulate action plans, and lead a balanced life. Asking questions that relate to values and beliefs can help to raise the learners' self-awareness of how their feelings and behaviours are affected by actions and events that support or challenge their values. The following are examples of questions a coach-mentor might use in a conversation to achieve this:

- Can you describe the values that drive you?
- Which are those things that are really important to you?
- How could you harness those values to help your own fulfilment and the wellbeing of those around you?
- What do you think are your strengths?
- Do you know what is at the main source of your energy and enthusiasm?

Culture and diversity

A culture can provide specific ways to see the world and is influenced by many things. For a nation, these influences will include their history, geography, ethnicity and politics. For an organization, culture will be shaped by its founders, leadership, working conditions and competitors, among other things. These cultural influences will be a part of the background of the learner who, it can be seen, may well belong to several cultural groups, and the coach needs to take this into account. In his book *Coaching across Cultures* (2004), Rosinski provides some useful insights and frameworks to help a coach take a multicultural approach to his or her practice and it is well worth reading if you wish to broaden your understanding of this area.

Coaching is, by its very nature, a one-to-one process where personal traits and characteristics come to the fore. Therefore, a coach-mentor needs to take into account other aspects of diversity as well as culture. These include: ethnicity, religion, age, sexual orientation, physical and mental disability and gender, the last of which is explored in more detail in the next section. However, if coach-mentors are not attuned to their own cultural and diversity issues there is a risk this may influence their coaching. Indeed, ignoring these differences in coaching for the sake of being politically correct, or because of our own discomfort, can block learning for both the coach-mentor and the learner.

Coach-mentors can also be at risk of assuming a similarity in cultures that may block the learning for their learners. It is wise to follow the advice of Adler (2002), a writer on cross-cultural issues, when she says: 'Assume difference until similarity is proven.' Often there are different ways of achieving the same common understanding. The coach-mentor should try to sensitively help the learner find alternate approaches that will work sympathetically within the specific culture or diversity while retaining the learner's own identity.

Gender

Many coach-mentors believe that coaching men and women requires different approaches. The dynamics of gender difference have been discussed in many books: Tannen (2007) and Gray (1992) are notable authors in this field, while Thomson *et al* (2005) have related gender to the subject of leadership. They offer the following observation:

> In our view, men and women lead differently; for historical reasons, business organizations bear the imprints of masculine values, norms and patterns of behaviour and that, as a result of this, the cultures of companies frequently don't 'fit' women, particularly at senior levels where women remain thin on

the ground... A new compact between the sexes must be reached about how our large companies are organized, managed and led, that makes them better adapted to and more welcoming for women.

SKAI Associates' research (Sobolewsha, 2007) in the UK makes a similar observation:

Given that most organizations are more male dominated it's useful to ask the question, 'What would the female traits, if nurtured, bring to the organization?' Successful coaching will... find ways to have a woman's natural traits and abilities deployed at scale in the workplace. Would it be a legitimate objective for coaching in organizations to reduce the domination of traditional 'male' traits and increase the influence of 'feminine' traits?

If it is acknowledged that men and women have different traits, then SKAI Associates suggest the implications for coaching might be understood as laid out in Table 5.1

Table 5.1 Possible coaching intervention

	Things learners will stretch themselves with	**Things that limit learners' potential**
Men	• Being a lead – taking on the mantle of making and implementing decisions • Solving gritty problems	• Disregard relationships • Don't like/can't be bothered with collaborating • Too much operational interfering
Women	• Creative effective relationships • Working with personal independent freedom • Expressing themselves well/being open	• Talk down personal ability – to self and others • Tend to think small(er) • Dislike confrontation

These are important issues that we recommend everyone should reflect on because it is not immediately obvious to us that it is appropriate for a coach-mentor to treat male learners differently to female learners. We believe it would be better to treat each learner as an individual and not stereotyped by gender.

Philosophies

As we have shown in the previous chapters, you don't need to be a psychologist to know that learners' motivations are a key factor in their successful learning and effective change. As the cliché says: 'You can lead a horse to water, but you cannot make it drink.' Even when people are motivated to change, it can be all too easy for them to slip back into their old habits or resign themselves to a situation because it is part of their personality or the way they see the world.

Another way of saying 'the way they see the world' is to describe it as a personal philosophy. We believe that philosophy can be defined more fully. In our own words: 'Philosophy is the examination of basic concepts such as truth, existence, reality, causality and freedom. The combination of these basic concepts forms a person's guiding or underlying principles.'

There are many published philosophies, some more accepted and/or well-known than others. There used to be a clearly defined demarcation between what were collectively known as 'Western' and 'Eastern' philosophies, but these now appear to be coming together, with the recognition that both have value. There are also a number of theories of human nature that seek to make sense of the similarities and differences between people. Many of the ideas developed by the historical and modern personality theorists stem from the basic philosophical assumptions they hold.

The following seven categories describe some of the fundamental questions that are at the root of most philosophies:

1 Hereditary versus environment – is personality largely determined by genetics/heredity (nature), by environment and experiences (nurture), or by both?

2 Freedom versus determinism – do we have control over our own behaviour; can we direct our own actions and understand the motives behind them or is our behaviour basically determined by some other force over which we may not have control?

3 Uniqueness versus universality – are we all unique or are large groups of humans basically similar in their nature?

4 Proactive versus reactive – do we primarily act through our own initiative, or do we react to outside stimuli?

5 Optimistic versus pessimistic – are we basically positive or negative? Can we alter our personalities or do they remain the same throughout our whole lives?

6 Past versus present – is our personality created and set by early events in our lives, or can we develop our personality in response to current experiences?

7 Equilibrium versus growth – are we motivated simply to maintain a psychological balance, or are we driven by an urge to grow and develop?

You might like to take a few moments to consider and answer these questions for yourself to help to describe your own philosophy. To assist you, we have provided a framework listing the seven philosophical questions in Figure 5.1. Consider each one in turn and mark the relative point on each line to represent your own philosophical perspective.

Figure 5.1 Philosophical perspectives

Factors	My philosophical perspective	Factors
Hereditary	←- -→	Environment
Determinism	←- -→	Free will
Universality	←- -→	Uniqueness
Reactive	←- -→	Proactive
Pessimism	←- -→	Optimism
Past	←- -→	Present
Equilibrium	←- -→	Growth

Existential philosophy

One philosophy that we believe is particularly appropriate and relevant to coaching is existentialism. This is a fusion of philosophical and psychological thought mainly founded by Søren Kierkegaard (1813–1855). Existentialism, broadly defined, is a set of philosophical systems concerned with free will, choice and personal responsibility: because we make choices based on our experiences, beliefs and biases, those choices are unique to us. The key concepts are that:

- everyone has free will;
- life is a series of choices that creates stress;
- few decisions are without any negative consequences;
- some things are irrational or absurd without explanation;
- if one makes a decision, one must follow through.

This leads us to the well-known phrase by Jean-Paul Sartre (1943): 'We do not choose to be free. We are condemned to freedom.'

The existential view holds that people have no inherent characteristics and instead are endlessly remaking or discovering themselves in a movement towards self-realization – a progression of discovering who the real 'you' is. Anxiety comes from pretending to be 'a character' by identifying ourselves with our roles, refusing to take responsibility for our choices, and taking our social attributes as 'wired in' rather than chosen. Crisis is inevitable and to be welcomed as positive because, existentialists believe, a crisis only occurs when you are equipped and ready to deal with it.

The main implications of existential philosophy for coaching are:

- The emphasis on 'being' rather than 'doing'.
- The recognition that we cannot always resolve conflict but must learn to accept and live with it.
- We should face uncertainty – acknowledge that change is constant – and strive to keep a balance.

Typical existential coaching questions would include:

- Do you like the direction of your life? If not, what are you doing about it?
- What are the aspects of your life that satisfy you most?
- What is preventing you from doing what you really want to do?

Ontological coaching

In the latter part of the 20th century, the integration of significant developments in the fields of philosophy and biology produced a new discipline with the general name of 'ontology of the human observer'. As a discipline it is grounded in recent developments in existential philosophy, the philosophy of language and the biology of cognition.

Ontology is the study of being and is an inquiry into the nature of human existence. It encompasses major existential issues of meaning, fulfilment, happiness and worthiness in our personal and professional lives. The concept is built around two key questions: what is it to be a human being, and what does it mean to live and work well? Ontological coaching focuses on exploring a person's 'way of being', referring to how they are at any point in time, and in particular refers to how they observe or perceive the world. The way of being is a dynamic interrelationship between language, emotions and physiology. Ontologists believe that:

- Humans are continually speaking and listening. The conversations that we participate in and the actual words we choose to use, internally and externally, form an important part of what is real for us.
- Humans are also emotional beings: their moods and emotions colour how they see the world and how they behave.
- Human physiology is the combination of the physical body, our posture, and the working of our internal systems and organs.
- Change happens only when there are shifts in all three domains, and when this occurs a different world is observed and new possibilities for action become available to the learner.

An ontological coach-mentor seeks to facilitate learning and change by working on a combination of all three areas of the learner's language, emotions and physiology. Working on all three dimensions can not only lead to effective behavioural action, but also help to build a more meaningful life. James Flaherty is a well-known author who coaches from a principle-shaped ontological stance. He suggests that coaching should follow these five operating principles (Flaherty, 1999: 10–12):

1 The relationship is the most important principle and forms the background to the coaching efforts. To be mutually satisfying, the relationship must be based on mutual respect, trust and freedom of expression.

2 The coach-mentor should be pragmatic in being willing to continually learn from experience, innovate and correct what is not producing the desired practical outcome.

3 A 'two track' approach requires the coach-mentor to divide themselves into two people: the one who acts in life and the one who watches (the observer). The coach-mentor should observe themselves and question their own assumptions and guard against their own blindness, prejudices and stubbornness.

4 The coach-mentor should acknowledge the learner is always/already in the middle of their lives. They will already have their own way of doing things and the coach-mentor must adapt their approach to fit the learner.

5 Using only techniques doesn't work. Techniques can prevent the coach-mentor from engaging fully with the learner with openness, courage and curiosity. Techniques cannot replace the human heart and creativity in coaching.

Psychological influences

The various branches of psychology attempt to explain how and why humans behave as they do, based on different philosophical standpoints. These psychological concepts bring with them a host of theories and models that explain the coaching and mentoring relationship.

From works such as those by the psychologist Peltier (2002) we see that a good range of psychological therapeutic frameworks are being adapted for application in the coaching context. As we have already emphasized, to practise as a coach-mentor a degree in psychology is not necessary but we do believe it is important to have a reasonable fluency in the language of psychology and a level of general understanding of the main concepts.

However, recent advances in neuroscience are starting to understand how the brain creates the mind and consequently this section would not be complete without an exploration of cognitive and behavioural neuroscience and its potential relevance for a coach-mentor.

Cognitive and humanistic neuroscience

Cognitive neuroscience is an offshoot of human psychology – the study of cognitive processes and their implementation in the brain. The focus is to try to understand how the brain creates the mind. To identify the neural substrates of mental processes such as attention, memory, language, learning, reasoning and decision making. Cognitive neuroscientists use methods drawn from brain damage, neuropsychology, cognitive psychology, functional neuro-imaging and computer modelling.

Behavioural neuroscience is the study of how the nervous system influences behavioural effects in the areas of motivation, perception, learning and memory, and attention and motor performance. Behavioural neuroscience overlaps with psychology in seeking to understand the biological basis of a person's actions at the level of brain circuitry, neurons and neurotransmitters. Research in this area investigates the complex interplay between the brain, behaviour and environment, utilizing multiple levels of experimental analysis.

For a coach-mentor, the interest in this is the notion that if you want to know what makes people tick you start by trying to understand the physical processes that are taking place in their minds.

A breakthrough for many coaching clients is the understanding that the brain is not 'hard-wired' in childhood and that they can change their thoughts and feelings, and consequently change their behaviour.

Researchers used to believe that changes in the brain primarily took place in early childhood. Most people grew up believing (and many still do) that by early adulthood the brain's structure was fixed. Neuroscience research in recent years has shown that the brain continues to create new neural pathways and alter existing ones in response to new experience throughout our life span.

Coaching and mentoring provides opportunities, possibilities and context for change. The science suggests that new learning and experiences create new neural networks. The implication is that using neuroscience as one part of a coaching practice can re-enforce and strengthen behavioural changes.

Ongoing research in the field of neuroscience is regularly changing the understanding of human dynamics. Coach-mentors do not need a degree in brain science to learn the basic, practical principles that can influence their approach to motivation and behavioural change. There is growing evidence that learning a little about how a client's brain (as well as your own) works can make you a better coach-mentor.

Having considered the recent advances in neuroscience, it is appropriate to examine three principal psychological schools or origins: psychoanalytical, behavioural and humanistic. Each of these is subdivided into more specialized concepts. In this section we briefly explore some of the most widely used theoretical influences that inform the coach-mentors' approach to their practice. Most relate to an existential philosophical perspective.

Humanistic

Viewing human nature as conscious, self-directed, self-actualizing and healthy distinguishes the humanistic psychology from psychoanalytic and behaviouristic psychology. Although there is no single accepted theory of what humanistic psychology actually is, there are some very consistent themes running throughout the concept. The major theme is that of change: the process of change; how humans strive for change to become more fulfilled and achieve their potential. Leading psychologists in the development of humanistic psychology were Abraham Maslow (1908–1970) and Carl Rogers (1902–1987). Humanistic theories emphasize:

- Growth and fulfilment of the self through self–mastery, self-examination and self-expression.
- Our purpose in life is to progress on a continuum of development – one that starts in early childhood but often gets blocked later on in life.
- The optimistic belief that all humans are naturally good and trustworthy.

The core implications for this approach are:

- The learners know best.
- They know what is wrong.
- They know how to move forward.

Coach-mentors using a humanistic person-centred approach need to:

- Be genuine or congruent in themselves – be transparent about their motivations and have a high level of self-awareness.
- Have unconditional positive regard or non-possessive warmth – respect and accept the learner.
- Have empathetic understanding of learners – their perceptions and the ability to stay with their emotions.
- See quality listening as an effective route to in-depth understanding.

Cognitive behavioural

Cognitive behavioural therapy (CBT) comes from a behavioural origin rather than humanistic. Its essential concept is that how people interpret an event or situation affects the way they feel about that situation and how they behave: ie it is not the situation itself that creates emotions, but rather how a person interprets that situation. This naturally leads on to the notion that if you change the way a person thinks, this will change the way a person feels and acts. Thus the route to emotional change, it is argued, is through cognitive and behaviour change.

CBT does not offer any quick fixes to achieve personal change or 'magic away' personal difficulties. Instead it emphasizes that sustained effort and commitment are required for a successful outcome to your life challenges.

CB coaching is based on a collaborative relationship that helps individuals to focus on problem solving in a structured and systematic way. Using a Socratic and non-directive approach encourages individuals to 'pull out' from themselves problem-solving strategies rather than have them handed over by the coach-mentor. CB coaching is characterized by:

- An emphasis on the achievement of clear short-term goals.

- Drawing on and adding to their existing skills help individuals to build greater self-reliance and confidence in managing change in their lives.

- The ultimate goal is for the individual to become his or her own coach-mentor.

Transpersonal psychology

The *Journal of Transpersonal Psychology* describes transpersonal psychology as 'the study of humanity's highest potential, and with the recognition, understanding, and realization of intuitive, spiritual, and transcendent states of consciousness'.

Transpersonal psychology embraces a range of values such as altruism, humanitarianism, aesthetics and ethics. It is about helping an individual identify a deeper purpose, realize his or her full potential, as well as serving the wider needs of the organization and of society. This approach also emphasizes the spiritual dimension to a person's functioning, which is called the 'higher' or 'transpersonal' self and is seen as a source of wisdom and energy. It is this reference to energy, combined with values, which is most relevant in understanding the role of transpersonal coaching and how it chimes perfectly with the perception of coaching as a positive, as opposed to remedial, activity. As Whitmore (1997) says: 'If we look for where the positive energy is, the vitality, and the spirit, and explore and build on it, then this is what will grow within an individual or a company.' In turn, this will lead to transpersonal coaching being 'an empowering process'. According to Whitmore this is because 'drilling into an individual's core values allows the coach to unearth the coachee's core strengths and creativity'.

Transpersonal coaching goes beyond the person by taking a systems approach, encouraging individuals to see themselves as part of a team, organization, family and community. A transpersonal approach to coaching would include:

- Focusing on the quality of the relationship rather than tools or techniques.
- Trusting the coaching process and respecting your intuition.
- Looking beyond the presented situation for its deeper meaning and wider implications.
- Seeing the individual as part of a complex system.

Positive psychology

Positive psychology is a relatively young branch of psychology, with Martin Seligman as its best-known advocate. He has criticized other psychologies as primarily dedicated to addressing mental illness rather than mental 'wellness'. He states in his book *Learned Optimism* (2005) that: 'The keystone of high achievement and happiness is exercising your strengths.'

Therapists, counsellors, coaches, and various other psychological professionals now use these new methods and techniques to build and broaden the lives of individuals who are not necessarily suffering from mental illness or disorder. Practical applications of positive psychology include helping individuals and organizations correctly identify their strengths and use them to increase and sustain their respective levels of wellbeing.

The positive psychology concept when applied to the world of work says that a great organization must not only accommodate the fact that each employee is different, but also capitalize on these differences. It must identify each employee's natural strengths and talents and then develop them so that his or her strengths can be used for the benefit of the individual and the organization.

Questions a coach-mentor may ask when using a positive psychology approach include:

- What are the things that you do best?
- How do you know when you are at your best?
- Tell me about a time when you were successful at doing this before.

A potential drawback of this approach is the prevailing ethos adopted by many managers and the mindset adopted by many employees: namely, that you should tackle the person's weaknesses and the strengths will take care of themselves. However, there is a growing body of evidence that suggests the opposite. The area of potentially greatest growth is in the individual's greatest strengths. Focusing on weaknesses demotivates, resulting in reduced strengths, and does not significantly improve weaknesses.

Mindfulness

Mindfulness is a modern application of the ancient practice of meditation. Although based on ancient Buddhist principles, it is not specifically related to religion or silent retreats. Western healthcare professionals have adapted these principles into Mindfulness Based Stress Reduction (MBSR) and Mindfulness Based Cognitive Therapy (MBCT).

MBSR is designed to help people cope with prolonged periods of stress, suffering with symptoms such as anger, anxiety, sleeplessness, etc. Work is the third biggest cause of stress after divorce and bereavement. Research by Oxford University showed a reduction in anxiety of 58 per cent and a reduction in stress of 40 per cent (Krusche *et al*, 2013).

MBCT focusses specifically on people with recurring depression and is recommended by the National Institute for Health and Care Excellence (NICE) as an effective treatment. Research as shown a reduction in relapse of recurrent depression averaging 43 per cent (Williams *et al*, 2014).

However, mindfulness isn't only applicable for those stressed or depressed; it claims to help anyone enjoy a more restful, healthier and happier lifestyle. Studies show a range of benefits – people feel more engaged in their work, have an increased focus, are more energized, more attentive in meetings, less distracted, sleep better and have fewer of the physical symptoms of stress.

Mindfulness, it appears, can be very effective in a surprisingly short time period. In 2015 almost 700 academic studies looked at mindfulness's positive effect on stress, brain connectivity and a range of chronic medical conditions. In one study a small group of 15 volunteers were given a session of mindfulness training each day for four days. Brain scans were done before and after and results indicated that anxiety levels fell by 39 per cent (Zeidan *et al*, 2013). This seems to fit with the claim that mindfulness strengthens a person's ability to combat negative thoughts and feelings.

It combines elements of other approaches discussed in this chapter by encouraging people to focus on the present, disregard negative thoughts, let go of the past and not worry about the future. There is also a focus on greater self-awareness of a person's own body through meditation, basic yoga and other body awareness practices such as breathing exercises and muscle relaxation. There are a number of books, audiobooks, videos, online courses and apps on the subject as well as practice groups to join.

As a way of learning to cope with the stresses of everyday life, it appears to be trendy. So much so that marketing departments have jumped in with using it as a buzzword to market such diverse products as a diet, clothing, a brand of tea and a burger.

Solutions-focused coaching

This approach moves away from problem analysis but does not ignore the problem's existence. The focus is on finding the best solution based on existing strengths and looking at what already works. A solutions focus has similar approaches to positive psychology and appreciative inquiry. All three approaches advocate a move away from focusing on the problem and recommend looking to the positives for solutions. The basic assumption of solutions-focused coaching is that for each learner specific individualized solutions for problems work best and any person is competent to solve his or her own problems.

The structure of a solutions-focused approach might look like this:

1 Acknowledge problems.

2 Define the preferred future or solution.

3 Identify potential solutions or positive actions to achieve the solution.

4 Amplify, refine and prioritize the solutions to achieve the desired result.

Gestalt psychology

Gestalt is best known as a therapeutic approach originated by Fritz Perls (1893–1970). In this concept each person is regarded as an exploring, adapting, self-reflecting, interacting social and physical being in a process of continuous change. The person is seen holistically and as an open system because existence calls for versatility and for 'creative adjustment'.

The life of each individual is full of numerous gestalts: temporary models, shapes or patterns of a person's experience that form and, when completed, dissolve. This pattern is referred to as the 'cycle of experience' and problems occur when the cycle is not completed or is blocked for some reason.

The Gestalt approach has four key concepts:

1 Greater awareness of the body, the emotions, the thoughts, the self and the environment is seen as a goal in itself.

2 Focus on the here and now and personal experiments. Don't just think about it – experience it and feel it.

3 Take personal responsibility for whatever you are experiencing or doing. Don't blame the situation or other people.

4 Unfinished business or avoidance, unexpressed emotions and avoiding confrontation prevent you being fully alive.

'The paradoxical theory of change' (Biesser, 1971) is a gestalt idea that suggests that change does not occur by trying to be what you are not but, by fully embracing who you are, change happens only when you are truly yourself. Lasting change cannot be attained through coercion or persuasion.

Applying the principles of gestalt to the practice of coaching would include:

- The coach-mentor is part of the process; the method cannot be separated from the person.
- Focus on what is happening now, not solely on what is being discussed.
- The coach-mentor works with what is, not what should be, could be or must be.
- Resistance is seen as positive and healthy, to be worked with rather than against.
- Work with the here and now, notice where the energy is and go with it.

Transactional analysis

Transactional Analysis (TA) was developed by Eric Berne (1910–1970) as a form of humanistic psychology. It aims to simplify and improve understanding of how people communicate and interact in order to help people to make better-informed decisions. TA is an interactional concept grounded in the assumption that we take current decisions based on past beliefs – beliefs that were at one time appropriate to our survival needs but that may no longer be valid.

The basic assumptions in TA are that awareness is an important first step in the process of changing our ways of thinking, feeling and behaving, and that all of us are in charge of what we do. Others do not make us feel in a certain way; rather, we respond to situations largely according to our beliefs.

The main concepts within TA (Berne, 1973) are:

- Three ego states – parent, adult, child.
- The need for 'strokes'.
- Parent drivers.
- Games.
- Life positions and life scripts – I'm ok, you're ok.

A coach-mentor using a TA approach would:

- Advocate and explain the basic concepts and terminology to raise awareness.
- Carry out a 'script' analysis to clarify their life role.
- Expose the 'game playing' and inappropriate 'drivers' to try to achieve the I'm ok, you're ok position.
- Reject the childhood decisions and beliefs.

Systems theory

Systems theory was first proposed by Ludwig von Bertalanffy (1901–1972) who saw that systems are interrelated and interact with their environments, and through this interaction they evolve.

In systems theory it is necessary not only to understand the individual parts of a system, but also to understand the relationships between those individual parts. For example, it is not enough to consider how people think separately from their emotions – rather they must be considered together to understand the relationships between them.

An example that highlights how the systems theory works is the coaching process itself, as one session can very often create an immediate change in an individual. Whether this change is positive or negative, or whether it is apparent straight away or not, an individual who has changed will react to the environment in a different way, which then has an impact on the environment, as well as on the individuals who inhabit that environment.

Systems theory will become of increasing importance with the recent growth in team coaching. A team is a good example of a complex system. One possible implication of applying this theory is the suggestion that individuals should not be coached in isolation but always in the context of the team or group (system) in which they work.

How do we apply our understanding of differences to our practice?

Having accepted that everyone is different, thinks and behaves differently and needs to be approached differently, how can that understanding be used in practice?

Psychometric assessments

Psychometric assessments have been increasingly used as a means of building awareness about an individual's preferred approaches. Individual coaches may favour the use of particular psychometric tools, such as the MBTI, Firo-B, SDI and the Enneagram, to name just a few. Many coach-mentors also use various 360- or 180-degree feedback processes. All have the objective of enabling the coach-mentor and the learner to understand the individual better so that they may work together more effectively.

Advocates of psychometrics claim a number of benefits of using such tools, such as helping the individual to build self-awareness; highlighting motivations that may not be obvious; providing clarity about strengths; identifying the particular preferences for the way he or she perceives and makes judgements about the world. Once again in our view it is not necessary to be an expert in any single psychometric tool to become an effective coach-mentor. But it is important to have a general understanding of their potential use and to have access to a more qualified colleague if a situation appears likely to benefit from their expertise.

Modelling excellence (NLP)

If you wanted to become very good at achieving particular results, a simple and rather common-sense suggestion might be to copy the thinking and behaviours of other people who seem already to be performing at a high standard to achieve those results. If you studied enough people performing at these high standards, it should be possible to establish patterns of thinking and speaking that these 'experts' use repeatedly to obtain their results. It would then be relatively simple to train people to copy these patterns and therefore achieve similarly high results.

Two Americans, Grinder and Bandler, developed these ideas in the 1970s into a theoretical framework they christened Neuro-Linguistic Programming

(NLP). This has grown into a worldwide 'movement' and has a direct application to the coaching and mentoring community.

Bandler and Grinder (1990) believed that although 'experts' have developed many innovative and effective skills, the core of their effectiveness was primarily the attitudes, approaches and philosophies they had in common that made them capable of effective work. As such, NLP has developed its own methodology and philosophical approach towards being effective within the human world, born out of pragmatism rather than theory.

One part of the explanation of why NLP has become a 'movement' is that these theories have been developed in many ways and new adherents are usually taught to believe and operate from a core set of 'presuppositions'. A typical set might be any combination of the following:

- It is possible to communicate with a person's unconscious and this is the most powerful communication.
- It is impossible not to communicate.
- The meaning of communication is the response you get.
- The words we use are not the event or the item they represent.
- The mind and the body are one system and affect each other.
- The map is not the territory. There is a huge difference between the world as it is and the world as we experience it. We create a representation of the world that suits us. If one changes one's internal map, one changes one's experience of the world.
- One should respect another person's model of the world.
- Language is a secondary representation of one's experience. When we communicate we give only 1 or 2 per cent of what we have actually experienced. The language we use is 'twice removed' from the world as it is.
- The best-quality information is behavioural.
- All behaviour is oriented towards adaptation and has as its origin a good intention.
- The law of requisite variety states that the element of the system that has most choice is the element that controls the system.
- You are in charge of your mind and therefore the results.
- Each person has all the resources they need.
- The perceived frame around a situation gives it its meaning.
- There is no failure, only feedback.
- Human beings are more complex than the theories that describe them.

Many professional psychologists and other practitioners are very sceptical about NLP because of the lack of accepted scientific support. We understand those reservations but also acknowledge the positive views of people like Nick Blanford, a learning and development manager in a City of London legal firm, who summarized the debate well during an online discussion we recently participated in:

> I think that NLP does create quite polarized views. Before I embarked on my NLP studies I was very sceptical about it so decided to train as practitioner to find out more. I have witnessed some quite alarming uses of NLP, which I think is a real shame and I think some of the NLP evangelists do it a disservice.
>
> In short, however, I feel NLP is a set of tools and techniques which have the potential to be tremendously positive for the learner. For me, coaching is far wider than staying at the non-directive end of the spectrum, although this is the space I prefer to occupy most of the time. I do bring elements of NLP into my coaching, which includes some timeline work, hypnotherapy, certain questioning techniques and lots more.
>
> My challenge has been to blend these techniques into my traditional coaching, which I feel I have achieved. Used properly, NLP doesn't get the learner to dwell in a negative state, as some psychotherapy has a tendency to do. NLP is much more about understanding ourselves better and then looking forward rather than backwards.
>
> I have used NLP to help people look at very difficult situations and reframe the experience into a more positive one by seeing it from the perspectives of others. Sometimes this new level of awareness is the only thing that has helped the learner move forward. I have found NLP to be an exceptionally useful part of my toolkit as a coach and I think it has made me much more effective both personally and professionally.
>
> But as has been said, it's horses for courses; some will love NLP and some with loathe it. Either way is fine as long as you have fully explored it and come to your own conclusions based on facts rather than hearsay.

General conclusion on awareness of individual differences

While we have not explicitly evaluated each approach in terms of effectiveness or efficacy, we have found it difficult to quantify how a specific coach-mentoring approach compares with other psychology or philosophy models.

These approaches all provide valuable insights and we believe the good coach-mentor needs to understand the underlying psychology or philosophy in order to draw from them appropriately in his or her coaching practice. However, over-reliance on one approach can produce a one-dimensional style of coaching. There is value in multiple styles and the demonstrated flexibility of the coach-mentor.

A coach-mentor needs to be able to hold multiple perspectives in mind and to look at challenges and issues from different viewpoints. Underpinning this concept is the view that there is no single truth about what enables a person to change, but rather a series of constructions that are more or less useful for evoking change.

This leads us to a common-sense conclusion that successful coach-mentors will be guided more by the situation they face than by following any single theory or dogma. They will have the knowledge, skill and confidence to be able to adjust their style flexibly, even in the course of a single conversation, in response to the situation they are facing. To do this they will, of course, need to be able to understand, interpret, respect and sometimes apply techniques from all competing brands and approaches that contribute to the emerging coaching and mentoring profession. As Carl Jung (1998) said: 'Learn your theories as well as you can, but put them aside when you touch the miracle of the living soul. Not theories, but your own creative individuality alone must decide.'

Endnotes

Adler, N J (2002) Global Companies, Global Society: There is a better way, *Journal of Management Inquiry*, **11** (3), pp 255–60

Bandler, R and Grinder, J (1990) *Frogs into Princes: Introduction to neuro-linguistic programming*, Eden Grove Editions, London

Berne, E (1973) *Games People Play: The psychology of human relationships*, Penguin, Harmondsworth

Biesser, A (1971) Paradoxical theory of change, in I Fagan and J Shepherd (eds), *Gestalt Therapy Now: Theory, techniques, applications*, HarperCollins College Division, New York

Flaherty, J (1999) *Coaching: Evoking excellence in others,* Butterworth-Heinemann, Oxford

Gallwey, T (1974) *The Inner Game of Tennis*, Random House, New York

Gray, J (1992, new edition 2012) *Men are from Mars, Women are from Venus,* Harper Paperbacks, New York

Jung, C G (1998) *Psychological Reflections: A new anthology*, J Jacobi (ed), Routledge, London

Krusche, A, Cyhlarova, E, Williams, J M G (2013) Mindfulness online: an evaluation of the feasibility of a web-based mindfulness course for stress, anxiety and depression, *BMJ Open*, 3 (11)

Peltier, B (2002) *The Psychology of Executive Coaching: Theory and application*, Brunner-Routledge, London

Rosinski, P (2004) *Coaching Across Cultures*, Nicholas Brealey, London

Sartre, J-P (1943, new translation 1990) *Being and Nothingness: An essay on phenomenological ontology*, Routledge, London

Seligman, M (2005) *Learned Optimism*, Simon & Schuster, New York

Sobolewsha, I (2007) *Coaching Men vs Coaching Women*, Research Paper, SKAI Ltd

Tannen, D (2007) *You Just Don't Understand: Women and men in conversation*, William Morrow

Thomson, P, Graham, J and Lloyd, T (2005) *A Woman's Place is in the Boardroom*, Palgrave MacMillan, Basingstoke

Whitmore, J (1987) *The Winning Mind: Strategies for successful sailing*, John Wiley & Sons, Chichester

Whitmore, J ([1997] 2002) *Coaching for Performance*, Nicholas Brealey, London

Williams, J M G *et al* (2014) Mindfulness-based cognitive therapy for preventing relapse in recurrent depression: a randomized dismantling trial, *Journal of Consulting and Clinical Psychology*, 82 (2), pp 275–86

Zeidan, F, Martucci, K T, Kraft, R A, McHaffie, J G, Coghill, R C (2013) Neural correlates of mindfulness meditation-related anxiety relief, *Social Cognitive and Affective Neuroscience*, 9 (6), pp 751–59

Feedback that builds confidence and success

06

At its most basic, the success of coaching and mentoring depends largely on the quality of communication between the people involved. Workplace communication has long been recognized as an important topic, yet two decades ago it was treated largely as a matter of language and techniques. People were trained in presentation skills, letter or report writing and telephone techniques. Today this is recognized as inadequate. The topic, now often termed 'interpersonal communication', covers a wide area of understanding about how humans interact.

Effective communication still depends on the correct choice of words and methods. A logical structure with the right level of content, plus the manner, tone and pace of delivery, are still important. However, it is now recognized that more breakdowns in communication occur because of psychological relationships than because of the 'mechanics' of communication.

Put simply, in any communication situation people bring a whole range of important 'filters' that can distort the reception, understanding, acceptance and response to messages. Figure 6.1 aims to simplify some of these complex interactions by highlighting some of the key 'filter factors' that messages have to pass through on their two-way flow between senders and receivers.

The diagram is only two-dimensional and perhaps suggests a systematic and linear flow through the process. In practice, interpersonal communication is not so smooth and many of the elements interact with each other in different ways, depending on the specific situation. For our purpose of becoming effective coach-mentors, the main lesson is not to underestimate the sensitivity and care that are necessary to achieve mutual understanding, acceptance and motivation to respond positively to messages we send and receive.

Figure 6.1 Filters

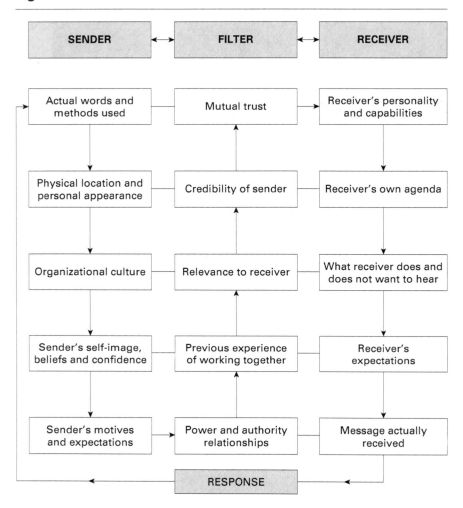

One definition of human communication is: 'The passing and receiving of messages between two or more people in order that both sender and receiver may act appropriately on their interpretation of the messages they receive.' The beauty of this definition is that it stresses that communication is a two-way process that leads to appropriate action. However, it also emphasizes the equal importance of responding to what is sent and that feedback is fundamental to effective communication.

In the context of coaching and mentoring to develop learners and their performance, it is not an exaggeration to describe feedback as 'the fuel that drives improved performance'. Feedback can drive motivation to continue and develop in two directions. Get it wrong and motivation goes backwards fast. Get it right and motivation goes steadily forward towards achieving the goal.

Feedback can be defined as communication with a person that gives information about how his or her behaviour is perceived by others and the effect it has on them. Feedback helps us to learn by increasing both the awareness of what we are doing and how we are doing it. Being able to seek and receive feedback about performance is therefore an important skill for learners too. If sought and accepted, it will greatly increase their self-awareness by helping to build a more accurate picture of how they are perceived, and it will help them to monitor the progress of their learning and development.

Observing performance

Coach-mentors will continually find themselves having to give feedback. Inexperienced learners often want to ask, 'How well am I doing?' or 'Have I improved my competence?' while an experienced learner, attempting to improve his or her performance still further, might say, 'If I do it this way, I think it will be better. What do you think?' Alternatively, a coach-mentor may be asked, 'I have the chance to apply for this new job, do you think I should do it?' Deciding on the appropriate feedback in these situations needs careful thought and should be based on the following principles:

1 To encourage the learner to articulate his or her own answer to the question.

2 To establish just how important or relevant the coach-mentor's feedback will be.

3 Having encouraged self-assessment, to give feedback which is clear, concise and constructive.

Constructive feedback increases self-awareness, offers options as well as opinions and encourages self-development. It does not mean giving only positive feedback on what a learner has done well. Feedback about poor performance, given skilfully, can be equally useful and important as an aid to development. Feedback may well result in people:

- understanding more about how they come across to others;
- choosing to change;
- keeping their behaviour on target to achieve good results;
- becoming more effective.

Potential barriers to effective feedback

There are several barriers to both giving and receiving effective feedback:

- Feedback can come as a surprise or shock when there are no clear objectives for the job or development, or when the learner and the coach-mentor do not share the same perception of these.
- The feedback may be delivered in a way that the recipient sees as concentrating on critical or unsubstantiated judgements, which offend the recipient's sense of fairness.
- There may be a problem of credibility; it is important that the recipient believes the feedback-giver is competent to comment on those points.
- Previous history of receiving negative feedback may make the recipient feel obliged to 'defend his or her corner'.
- People are 'afraid' to give feedback because they are not confident about handling the response and are concerned that feedback will damage relationships.

Sensitivity and stress

Many young people are shy and feel awkward and embarrassed in new situations where they have to perform alongside other experienced staff. More experienced people on a learning programme can also feel inhibited and unable to relax in the same way that they can in their usual work role. Helping people whose self-image may not be too high by guiding them towards early successes, encouraging positive behaviour and rewarding the efforts being made, will usually contribute towards the development of a positive 'I can do it' attitude.

Coach-mentors need to be sensitive to the mental state of the people they are working with. Of course, they must also be sensitive to their own mental state because feedback is a two-way process. In stressful situations, people react differently and not always in the most appropriate manner. It would be a mistake to underestimate how stressful some may find the coaching and mentoring session itself!

Transactional analysis

Transactional analysis (TA) is one approach to understanding the basics of the differing mental states that people have in relationships. A transaction can be defined as a signal or stimulus from one person to another, and the signal or response sent back in reply. One signal and its reply are followed by another, so that feedback becomes a series of transactions.

TA suggests that there are three predominant mental states and that we respond in any one of these states, depending on our mood and the pressure of the situation. The sensitivity of the transaction lies in recognizing, selecting or managing our own behaviour, thus responding in the most appropriate state to match both the situation and the mental state of other people involved. People continuously swap and change between the three states, which can be summarized as: parent (beliefs), adult (thinking) and child (feeling). Briefly, a description of each of these ego states is:

- Parent state – consisting of our beliefs, values, attitudes, standards and morals. We calculate and judge in this state. We can also adopt either a critical or caring outlook to the other person.

- Adult state – consisting of our rational, unemotional and analytical outlook. In this state we are happy to consider reality, facts and figures. We readily engage in problem solving and discuss calmly the implications of our decisions.

- Child state – consisting of spontaneous, fun-loving and natural reactions to events. We are curious, creative and jokey in this state. On the other hand, we may behave emotionally, irrationally, being petulant and sulky, just like spoilt children who can't get their own way.

Understanding the basics of TA and the ego states can help us to be aware of our mental state before or during a situation. This helps us respond in a way that is most likely to avoid the clashes that occur when transactions between ego states become crossed rather than complementing or parallel.

In constructive feedback, the aim is to get both people operating in their adult ego state. They can then review facts, examine solutions and implications without crossed transactions creating too many obstacles of beliefs and prejudices or feelings and emotions.

How would it feel to you?

A useful way to begin to understand how to give appropriate feedback in content, style and tone is to consider how you feel when you ask for or receive feedback. Ask yourself, when receiving feedback from another person, do you:

- Listen actively to their description of your behaviour or performance?
- Carefully consider what is being said, trying to see the situation from their point of view?
- Weigh up the positives and negatives of changing or modifying your behaviour?
- Enter into a calm discussion about your views on their comments?
- Mutually agree upon subsequent action?
- Ask for any support or help you think will be necessary?
- Thank them for their feedback?

Be honest. In many situations there are probably as many 'No' answers as 'Yes' ones. By reversing the role, it is easy therefore to see some of the difficulties we face as recipients of feedback. We may:

- Be afraid of what others think of us.
- Wonder about the motives behind the feedback. Is it honest? Can they be trusted?
- Fear a loss of face or independence even if we do recognize the need for help.
- Lose confidence and feel inferior.

If coach-mentors are sensitive to these issues and constantly remind themselves of them by 'looking in the mirror', they will avoid the pitfalls of insensitive and inappropriate feedback.

It may be all too easy for coach-mentors to take the relationship aspect of their roles for granted, particularly if they have been working with their 'learner' for some time. In the work situation, issues of power and authority often underlie working relationships: learners usually understand only too well that they are in a dependent and somewhat subordinate role vis-à-vis their coach and mentor.

It is not always easy therefore to create a relaxed, informal and supporting relationship. This is particularly true if the culture of the organization is bureaucratic or aggressively hierarchical and results-oriented. Recognizing the reality of pressures from the organizational culture is important since it will help both parties to develop realistic expectations. It is also important to appreciate the effects that differences in age, gender, educational background, ethnicity and culture can have. This is not to say that these are necessarily or inevitably obstacles, but simply to point out that lack of awareness and sensitivity of such issues may make feedback sessions strained and unproductive.

Feedback that builds confidence

During a development process, one of the best ways to build confidence is regularly to monitor progress. 'How am I doing?' is a reasonable question that the learner will want to ask. For development to occur, the learner often needs to be reassured that he or she is beginning to perform closer to the standard or goal agreed earlier. Regular reviews act as a vehicle to reinforce effective performance, highlight areas for improvement and recognize developing strengths and potential weaknesses. Obstacles or barriers to performance can also be discussed and joint actions planned to overcome them or, if necessary, the development programme can be modified.

Whenever a development review takes place, it should start by agreeing exactly what it is that the learner wishes to discuss in relation to achieving his or her goals. If a qualification is the goal, how is the learner progressing against the syllabus or development plan? What do results from tutors' reports indicate? If the acquisition of new knowledge or skills is the goal, how has the learner performed in post-learning tests or in applying the information gained? A consistent, well-organized and systematic approach by the coach-mentor is one of the surest ways to build confidence in his or her learner.

Retaining control over situations or events for the duration of the development plan is crucial for it to be successful, but some things are often outside the learner's control. For example, a learner may find it difficult to resolve any conflicts caused by short-term reassignment of his or her work priorities and completion of the development plan over the original timescale. His or her manager may be under considerable pressure to achieve short-term results and find it difficult to give immediate priority to what he or she (the manager) may see as the learner's medium-term development needs.

To maintain progress and help to encourage a positive attitude, it is necessary to help learners to develop strategies to marry their needs with the organization's pressures. Review sessions should also get the learners to highlight achievements and reflect on difficulties that have been overcome. Comparing progress to the original plan and recognizing the passing of milestones helps to show real step-by-step achievement. This also provides an excellent opportunity to reward and celebrate successes. This will, in turn, reinforce the growing confidence in the learner.

Aspects that the learner has had difficulty with should be discussed honestly. Was it the method or style of instruction or coaching that caused problems? Were the targets for achievement set too high? Was the learner trying enough or perhaps trying too hard? Were there sufficient chances to practise before starting the activity? By breaking down what may appear to the learner to be an insurmountable and complex problem into smaller chunks will allow each part to be simplified and dealt with separately and more successfully.

Observing performance

Successful coach-mentors should look at both the 'what' and the 'how': they should consider the results the learner achieves and the process he or she used to achieve the result. One of the most effective ways to do this is to actually watch the learner in action. This allows the coach-mentor to observe his or her performance directly, rather than depend on the second-hand information of others, who might have added their own interpretation to the behaviour. Sometimes the learners themselves have only a partial understanding, or even a misunderstanding, of how they perform or behave. Direct observation enables the coach-mentor to be precise in identifying specific behaviours, techniques or skills for further development.

Observing performance is best done on a regular, recurring basis to offer ongoing validity to your coaching feedback. A little feedback and guidance close to the activity is more effective than storing up the feedback for the once or twice a year formal performance review. However, learning how to observe your learners without making them feel intimidated or uncomfortable is a skill in itself. Here are some tips to consider when planning to observe behaviour.

Simplicity tips – how to observe

1 Start by explaining, or confirming if previously agreed, why you are observing the learner – you are there to help him or her improve, not to catch him or her out. Make sure you also explain your purpose to any other people directly involved.

2 Be aware of your influence on the learner's performance and position yourself as unobtrusively as possible. Consider how you would feel if someone was watching you do something.

3 Observe the process the learner is using to carry out the activity.

4 Observe the quality or standard of the final outcome or end result achieved.

5 Don't interrupt the interactions or activity, or distract the learner or any other participants during the observation.

6 Ask questions to verify your understanding, but only when you are sure you are not affecting the activity or process.

7 Observe the interaction or behaviour several times in different contexts if possible.

8 Make notes at the time for discussion later.

9 Compare what you saw with any 'standard' procedures or with what you may have previously been told.

10 Observe other people carry out the same process or behaviour for comparison purposes if relevant or appropriate.

Observing a team

In recent years there has been an increase in coaching complete teams rather than individuals in isolation. There is an argument that all coaching should ideally be done in the context of the 'team', since most business activities are now done as some form of teamwork. Trying to coach individuals while ignoring the context of their 'team' or 'teams' is likely to be limited in effectiveness. The power and influence of the rest of the team are such significant factors that they cannot be ignored. Therefore, most individuals should be coached as part of their team and ideally the whole team could be coached together.

When coaching and observing a team rather than an individual, there are several additional factors to take into consideration. As the coach-mentor, you will probably be observing the whole team in action, performing their function as a team. When observing and giving feedback to a team, it helps to consider this four-stage process:

1 Contract: What role do they (the team and the sponsor) want me to play? Am I clear on what I am looking for?

2 Observe: How do I behave when watching the team's behaviour?

3 Diagnose: Do I understand what I am seeing?

4 Intervene: Should I intervene now? How? Why?

Considering this process in more detail raises a number of important questions that coach-mentors should ask themselves at each stage.

Stage 1. Contracting

Who are the stakeholders?

The first thing to consider is that in a team situation the client may or may not be a member of the team. You may have been brought in by a senior manager to work with one of his or her teams. You may have been brought in by the leader of the team or a team member who is not the designated leader. Alternatively, you may be the leader or a member of the team who wishes to, or has been asked to, take on a coaching role for the benefit of the whole team. In all cases it is important that you are clear at the start what the current situation is and what is expected. So ask yourself: who is the client? Who are the stakeholders? What is their stake?

- The team leader? Is their leadership in question?
- All the members of the team? Is the team united? Do they all accept the need for coaching?
- The sponsor? If they are not part of the team, are they part of the problem?
- All or some of the above? In some cases, the coach-mentor may be working with a combination of the above.
- Are there any conflicts or contradictions? Do all parties want the same thing?
- Do you have a clear contract? Be clear that you understand what each stakeholder believes is the situation and what needs to be done.

What is my contract?

The next part of stage 1 is to consider what the team are willing and prepared to work on. There are five levels of interaction associated with any team that need to be considered before starting to work with the team members. The five levels are of increasing sensitivity and require increasing levels of diplomacy and tact from the coach-mentor:

1 Structural-functional: focuses on the attitudes, values, beliefs and perceptions about the roles and functions of members with little regard for individuals' characteristics.

2 Performance goal: focuses on the appropriateness and commitment to the performance goals of the team.

3 Process: focuses on processes and looks at the changing work behaviour and work relationships between members of the team.

4 Relationships: focuses on attitudes, feelings, values, beliefs, perceptions and behaviours of the individual members and the relationship they have to other members of the team.

5 Intrapersonal: focuses on self-awareness, the attitudes, values, beliefs and perceptions that each member has about themself. This level of intervention is usually best handled individually in one-to-one sessions separate from the team.

Stage 2. Observation

Once you are clear on what you are looking for and this has been agreed with all concerned, it is necessary to prepare for the actual observation and consider the following:

- Do I join the team or keep out of the way? Are you expected to take part in the discussion or activity of the team? If you are the team leader or a member of the team, not taking part might be difficult and disrupt the normal working of the team. On the other hand, can you objectively observe what is happening and focus on the interactions while also performing a team function? It may be advisable to agree with your team colleagues that you 'step out' of the activity in order to give more comprehensive feedback. It is easier for a coach-mentor who is not normally a member of the team to take a passive observer role.

- Am I keeping an open mind? When observing a team in action, it is important not to prejudge people, jump to conclusions, argue or interrupt. Teams have their own culture and dynamics and their own way of working.

- Am I aware of my own emotions? Try to listen and observe objectively, even when you might disagree with what is being said or done. It is vital to suspend your own prejudice and not allow the fact that you disagree with what is happening to influence your observations.

Stage 3. Diagnosis

The purpose of your observation is to infer the correct meaning in what you are observing. Therefore, it is important to ask the following questions before considering a suitable intervention:

- Have I observed the behaviour for long enough to make a reliable diagnosis? Is this a persistent behaviour or a one-off? Be aware that feedback will not be accepted if the team can dismiss it as an aberration from their normal behaviour.

- Is my diagnosis within the boundary of my contract? Is what I have observed appropriate to the level of interaction I have agreed to provide feedback on? The team will resent feedback at an inappropriate level.

- Can I describe my observations without judgemental comment or tone? Can I say what I have noticed without implying what I observed was wrong or inappropriate? If the team believe they are being criticized, they may respond defensively.

- Am I articulating something the team members have recognized for themselves? Do the team seem to be aware of what is happening? If you describe something they have noticed for themselves your feedback is more likely to be accepted as valid.

Stage 4. Intervention/feedback

Having decided there is something worth feeding back, you need to consider the best time to give your observations. Ask yourself:

- If I do not intervene now, what is the probability that I can intervene later and still help the team avoid the negative consequences of continuing the dysfunctional behaviour?

- If I do not intervene now, will another team member intervene? If this happens, is it likely to make the situation better or worse?

- Is the observed behaviour central enough or important enough to warrant intervention?

- Have I already contracted with the team to make this type of intervention? Do I have their permission?

- Will it help or hinder their learning and/or the performance of the team?

- Should this intervention be handled individually or would it be best to speak to them privately?

- Do the team have sufficient experience and knowledge to use the intervention to improve their effectiveness, or would it just confuse and frustrate them?

- Are the team mature and open enough with each other to handle the intervention positively, or would the intervention cause more friction and dysfunction?

- Do the team have enough information (or can I give them enough information) to make an informed choice on how to respond to the intervention?

- Will the team have time, or are they too overloaded, to process the intervention?

Handling the feedback session

There is clearly a range of ideas and techniques that can be used to build confidence and the will to succeed, and the key is deciding when any of them might be appropriate. How feedback is handled on a day-to-day basis is therefore crucial.

It is important for the coach-mentor to always be aware of the necessity for giving negative messages with positive ones wherever possible. Strengths should be balanced with weaknesses and the aim should be to be fair as well as totally honest. It also helps to keep feedback as immediate as possible. The question of timing is crucial, particularly if the session is likely to be disappointing – don't delay it and don't give feedback in small amounts. You needn't mention every single fault, but you should concentrate mainly on the essentials. If you start with 'picky' less significant points, you may create an atmosphere that makes the discussion of more important topics unnecessarily difficult.

If, as we have previously discussed, you are asked for your advice, you should give it, but remember that some of us like to give advice because it makes us feel important. Sometimes this only serves to satisfy our ego. Similarly, you should avoid trying to persuade or even argue. If the other person becomes defensive or obstructive, try to discover the reason for this reaction and build on that towards a positive action.

Be aware, too, that over-praising is often dangerous as it can confuse the situation. Being supportive does not mean constant praising, but rather creating an atmosphere in which learners can admit faults or fears, knowing they will be understood if not necessarily endorsed.

Always strive to be sensitive to the other person and avoid unwittingly denying the individual his or her feelings with hasty comments like, 'You don't mean that' or 'You have no reason to feel that way'. It helps, too, if you can keep your comments as descriptive as possible and avoid making value judgements or giving the appearance of making a personal attack. Avoid saying, 'What a stupid way to do it'; try rather, 'On reflection can you think of a better way of doing it?'

Some tips are easier to give than to apply, but they will all produce a positive response. It is equally important to recognize that other behaviours have the potential to destroy the value of the feedback you give. For instance:

- being quick to disagree;
- being overly critical;
- being distant or aloof;
- interrupting repeatedly;
- ignoring comments, ideas, feelings;
- not asking any questions at all;
- appearing to be in a hurry to finish the session.

There are a number of things, too, that learners can do to ensure that they get quality feedback:

- Identify who is best placed to provide them with feedback – managers, coach, mentor, suppliers, customers, colleagues. The concept of 360-degree feedback encourages an all-round look.
- Agree an appropriate time and place when they will be able to have a constructive discussion.
- Be clear about the areas on which they need feedback.
- Try not to cover too many things in one discussion, but focus on the key issues only.

- Challenge the person giving feedback if they feel they are not being completely honest or specific enough for the information to be useful.
- Ask probing questions of the coach-mentor to identify what behaviour they should continue doing or stop doing.

Be aware that, although giving feedback is a difficult and unfamiliar process for some people, most will welcome the fact that you have sought their views and are willing to help.

Having sought feedback from their coach, mentor or another person, learners must ensure that they receive it skilfully and assertively by:

- listening actively, concentrating and being receptive; this will make it easier for the giver to be honest;
- clarifying and testing their understanding of what is being said;
- not reacting defensively or trying to justify their behaviour;
- spending some time reflecting on the feedback received;
- thanking the person for the feedback.

Visualizing successful performance

An extremely powerful way of increasing motivation and enhancing the will to succeed is to teach learners how to visualize themselves performing an activity successfully and smoothly. Before attempting the task, encourage them to use their mind's eye and project themselves forward in time to see themselves doing the task in the way they would like to perform.

Sportsmen and women often use this technique and visualize themselves carrying out each action in slow motion. They concentrate on mentally rehearsing each step and then grooming it until it is perfect. Whenever the action is unclear or hazy, they re-run this mental video until a perfect sequence is logged in their memory bank. This allows them to relax when they actually perform and rely on their memory to steer them to a successful result.

In a business context, this technique can be adapted to help nervous presenters. Get them to visualize themselves:

- talking fluently to the audience;
- hearing their words putting a point across persuasively;
- seeing their gestures adding emphasis;
- watching their amusing anecdote draw smiles and appreciation from the audience.

This will help build up the confidence that they will be successful when they come to perform in 'real time'.

Harnessing the essential mental qualities

Building confidence, then, is about harnessing the mind of the learner. In Gallwey's book *The Inner Game of Tennis* (1974) he talks about the two 'selfs' that are part of a performer's character. Self one is the 'teller' who instructs, evaluates and tries to control the performance. Self two is the 'doer' who actually performs the task, often unconsciously and automatically.

In Gallwey's sporting analogies, you can often see and hear the two selfs having a conversation. Self one is usually exhorting self two to try harder and to do specific things, as well as criticizing what is happening. This can get in the way of self two's natural flow and ability by creating a 'busy mind' and distracting the performance.

For the learners, the danger may be that they try too hard and so complicate and confuse themselves with too many of their own instructions. Poor results then encourage self-doubt to creep in, which can begin a downward spiral. The secret is for self one to trust its other half and simply let it perform. Self one demands a role, however, so the learner must programme it with images of the task and of performing it successfully. Holding back on criticism and replacing this only with observation allows self two to make subtle adjustments and perform better.

Whitmore, in his book *The Winning Mind* (1987), takes this process further. He has developed a list of what he describes as the 'essential mental qualities':

- Responsibility: taking personal responsibility for both successes and failures and not blaming other factors. Responsibility empowers the learner to take action, not wallow in recriminations.

- Awareness: most simply described as focusing on what is going on around you while performing. Being conscious of all factors in the environment and in the body allows learners to self-correct their actions.

- Concentration: involves remaining in a passive state while focused on the task, but staying receptive to ideas and thoughts. By not trying too hard, learners avoid the anxiety and pressure on themselves.

- Relaxation: aids containing self one by keeping the chatter and instructions to a minimum. When learners let concerns about the future or regrets about the past into their mind, they also let in anxiety.

- Detachment: involves learners standing apart mentally from the activity and observing their actions. Maintaining a free and flexible state keeps self one at bay.

- Commitment: encapsulates the will to win in three steps. First, the goal must be achievable to the learner. Second, obstacles to achievement must be eliminated. Finally, the will must be supported by 100 per cent honest effort.

- Trust: by being fully prepared, learners can trust their own mind and body to reproduce the action or task. Self two takes over the driving seat and lets self one merely observe how well the performer has done – without judgement.

These concepts, although relatively easy to explain, are really quite sophisticated to apply and require careful study and practice. However, they are important ideas to master and employ.

A final tip for the learner, which Whitmore advocates, is to find a personal stimulus that creates a positive and relaxed mind and to use it either as an outlet before or during the activity. Examples might include listening to a favourite piece of music on a personal stereo or recalling an inspirational poem. Physical activity, such as a visit to the gym or a short run, can have a relaxing effect too. All of these techniques, Whitmore believes, help people to understand and capture the essential qualities of the mind and support a confident and positive approach by the learner.

Making winners

Giving feedback that helps to build confidence and success is not simple. Done effectively, feedback is about the making of winners. It fuels the motivation to learn how to improve performance – your main aim as a coach-mentor. Think carefully before you start to give feedback. Remember, it is fundamentally a two-way process. When in doubt, try to put yourself in the recipient's place or, to quote the proverb: 'Do unto others as you would be done by.'

The following checklist should help you to apply the essentials of giving effective feedback.

Essentials of effective feedback

1 Remember you get more out of people if you are sensitive to their situation and treat them as adults.

2 Imagine how you would feel if you were on the receiving end.

3 Make your feedback honest as well as fair.

4 Balance negative and positive messages.

5 Don't avoid weaknesses, but always balance them by emphasizing strengths as well.

6 Choose the appropriate time and place as well as the appropriate tone and language.

7 Keep criticism simple and constructive by concentrating on behaviours, not personal attitudes or beliefs.

8 Encourage people to take responsibility for their own development.

9 Be well organized yourself and hold regular progress reviews.

10 Recognize that you may be taken as a role model, so practise what you preach.

Endnotes

Gallwey, W T (1974) *The Inner Game of Tennis*, Random House, New York

Whitmore, J (1987) *The Winning Mind*, Fernhurst, Steyning

Observant listening 07

There is an old saying that God gave us two eyes and two ears but only one mouth so that we could look and listen four times as much as we speak. Certainly, we have increasingly realized that talking is not the main part of the communication process. Not everyone appreciates this, however. How often have you attended communication courses where the tutor spends most of the time explaining how you can structure your presentation or use visual aids but little, if any, on improving your listening skills?

More attention is also often paid to developing your observing rather than listening skills. If you have ever participated in games or exercises where several people are shown the same picture and asked to describe what they see, you will know that it often results in contradictory interpretations. All kinds of obstacles impair visual communication – and not just poor eyesight! People's expectations, assumptions, prejudices, values and wishes, all influence the messages they receive from observing and listening. Coach-mentors rely heavily on these skills and therefore need to be able to apply them effectively.

A coach-mentor using a 'hands-on' style needs, for instance, to listen to a learner's reply not only for accuracy, but also for the note of confidence or hesitation in the learner's voice. It is this that will confirm whether he or she has really understood the coach-mentor's message. Confidence and other emotions are most likely to be expressed as much in the tone of the response as in the actual words themselves.

A coach-mentor using a 'hands-off' style relies very heavily on questioning skills. As soon as the question is asked, the coach-mentor has to listen to and interpret the response and at the same time decide very quickly on the next appropriate question. Pausing to reflect on the answer is often a sensible technique, but having to ask for the answer to be repeated because of lazy listening will damage the coach-mentor's credibility and effectiveness.

Coach-mentors will sometimes hold sessions in their own office. Failure to take the elementary precaution of arranging for phone calls to be diverted can result in unnecessary interruptions to listening, as well as signalling a certain lack of interest in the purpose of the session. A coach-mentor focusing on developing a specific skill often has to observe and judge actual performance in the workplace against a clear framework of competence standards and then immediately follow the observation with questions to check understanding. If awarding a qualification for the skill is involved, and is to have credibility and validity, it is essential that any number of coach-mentors observing the same demonstration of performance and listening to the same answers would make the same judgement as to the competence of the performer. So the consistent application of these skills to a high standard is a requirement for effective coaching and mentoring.

It isn't simple to observe

The first rule of observation must be: 'It isn't as simple as you might think.' Observing is not necessarily a step-by-step easy-to-follow process, but is often continuous, with lots of things happening at once. Take the example of the coach-mentor during a session with a horse rider preparing for a competition. Just imagine what that coach-mentor would have to observe while the rider was practising even a simple movement:

- What aids did the rider use?
- How did the horse respond?
- What went well and why?
- What went wrong and why?
- How could it have been improved?
- Was the pace right?
- Was the rider's position right?
- Did the horse keep a correct outline?
- Did the horse resist and why?
- What was the general overall impression?

Take another example of a coach-mentor observing a salesperson in a sales interview:

- How did he or she greet the customer?
- What was the initial reaction?

- What type of questions were asked?
- How well did the salesperson listen?
- Which products were presented and in which order?
- To what extent was the customer involved?
- How were the sales aids used?
- Did the salesperson handle technical questions knowledgeably?
- How did the salesperson gain commitment or take an order?
- What was missing?
- How did the customer react throughout the interview?
- Which aspects of the interview went well?
- What could have been done better?

These and many other observations have to be noted as they occur. Learning to concentrate and interpret what you see is really hard work. Working with a checklist prepared in advance helps enormously. Note-taking is also essential: relying on memory means that important points are sometimes missed.

Taking notes is not easy for some people but, with practice, the skill can be acquired. Noting key words or phrases is one technique, while using mind maps is another. Having a sensible-sized pad and a pen available is an obvious tip that is sometimes forgotten.

These two examples of a coaching situation also illustrate another difficulty associated with observing. Had the coach-mentor become actively involved with either of the instances described, it may have reduced the validity of the observations and subsequent feedback or assessment. Unobtrusive observation and restraining the impulse to intervene and take control when things are not going exactly as you think they should are therefore also important skills to develop if you really want to help people to learn from their own experiences.

Another danger to be aware of is failing to distinguish between an observation of behaviour and making an inference, or drawing a conclusion, about the cause of the behaviour. The examples in Table 7.1 illustrate the potential pitfalls.

These simple examples show how easy it would be for a coach-mentor to misread the situation. The guiding principles are that observations must be objective – make an accurate record of non-judgemental, actual behaviour – and that inferences are subjective; avoid drawing conclusions and stick to descriptions of what you see.

Table 7.1 Observation vs inference

Observation	Inference	Real cause
John attended the meeting in shirt sleeves	He is unprofessional	He got soaked in a rainstorm
Wendy always leaves work right on time	She is uncommitted	She has a difficult childminder
Ken entered the figures in the wrong column	He is careless	The forms are poorly designed
Anne disagreed strongly	She is bad-tempered	She is under severe stress at work and at home

The importance of observing body language

Imagine a situation where you, as a coach-mentor, choose to hold a session with two people at the same time. This could be at the end of a project or before a programme starts. One of them sits with his or her arms folded, feet tapping and replies in a terse but perfectly accurate way. The other person is sitting forward comfortably, arms on the table, looking you straight in the eyes and answering calmly but in an equally accurate way.

If you are listening only to the verbal answers, you will receive one set of messages and quite possibly only gain a partial view of the whole picture. However, by observing consciously at the same time, you will also receive what are described as 'non-verbal' messages. These messages can be equally important and may give clues to either unspoken frustrations or important development needs.

To help resolve these dilemmas, it is important to appreciate the basics of non-verbal communication, or 'body language'. Facial expressions, gestures, posture, eye signals, body movements, all transmit a message. A useful book that gives more information on observing body language is *The Definitive Book of Body Language* (Pease and Pease, 2004). Body language, it is claimed, can be a window to our thoughts; indeed, it often speaks louder than words – we may say one thing, while our bodies say another.

Some of the key non-verbal signs are as follows:

- Empathy can be signalled by smiles, open and positive gestures, standing or sitting close, eye contact or nodding and tilting the head.

- A defensive or distrusting attitude can be signalled if someone sits with his or her crossed leg towards you, while a willingness to trust can be signalled if the crossed leg is away from you.

- Anger or aggression can be signalled by a rigid or tense body posture, staring eyes, clenched fists or clasped hands, tightly folded arms, foot tapping and finger pointing.

- Nervousness can be signalled by downcast eyes, hand over the mouth or frequently touching the face, shifting weight or fidgeting.

- Boredom can be signalled by picking imaginary fluff from sleeves, pulling at an ear, stifled yawning or gazing around the room.

One word of caution, however: you will note that we have said only that these signals can indicate the different emotions. One gesture on its own almost certainly won't be enough to give the full picture. Rather, it is a combination of non-verbal signals that you need to learn to interpret. When the combination of non-verbal signals appears to suggest a specific emotion that matches the words, this is known as 'congruence'. Where there appears to be a mismatch between the non-verbal signals and the language used by the learner, this is described as 'incongruent' and, as such, is a possible cause for concern. Of course, not only must we recognize all these gestures in others, but we must equally be aware of our own body language as it may be interpreted by others in the same way!

It is also important to remember that, although people in the same culture or from the same country send and receive similar non-verbal signals, people from other cultures or countries may interpret them differently. For example, in the UK, people signal numbers with their fingers by using the index finger as number one. However, in Germany, if you put up your index finger for a beer in a bar, you're likely to be served two – they use the thumb to signify number one. Another example of cultural differences is that an ok signal formed by creating an 'O' with your finger and thumb means ok to the English or Americans, but to the French it means zero or no good at all! As an example of cultural differences, the eye contact rules used by Africans for showing interest and paying attention are opposite to those of Europeans, who often misinterpret this different behaviour as rudeness or sullenness. Styles of spoken communication can also differ markedly. Certain Asian groups tend to give very detailed responses, which are sometimes considered by non-Asians to be irritatingly long-winded.

One also has to be careful about other people's speaking delivery, which may be affected by simple awkwardness rather than any attempt to mislead. If someone has an irritating or squeaky voice or speaks slowly or in what you find to be a boring manner, it will be even more important to listen to the message rather than be distracted by the delivery. It is the message that has to be judged, not the way it is said, and this can sometimes be an incredibly difficult discipline to achieve. 'It ain't what you say but the way that you say it' can be dangerous advice to the listener!

Awareness of personal space

There is another aspect of body language that should be considered within our context. This is the need to be sensitive to the area or space that people claim as their own, as if it were an extension of their body. People tend to regard their office, desk, chair and the space surrounding any of their possessions as 'their territory'. To make yourself at home by immediately sitting down and placing your belongings on their desk may well be offensive and invasive to that person.

Therefore, coach-mentoring learners in their office or 'territory' may make it difficult to take them out of their comfort zone, when appropriate, as they may feel too mentally comfortable. Conversely, a coach-mentor should consider the effect on both him- or herself and the learner of running the session in the coach-mentor's own office or 'territory', as the learner may feel intimidated or mentally unsafe.

There are also what are termed 'personal zones' or 'interpersonal space': an invisible ring or sphere in which we live as individuals, within which we don't want others to encroach or come too close. These are often determined by culture or personality and therefore the size of this space will differ between individuals. As a rule, this space is jealously guarded by us all. Move within the interpersonal space of somebody and he or she may well immediately feel uncomfortable and even threatened – unless of course you share an intimate personal relationship! Research has shown that people from the country need greater interpersonal space than people from towns and cities. Another example is entering a crowded lift. You will notice that often, if it is very crowded, people tend to look up at the floor level indicator light, or down at the floor, rather than at each other, mainly because they feel too close together. Research suggests that these behaviours relate to the very strong reactions that such invasion of body space can cause. If you want people to feel at ease in your presence, keep to the distance within which people feel most comfortable. An arm's length is a good guide.

It is also important to think carefully about the positioning of desks, tables and seating arrangements for a mentoring or coaching session. A competitive or defensive position may be created when a desk or table forms a barrier between two people sitting directly opposite each other. They are forced quite literally to take sides. This does nothing to enhance openness, trust and harmony. To avoid this, salespeople are often encouraged to move round to the customer's side of the desk when demonstrating or illustrating a particular point. This is done to create a feeling of togetherness as opposed to a 'you-and-us' relationship. It also allows customers to avoid the salesperson's face so that, if necessary, they can look away with ease. This sales technique has to be handled with care to avoid the negative reaction of invading personal space, but it is a useful technique for coach-mentors to be aware of.

Trust and distrust

Eyes often give the most accurate and revealing signals of all. The expression 'we see eye to eye' indicates that agreement can be signalled by eye contact. Acceptable eye contact is usually in the area of 60–70 per cent during the course of a conversation. If the other person either hardly looks at you or alternatively stares intently at you all the time, there is a tendency to immediately regard him or her with distrust and suspicion.

It is claimed that body language can be the most important part of any message. Some estimate that it accounts for 55 per cent or even more. When the words spoken conflict with the body language, it is claimed that the receiver tends to believe the non-verbal message. For example: you are busy but a colleague asks you for a few minutes of your time. You easily agree: 'No problem, I've always got time for you.' Soon, however, you are looking at your watch and shifting in your seat. All the signals suggest you haven't got the time, despite what you have said. If your colleague is alert and sensitive to these gestures, he or she will curtail the conversation and leave rather than risk upsetting your relationship. Similarly, how many times have you seen a child look at the floor and deny that he or she has 'done wrong'? You may be strongly inclined to believe the stance and gestures, not the verbal denial.

Myths and prejudices

It is also important to guard against your own prejudices and to avoid stereotyping people when interpreting visual and verbal messages. Some people, for instance, believe that people with public school accents or who wear glasses are automatically cleverer than other people. Another common myth or fallacy is that older people find it harder than young people to learn new things, or that women managers make emotional decisions while male managers act only on logical and rational interpretations of factual information.

When you stop to think about these issues, it soon becomes clear that they are highly unlikely to be true, but there is a real danger of allowing stereotypes, or simply first impressions, to affect your judgement. In a situation where you are assessing performance against a standard, this can be particularly dangerous, as you need to listen and observe throughout the session to make an objective judgement.

Of course, people can try to mislead you. Someone who answers in a confident manner or appears to agree with everything you say may create a more positive impression on you than his or her level of performance deserves. There is a well-used term called the 'halo effect', which describes this possibility. This warns of the danger of allowing one impression or element of the skill being demonstrated to create an overall impression that 'clouds' all the other evidence. It is suggested that we are all open to this type of misjudgement, particularly where one strong negative impression blinds us to an accurate and objective interpretation.

Active listening

We have concentrated so far on observation skills, but many of these issues also relate to listening. So let's discuss listening in more detail. It is useful to recognize that there are different levels of listening:

- *Peripheral* listening is done at a subconscious level and can occur in formal or informal situations. For example, you may be in a busy restaurant talking to people at your table, but also picking up snippets of conversation from another table.

- *Apparent* listening is what we all do most of the time. We look as if we are listening, but in fact we are not really concentrating.

- *Active* or effective listening is often what we should be doing. This involves really concentrating on the message being transmitted by trying to understand not only what is being said but how and why it is being said.

It is the ability to listen 'actively' that separates the good communicators from the poor. Like any skill, effective listening requires self-discipline and practice and it is certainly hard work. It is estimated that most people talk at a rate of 125 words per minute, but that they can think at up to four times that speed. This means that as a listener you have spare mental capacity which, if you do not discipline yourself, results in your mind wandering and a lack of concentration.

We have probably all experienced ourselves tuning in and out of conversations or discussions and then having to ask for something to be repeated because we have missed a key point of the message. A listener can, however, use his or her speed of thought to advantage. You can learn to use the time to summarize mentally what the speaker has said, to ensure you have understood the message fully and to consider whether you need to ask any further questions.

Success as a coach-mentor depends to a large extent on the ability to concentrate efficiently on what is being said, often for long periods. You may well make the other person feel unimportant or insignificant if he or she senses that his or her ideas and feelings are not being paid close attention to. The relationship will then undoubtedly suffer. The temptation to only half listen is, of course, very real. Having asked a question, if you get an early indication that the answer is going to be correct, or is exactly what you were expecting, there is an inclination to switch off before the end of the response. By doing so, you risk missing some enlightening new information or ignoring additional information that shows that your initial assumptions were incorrect. Similarly, you may be so preoccupied formulating your next question that you miss at least part of the response to your current question. Therefore, to be able to actively and deeply listen, you must ensure your own mind is quiet, with your whole attention focused on the person speaking. You should be fully present but not trying to anticipate what is being said or influence the direction of the conversation. This state for a coach-mentor is sometimes described as 'simply being and not doing'.

So what does active listening involve? What do we mean by active listening? This deep level goes beyond simply listening to what the other person said, into the area of intuition, insight and almost telepathy. Understanding this process will help you to adopt a disciplined approach to active listening. The process is as follows:

1 Having received a response there is interpretation of what was heard.

2 This leads to understanding.

3 Then comes evaluation, or weighing the information, comparing it with existing knowledge and deciding what to do with it.

4 Based on your understanding and evaluation, you react by planning your reply.

5 Finally, you respond.

What cannot be ignored in this process is, of course, the way in which a response is delivered. It is estimated that tone counts for as much as one-third of a message. Active listeners must be alert to any emphasis on certain words, also to fluency, or lack of fluency, as well as any emotional language. In the same way, they must listen for the meaning behind the words. If a learner says, 'The main reason is...' this could imply there are other considerations that may need exploring. Only by active listening will it be possible to identify and evaluate what is not being said.

Active listening requires planning and practice. We have to work at it and, like all other skills, we need to be interested and motivated enough to want real results from our efforts. So, how do you go about putting all this into practice? Let us suggest a three-stage process for efficient listening.

Stage 1. Carefully select the location (whenever possible)

- Choose a quiet room or area free from the distraction of other people and noise.
- Arrange seating to avoid any physical barriers, such as a desk, but don't sit too close.
- Set aside any other work you are doing.
- Arrange for telephone calls or messages to be diverted.
- Remove or ignore any other distractions.
- Shut the door, if possible.

Stage 2. Create the right atmosphere

- Make sure the speaker knows you want to listen to him or her, look interested and maintain eye contact without staring.
- Give the speaker your full attention.
- Address the person by the name he or she wants to be called, usually his or her first name.
- Be patient – allow the person time to say all he or she wants to say (within reason).
- Maintain a relaxed posture and encourage the speaker to feel relaxed.
- Be encouraging by leaning forward, nodding, putting your head to one side, smiling whenever appropriate.
- Empathize as necessary if something difficult or painful or different from your own beliefs is being discussed.
- Don't take any views personally and try not to be defensive.

Stage 3. Practise helpful listening behaviour

- Make listening noises: eg 'Mmm', 'Yes', 'I see'.
- Pause before responding to indicate that you are digesting what has been said.
- Keep an open mind – do not prejudge people, jump to conclusions, argue or interrupt: other people may have a different point of view.
- Be aware of your own emotions; listen carefully even where you might disagree.
- Suspend prejudice; don't allow the fact you disagree make you turn a deaf ear to what is being said.
- Concentrate on what matters by trying to get at the core of the response.
- Be sensitive to mood, facial expressions and body movements to understand the full meaning of what is being said.
- Plan to make a report to someone else following the meeting and imagine he or she is the sort of person who likes to know all the details of what you have heard.
- Seek more information by summarizing, asking questions, repeating or paraphrasing.
- Summarize to check your understanding.

Finally, make a habit of taking notes. As we have seen, listening only occupies something like one-quarter of our available mental capacity. The remaining three-quarters of the mind will wander if not otherwise used. More importantly, note-taking gives you a record of what you are hearing and helps to emphasize the importance you are placing on what is being said to you. Many of the helpful behaviours we have listed will be made easier by good and accurate note-taking, but it helps if you explain to the other person why you are taking notes.

Telephone coaching

Increasingly, coaching and mentoring are being done over the telephone because of the pressures of time and the additional cost of travelling to a common meeting place. Also, remote working is becoming more common in organizations, which means that many people are using the telephone as the 'normal' form of communication with colleagues, customers and suppliers. Telephone coaching has the benefit of not being location-dependent and so can be done across different countries or even continents. This form of coaching offers increased flexibility for both learner and coach-mentor but would appear to make active listening much more difficult. Many coach-mentors say they could not possibly do telephone sessions, as the vital component of being able to see, and react to, the learner is missing.

We would challenge this assumption. Until the widespread use of video telephones or web-cam technology, it was true that you could not actually see the learner during a session. However, you can still fulfil nearly all the requirements of active listening over the telephone. By ensuring the session meets the requirements of the three-stage process described earlier, the coach-mentor and learner can experience a totally satisfactory session. Let us consider those same three stages.

Stage 1. Location

- All the requirements apply, apart from don't sit too close!
- An addition requirement is a hands-free telephone, or headset. It is not advisable to hold a conventional telephone to your ear for an hour or more!

Stages 2 and 3. Atmosphere and behaviour

- Again, all the requirements apply, with the exception of maintaining eye contact without staring.

- We would say that you will need to increase the verbal cues as a reinforcement for the non-verbal signals. Comments such as, 'Yes, I am still listening', 'Go on', 'I'm still here', will encourage the speaker to continue to talk and to reassure him or her that you are still on the line.

- You may think some of the requirements are not important or irrelevant in this section, since the other person cannot see what you are doing. However, it is amazing how much of a person's body language can be detected by actively and deeply listening over the telephone. We believe that continuing the body posture and non-verbal mannerisms you would normally adopt when actually facing the person should be maintained. In this way your concentration will be increased and something of these supporting behaviours will be detected by the learner. Some coach-mentors find placing a picture of the learner or a suitable object in front of them to focus on aids this process. Others find closing their eyes to minimize the distractions of their own surroundings helps their concentration.

We believe that coach-mentors need to feel comfortable with, and competent in, using the telephone as an integral part of their practice. Telephone coaching should not be seen as a poor substitute for the real thing to simply save time or money. It should be seen as an equally valid alternative to face-to-face sessions and offered as an integral part of the relationship with the learner. For example, some learners said they preferred telephone sessions because they felt able to be more open and reveal more of themselves without the embarrassment of being 'looked at' by the listener.

However, having said that telephone sessions are just as effective as face-to-face sessions, we do strongly recommend that the first session with a new learner should be face-to-face if at all possible. We would also recommend the last session should be face-to-face if possible and practical.

Whether you are a coach or mentor, effective observing and listening are key to both roles. If you listen actively, your learner will feel listened to. The coach-mentor will want to encourage responses that guide learners to work out the best way forward for them. The following checklist should prove a useful guide to improving the way you use your eyes and ears.

Simplicity tips – effective observing and listening

1 Non-verbal signals are important and you should learn to recognize them to get the full picture.

2 Beware of cultural differences in communication habits.

3 Recognize that your own emotions affect the signals you send.

4 Don't let your own values, attitudes and beliefs get in the way.

5 Concentrate and pay attention to details.

6 Take accurate notes to avoid misunderstanding.

7 Tone of voice is often as important as what is said.

8 If you want to understand, you must be prepared to listen and show you are listening actively.

9 Establish the performance criteria before you begin to observe or listen to the performance.

10 Plan in advance to avoid distractions.

Endnote

Pease, A and Pease, B (2004) *The Definitive Book of Body Language: The secret meaning behind people's gestures*, Orion, London

Questioning 08

One of the oldest jokes we can remember is the story of the little boy standing outside the door of a house. A door-to-door salesman approaches him and asks, 'Son, is your mother at home?' 'Yes,' replies the little boy. The salesman knocks on the door but receives no reply. After several minutes of knocking with no response he turns angrily to the boy and says, 'Hey, I thought you said your mother was at home.' 'She is,' replies the boy, 'but I don't live here!'

The moral of that story is that if you don't ask the right question, you probably won't get the right answer. The combination of asking the right question because you know the subject matter well, and asking the right question in the most appropriate way, lies at the heart of skilled coaching and mentoring.

Coach-mentors should bear in mind that their primary role is to help and encourage their learners to develop. This cannot be achieved if they create undue pressure or confusion by inept questioning. A meaningful coaching or mentoring session depends on using questions that provoke a response that enhances learning. It is important to build a relationship that is open and honest, so that the learner can accept the sometimes painful process of being stretched by difficult questions. Asking embarrassing questions is likely to lead to defensive, negative responses and a deterioration of the relationship.

Developing good questioning skills is vital to successful coaching and mentoring. Many managers will, during the course of their work, have received training on asking questions on interviewing, appraising and counselling courses. There are also plenty of written materials and learning packages available. Let us nevertheless look at various questioning techniques, which every coach-mentor should know about and try to apply.

Understanding the basic types of question

The importance of recognizing that there are two main types of question – open and closed – is a significant basic theoretical concept of questioning.

A closed question is one that may be answered by a simple 'yes' or 'no' and usually begins with 'do you', 'are you', 'have you', and so on. It may also be a question to which the respondent is offered a choice of alternative replies, such as 'Which of the following three alternatives would you choose...?' Open questions are aimed at provoking an extended 'free' response and might start with 'what', 'where', 'which', 'why', 'how' or 'when'.

Closed questions are appropriate:

- where a straightforward 'yes' or 'no' is enough;
- to gather or verify information;
- to confirm understanding of facts;
- to confirm agreement or commitment;
- to get a decision when there are only two alternatives.

The repeated use of closed questions needs to be avoided, however. A series of such questions can become very wearing on the respondent and can quickly turn a discussion or session into an interrogation.

A more difficult skill to develop, but one that is essential to guiding and supporting a learner, is to use open questions. These enable the questioner to:

- establish rapport and put the other person at ease;
- free up respondents to answer as they choose and in their own words;
- encourage uninhibited feedback;
- help to explore opinions and values in more detail;
- create involvement and commitment;
- check out the learner's understanding more comprehensively.

For example, if you wanted to ask someone his or her opinion on, say, the merits of the local football team, you wouldn't say 'Do you agree that the local team is a good one?' This invites a simple 'yes' or 'no' response. On the other hand, if you had phrased the question 'What do you think are the good points about the local team?', you would instead invite a response that required the candidate to express an opinion. If there were no good points, you then have the opportunity to follow up with 'Well, can you describe their weak points?' The benefits of using appropriate open questions are that you obtain more information and encourage the candidate to think more – a win–win result.

A variety of useful question types

Coach-mentors need to exercise care in selecting the best type of question to use in different situations. First they need to ask themselves some basic questions about the purpose of their questioning:

- Are they helping learners to explore their situation in more detail?
- Are they encouraging them to move from an overall analysis of their performance to a more detailed one?
- Are they looking to help learners to identify strengths and weaknesses that could be capitalized upon or improved for better performance?
- Are they working to increase personal awareness and responsibility?

There are several different types of questioning that are appropriate for different purposes, discussed below.

Awareness-raising questions

If coach-mentors want to encourage learners to develop their performance, they also have to help them to develop self-awareness, a sense of responsibility for future action and a commitment to persevere with the action. You will find that open questions like, 'What happened?' and, 'Why did that happen?' tend to produce descriptive and potentially somewhat defensive responses. On the other hand, questions like, 'How did it feel when you were doing that?', 'What do you imagine it would look like if you did it differently?' and 'What can you do to lift the performance still further?' will encourage responses that focus on positive ideas for future action. We would call these 'awareness-raising' questions.

Reflective questions

This type of question is a useful means of eliciting clarification and confirming that you are listening 'actively'. By 'replaying' the words used by the learner or rephrasing and reflecting them back you, as coach-mentor, can both test your own understanding and encourage the other person to talk more. You can say, 'You said xyz..., can you explain in more detail please exactly what you mean there?' or you can use questions like, 'So is what you're saying...?' or 'Let me just check that I understand you correctly...'. These types of questions give the opportunity for the respondent to give additional information or to think of new ways of making his or her views clearer. It also assures him or her that you have heard and understood correctly.

Justifying questions

These questions provide an opportunity for further explanation of reasons, attitudes or feelings. Examples are, 'Can you elaborate on what makes you think that...?' and 'How would you explain that to someone else...?' This type of question can provide very useful responses, but can also appear rather confrontational, especially if delivered in a challenging tone or manner. Sometimes it is better to phrase them slightly differently: for example, 'You say this... am I right in understanding that what you mean is...?' or 'Could you help me to understand your explanation by putting it another way?'

Hypothetical questions

These are questions that pose a situation or a suggestion: 'What if...?', 'How about...?' These can be useful if you want to introduce a new idea or concept, challenge a response without causing offence or defensiveness, or check that you fully understand the implications of an earlier answer. Hypothetical questions can be very powerful and stretching in coaching and mentoring situations. However, they should only be asked when it is reasonable to expect the other person to have sufficient knowledge or understanding of the situation you are asking him or her to speculate about.

Probing questions

Effective questioning usually begins broadly and then becomes more focused on detail. Probing questions are those supplementary questions where the full information required has not been given as part of the initial response. The reason it has not been offered may be because the initial question was inappropriate, unclear or simply too general. Alternatively, the respondent may deliberately not be replying fully. Probing questions can also be used to discover motivations and feelings, where they have not been offered.

Probing questions are among the most difficult to ask and may, of course, involve asking a mix of open, closed, reflective, justifying and hypothetical questions. Their advantage is not only that they elicit more information where necessary, but they also help the learner to consider issues or factors that might be a little 'below surface'.

Two basic probing techniques are funnelling – where you start with large, broad questions and gradually narrow the focus down to the specific information you are seeking; and drilling – where you decide in advance the question areas you want to pursue and dig deeper and deeper until you strike the response you have been looking for.

Checking questions

Sometimes it is necessary to check what you are hearing or to correct an understanding. This can be done through a number of different open or closed questions, such as, 'Are you sure about that?', 'This may generally be the case, but I wonder if it is true in your situation?' and 'Why do you interpret it that way?'

It is crucial, however, that the coach-mentor does not dictate the route of the discussion by 'forcing' its direction or be seen to be 'testing' through inappropriate questioning. Questions should be used to help learners to work on their own goals and needs and to take responsibility for them. Questioning should not be used simply to satisfy the curiosity of the coach-mentor. Questioning is about helping learners to explore possibilities and reach their own decisions; it should also be used to encourage self-development.

It is obvious, therefore, that coach-mentors should always use simple, uncomplicated and understandable language and also make sure they do not make unfair or unrealistic assumptions or jump to conclusions.

Types of questions to be avoided

There are several types of questions that are inappropriate for a coach-mentor to employ. These will not help to generate trust and they may provoke a negative, defensive or ambiguous response. Avoid asking:

- long-winded questions – they will probably be misunderstood;
- several questions rolled into one multiple question – people inevitably choose the easiest answers first and avoid the difficult one you really wanted to know the answer to;
- leading or loaded questions – they usually only demonstrate what you already know or think rather than what the respondent really understands or believes;
- trick questions unless you can explain the purpose – they can cause resentment and demotivation.

Questioning techniques

It is very difficult to give examples of the type of questions that might be appropriate for specific coach-mentoring sessions, since each session will be different and will need the coach-mentor to apply his or her general theoretical understanding and range of skills to meet the requirements of that specific situation. However, there are some techniques that may be helpful in the most common situations that a coach-mentor can face, such as:

- coaching an inexperienced learner to develop a new skill;
- finding time to help someone to sort out a problem when you as the coach are under pressure from a heavy workload;
- coaching an experienced and able learner who has the time and motivation to improve his or her performance;
- coaching a confused or unfocused learner who is unsure of what they need;
- coaching a learner who is uncertain or unwilling to face up to awkward or unpalatable options;
- coaching someone who has little confidence or self-belief;
- coaching someone who is struggling with his or her work–life balance.

For each of these situations different questioning techniques can be employed. We'll look at each of them in turn.

Coaching inexperienced learners

One technique that has been found most helpful in these situations is called the 'practice spiral' (once again, please remember that this is a model, not a set of instructions to be used in any and every situation).

The practice spiral starts with an initial explanation and demonstration stage. This is followed by a stage for reflecting on the learning achieved during the initial stage. Then comes a reviewing stage that focuses on drawing specific conclusions about how much progress has been made towards achieving the eventual goal. The final stage involves planning to practise again. This, of course, leads to another new experience, but this time at a slightly higher level of performance. The whole process begins again and continues to spiral towards higher and higher levels of performance after each new practice session. The process is shown in Figure 8.1.

Figure 8.1 A practice spiral

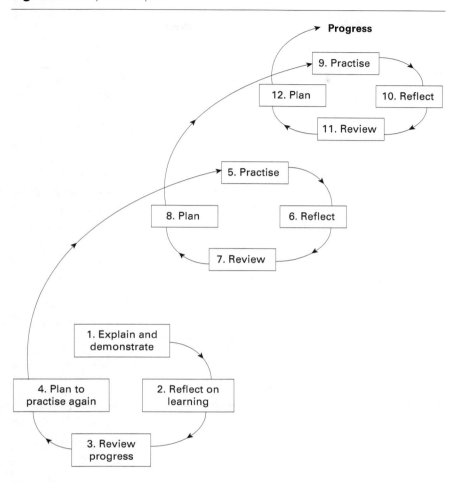

There are a number of key points for the coach-mentor to follow at each stage of the spiral.

Stage 1. Explain and demonstrate

At this stage the coach-mentor should:

- summarize what is about to be explained and demonstrated;
- emphasize why it is important;
- outline how it is going to be done;
- explain and demonstrate, following a logical sequence;

- summarize, re-emphasizing why it is important;
- allow time for questions, clarifications and feedback to check understanding.

Stage 2. Reflect on the learning

This stage should be deliberately timed. Often, simply allowing a few minutes' private thought, note-taking or handling of a piece of new equipment is all that is required.

Stage 3. Review progress

At this stage, the coach-mentor needs to remind learners of the ultimate goal of the learning programme and to encourage them to articulate the progress they feel they have made so far. Skilful questioning can help learners to identify any barriers to learning they are experiencing, as well as enabling them to clarify any areas of misunderstanding that may have arisen.

Stage 4. Plan to practise again

Opportunities to practise what has been learnt are crucial to ensure that the required competence standards are achieved. The coach-mentor should ensure that there are three types of practice sessions:

1 *Risk-free opportunities*: where mistakes can easily be made and remedial action taken with no damage done or blame expressed.

2 *Close-observation opportunities*: where learners can practise in real-life situations with the coach-mentor in close attendance to be able to intervene to help to correct any faults and to build confidence with constructive feedback and praise.

3 *Spot-check opportunities*: where the learner is free to operate in a real-life situation but with the knowledge that there will be occasional spot-checks by the coach-mentor to offer feedback and motivation.

As learners progress up the spiral, the type of practice session the coach-mentor will agree with the learner will obviously move from risk-free to spot-check. Note that although the spiral starts with a totally hands-on style, the coach-mentor moves steadily down the styles continuum towards a hands-off position.

The 'skills framework' technique

The 'spiral' technique works well when the inexperienced learner has to acquire a mechanical skill or has to master a new operating process. But when a 'soft skill', like presentation or influencing, has to be learnt or when a combination of process and soft skills, like interviewing skills and techniques, is required, it is more helpful to use a 'framework' technique.

This requires the coach-mentor to have a clear competency framework of the identified learning need on which to focus the development programme. As an example, let us choose the need to develop 'Appraisal interviewing skills and techniques'. This could develop the competency framework as in Figure 8.2.

Figure 8.2 Appraisal interview skills framework

Appraisal Interviewing Skills Framework		
Please tick appropriate column	Yes	Needs help
Process knowledge		
The learner understands:		
1.1 The purpose, benefits and limitations of appraisals		
1.2 The organization's appraisal process:		
• Principles		
• Practices		
• Paperwork		
Process skills and techniques		
The learner can:		
2.1 Collate and evaluate performance measures (before the appraisal)		
2.2 Prepare for the appraisal (in the weeks before)		
2.3 Brief the team members to prepare themselves		
2.4 Prepare for the appraisal (on the day)		
2.5 Follow a clear structure for the interview		
2.6 Provide feedback on performance during the interview		
2.7 Set objectives during the interview		
2.8 End an appraisal appropriately		
2.9 Help team members who have performance problems		
2.10 Provide ongoing support to achieve results		
Personal skills, style and attitudes		
The learner can:		
3.1 Communicate effectively during the appraisal		
3.2 Resolve conflicts during appraisals		
3.3 Display a positive attitude towards personal development throughout the appraisal process		

This framework is a general checklist, which would be backed up by a more detailed set of checklists, and provides both the learner and the coach-mentor with an opportunity for a rigorous self-assessment of exactly what the outcome of the learning programme should be. Those areas that the learner already understands and in which he or she can perform confidently can be ticked off, allowing the coach-mentor to focus on those issues that need detailed attention. The coach-mentor now follows the normal coaching process model to achieve the required results.

This technique has the benefit of clearly showing that different aspects of the skills and techniques of the development programme will require different learning opportunities to be taken. Some will involve individual study, others observation and practice. While it may be an advantage for the coach-mentor to be a skilled interviewer, it is not absolutely necessary. The framework provides the coach-mentor with a clear overall appreciation of the desired outcomes and, if necessary, the learner can be given access to alternative and more detailed expertise.

A coach who has used the 'framework' technique to develop customer service telephone effectiveness (combining soft and process skills) comments:

> I am involved in three different development situations. I coach my staff to manage their own learning and performance improvements; I coach-mentor a client to achieve a qualification; and I also coach others to develop specific customer service skills.
>
> Each situation calls for a different approach, and I find that a competency framework approach produces the best results when I am helping to improve performance in a specific skill area. It combines a rigorous analysis of the behaviour and performances that are required with an easy-to-use observation and self-assessment checklist. It also helps to ensure consistency of performance, providing all the coaches have a common understanding of the framework before they start coaching.
>
> Remember, that in call centre situations, we may be talking 100 coaches, each aiming for the same quality of performance and so consistency is important. To achieve this, there needs to be not just a common understanding of the competences, but for fairness as well. There is therefore a need for regular meetings in which the group of coaches runs check assessments to test for fairness and consistency.
>
> One approach we use is to listen to recordings of customer interactions and then independently complete the checklist. Each coach decides the coaching priorities and discusses them with the rest of the group. If we are doing the job properly, we should all be agreeing on the priority areas for both improvement and reinforcement. We also run role-plays of the coaching meeting to ensure that feedback is given in a constructive way.

Some trainers believe that coaching can be seen as the 'glue that makes training stick', particularly when the objective of the intervention is to improve something like customer service effectiveness over the telephone.

In these situations, the customer service representatives usually need a combination of product knowledge, technical dexterity to operate a computer program and personal skills. Knowledge can often best be imparted in a training context, but technical and personal skills require continual practice in real-life situations. Thus a combination of training and coaching will produce the best results. Organizations that try to save short-term costs by limiting the development to a training course alone usually find that it is an expensive mistake. They sometimes find themselves in a situation where coaching to improve performance is seen as a 'punishment'. The truth is more likely to be either:

- lack of the basic knowledge of how to do it;
- misunderstanding the competences or objectives;
- seeing no reward for doing the job;
- factors outside the control of the individual;
- being unaware of a performance problem.

As coaches, we have to be very careful to identify the root cause of the performance difficulty and work very hard to create the motivation to change behaviour. If the initial development programme had combined training with adequate coaching follow-up, these sorts of difficulties could have been avoided.

Coaching when you are short of time: the '3-D' technique

Even when an organization has followed the appropriate learning methodologies to develop its people, operational challenges still arise. For example, sometimes people ask for help at times inconvenient for the coach-mentor. Most managers are under increasing time pressures and may genuinely find it difficult to reorganize their priorities to meet the immediate needs of a member of their team. Experience has shown that coach-mentors who can cope with these situations are highly regarded by their colleagues and team members. Successful coach-mentors often express the belief that time spent in coaching to help with immediate problems is repaid many times over through the improvements in performance and higher levels of motivation.

The essence of handling these pressurized coaching sessions is to focus as rapidly as possible on potential solutions that the other person can recognize and take personal responsibility for implementing. The '3-D' technique is one that has been found helpful for these situations. It is based on recognizing a three-dimensional analysis, as illustrated in Figure 8.3.

Figure 8.3 The 3-D technique

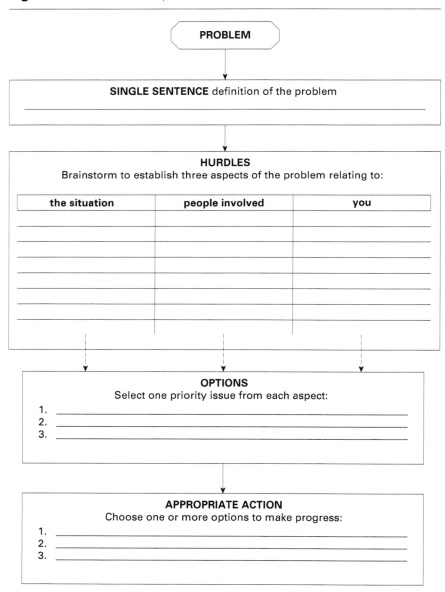

To use this technique, a coach-mentor simply needs a blank sheet of paper or a flipchart. The learner is asked to quickly define the problem in a single sentence. Careful questioning and using the 3-D analysis technique enable the coach-mentor and the learner to quickly identify three elements of the problem under each of three headings:

1 the situation – eg timescales, lack of resources, geography;

2 people involved – eg unhappy customer, impatient boss, unreliable supplier;

3 you – eg lack of technical knowledge, conflicting priorities, the learner's general attitude.

With these three dimensions or aspects of the problem identified, it is usually relatively easy to identify several options to choose from, even if most of them require actions related solely to the learner themself! The final stage is to choose the 'best-fit' option to actually implement.

Following this structured technique, it is possible to focus rapidly on potential actions. By relying almost entirely on questioning, the coach can help people to articulate most of the issues and options themselves. The coach-mentor will have enabled the learners to focus more clearly and can leave the responsibility for taking final decisions with them. With practice, this technique can work in 10–15 minutes.

It is also possible to use the 3-D technique to coach yourself through a problem. You can try it for yourself now:

1 Define a current problem in a single sentence.

2 List three general issues relating to the problem situation.

3 List three issues relating to the people involved.

4 List three issues that relate specifically to you and the problem.

5 Choose one issue from each of your three lists of three issues.

6 Now identify one or more options that are most likely to make progress in solving the problem.

It may seem quite simple, but it works. The technique works best when the coach-mentor relies entirely on questioning to encourage the learner to work through the process.

Coaching an experienced and motivated learner: the 'GROW' technique

The GROW technique has its origins in sports coaches who have been influenced by Tim Gallwey's book *The Inner Game of Tennis* (1974). The technique relies heavily on using skilful questions and following a clear structure.

The idea of the GROW framework is to use a simple set of questions to guide the discussion through four stages of a coaching session or event. By going through the different stages, asking a variety of questions at each, you will be getting the individual to think about the issue/problem at hand and identify a possible solution, or range of solutions.

First, the questions focus on the 'Goal' the learners want to achieve in the immediate coaching session. Next, the focus is on the total 'Reality' in which the learners are operating. This is followed by questioning the practical 'Options' that the learners might choose, to achieve the goal that they have set themselves. Finally, the focus is on the 'Will' to actually take specific action to implement one or more of the options previously chosen. An easy way to remember the structure is to use the mnemonic that summarizes the GROW technique as:

establish the Goal;

examine the Reality;

consider all Options;

confirm the Will to act.

Note: it might be necessary to retrace your steps through the stages if you realize the conversation suggests you did not fully explore a previous stage.

This type of approach is far more effective than simply telling learners what to do because it gets them to think about what they need to do and why they need to do it. The end result is that they feel more ownership of the solution, and therefore more accountability for taking it forward and making it work.

GROW is a powerful technique when you are coach-mentoring learners who already have a basic knowledge, expertise and enthusiasm for the issue involved. This is generally true in a sports context, but is often not the case in work situations. With inexperienced learners – or coach-mentors for that matter – the GROW technique is, in our experience, often too time-consuming and sophisticated for practical day-to-day work-based coaching situations.

However, where the coach-mentor has the time, patience and skills, the GROW technique is an excellent coaching technique for the 'hands-off' coaching style, with a proven record of success. The key is asking effective questions and systematically following the GROW structure during the coaching session. It is often an interactive process and cannot easily be rushed. The end result of coaching with GROW can be a highly focused and motivated learner.

Here is a selection of the types of questions that could be asked of such a learner, adapted slightly from the work of both Whitmore (2010) and Downey (2014).

Goal

To help establish the 'goal' that the learner wishes to focus on during the session, the following questions might be appropriate:

- What is the issue on which you would like to work today?
- What would you like to achieve by the end of this coaching session?
- How far and how detailed would you like to get in this session?
- Is your longer-term goal related to this issue?
- Is your goal SMART?
- Can we achieve what you want today in the time available?
- Are you sure you have defined your goal for this session?

Reality

To help the learner to understand more clearly the 'reality' of his or her own position and the context in which he or she is operating, the following questions might be appropriate:

- What is happening at the moment?
- How sure are you that this is an accurate representation of the situation?
- What and how great is your concern about it?
- Who, other than yourself, is affected by this issue?
- Who knows about your desire to do something about it?
- How much control do you personally have over the outcome?
- Who else has some control over it and how much?
- What action steps have you taken on it so far?
- What stopped you from doing more?

- What obstacles will need to be overcome on the way?
- What, if any, internal obstacles or personal resistance do you have to taking action?
- What resources do you already have – skill, time, enthusiasm, money, support, etc?
- What other resources will you need? Where will you get them from?
- If I could grant you one wish related to the issue, what would it be?
- Do you need to redefine your immediate or your longer-term goal? (If the answer is 'yes', you will need to start the process again.)

Options

To help the learner to fully explore a range of possible courses of action that are open to him or her, the following questions may be appropriate:

- What are the different ways in which you could approach this issue?
- What are the alternatives, large or small, open to you?
- What else could you do?
- What would you do if you had more time, a large budget or if you were the boss?
- What would you do if you could start again with a clean sheet, with a new team?
- Would you like to add a suggestion from me?
- What are the advantages and disadvantages of each of these in turn?
- Which would give the best result?
- Which of these solutions appeals to you most, or feels best to you?
- Which would give you the most satisfaction?
- Do you need to redefine your immediate or your longer-term goal? (If the answer is 'yes', you will need to start the process again.)

Will

To help a learner to reach a decision on the course of action that best meets his or her situation and to establish the learner's genuine commitment to follow through with action, the following questions may be appropriate:

- Which option or options will you choose?
- What are your criteria and measurements for success?

- When precisely are you going to start and finish each action step?
- What could arise to hinder you in taking these steps or meeting the goal?
- What personal resistance do you have, if any, to taking these steps?
- What will you do to overcome these resistances?
- Who needs to know what your plans are?
- What support do you need and from whom?
- What will you do to obtain that support and when?
- What commitment, on a 1–10 scale, do you have to taking these agreed actions?
- What is it that prevents this from being a 10?
- What could you do or alter to raise your commitment closer to 10?
- Is there anything else you want to talk about now or are we finished?
- When would you like to meet again?

We should stress that these are examples only, not a checklist of the exact number, type and sequence of questions that must be followed! Don't worry if you use different words – the idea is to empower the individual to take responsibility for his or her own actions. Remember – there is logic to the sequence of the stages. Do not be ruled by the process; move back and forwards as the conversation develops but ensure the session ends up at 'Will'.

Coaching for a confused or unfocused learner: the 'HELP' technique.

Often a learner will approach a coach-mentor, unsure what the problem is or what they want to do about a situation. Learners can sometimes not know, or not be able to express, what they really want to talk about. Coach-mentors will often hear common phrases such as 'I don't know where to start' or 'I don't know how it happened' or perhaps 'I don't know what to say'. As described earlier, techniques such as GROW can be too directive and challenging for unfocused or confused learners. For these situations, the use of the HELP technique is often very helpful.

This technique is based on the four-stage development cycle and an extension of the reflection note tool described in Chapter 4. As with the GROW technique, many people find the use of an acronym useful and this four-stage technique of sequencing questions is called HELP:

clarify what Happened;

surface the Emotions;

identify the Learning gained;

choose a Plan of action.

You could say the use of this technique in coach-mentoring would HELP people GROW!

What **Happened**?

As Hercule Poirot might say – 'just tell me what happened'. This is usually a good place to start because you are simply asking them to recall the facts of a specific situation, event or incident. Most learners would find this easy because it simply requires them to remember what happened and in what sequence. The type of questions asked in this first section are simply to get the learner talking. This level of recall reconnects the learner with the previous event and they start to relive the experience. The role of the coach-mentor at this stage is to encourage the full exploration of the facts and perhaps to coax the learner to reveal more than they are initially saying. An in-depth examination of the event can take some time and should not be rushed or taken lightly. By the coach-mentor holding a non-judgemental 'safe space' the learner should feel able to share all the details without getting defensive or evasive.

Typical questions for the coach-mentor to ask at this stage might include:

What happened then?

What happened next?

What did you do?

What did they do?

Why do you think it happened like that?

Why do you think they/you behaved that way?

What **Emotions** were involved?

Many people find it easier to talk about the facts than to talk about feelings. Only by surfacing the feelings and emotions evoked by an event can effective learning begin to take place. It is sometimes insightful for the learner to try to put themselves in the other's shoes and consider how the other person's feelings and emotions during the events being described may have influenced the outcome. The role of the coach-mentor is to encourage the learner to separate what happened from what their feelings and emotions were at the time.

Typical questions for the coach-mentor to ask at this stage would include:

How did you feel, before/during/after the event?

How do you think they felt before/during after the event?

What emotions were evoked by you/by them?

Why were you feeling like that?

Why do you think they felt that way?

What emotion would you have liked to have felt?

What have you **Learned**?

This question is designed to encourage the learner to start reflecting on what happened and what emotions were evoked by all concerned. It is believed that the most insightful way to reflect on past experiences or incidents is to try to make connections between the behaviours of the people involved and the emotions and feelings being felt. Therefore, asking the learner to reflect on the previous two questions should enable them to view the event in a different light. Some people find it easier to talk about their emotions, some find it easier to talk facts. By encouraging a learner to fully explore both aspects of a situation, their learning should be deeper and more meaningful.

Typical questions for the coach-mentor to ask at this stage would include:

What have you learned about yourself?

What have you learned about the other people involved?

What have you learned about the situation/what conclusions can you draw?

Can you see/describe the event differently than you did before?

Do you have a different perspective on things now?

Does it make more sense than it did before?

Does this relate to any other events/situations in which you have been involved?

Is there a pattern starting to emerge?

What do you **Plan** or **Propose** to do?

This final question is the one that moves the learner forward. Only when there is movement in the learner's thinking can a coaching or mentoring session be considered successful.

The role of the coach-mentor is to help the learner reach a decision or decisions and gain their commitment to action or actions that seem appropriate to the situation.

Typical questions for the coach-mentor to ask at this stage should include:

What do you plan/propose to do about this situation now?

What do you plan to do next time?

What else could you do?

How are you going to take this forward?

How are you going to resolve the situation?

How confident are you that your plan will achieve what you need?

What will you do to prevent this happening again?

How can you ensure this does happen again?

As with the other techniques described in this chapter, these questions are simply suggestions indicative of the type of questions to be used at appropriate stages. The skill of the coach-mentor and the needs of each individual learner will define exactly how to apply this, and other techniques, effectively.

Uncertain or unwilling to choose: 'transfer' technique

It is not uncommon for a coach-mentor to be faced with a situation during a session when it becomes clear that the learner is consciously and/or deliberately choosing to avoid answering questions that will make him or her face an awkward or unpalatable course of action. The action may involve the learner upsetting a close friend or colleague, disciplining a member of the team, or accepting that their personal ambitions are unrealistic or that their job is never going to be satisfying for them. In these types of situations, the coach-mentor may believe that the learner's future positive development will only be possible if the uncomfortable truth is openly acknowledged.

The transfer technique involves transferring the responsibility for asking the awkward or unpalatable questions to the learner by using a phrase like: 'Can you help me by putting yourself in my position? If you were facing the situation where a learner was responding as you are, how would you handle the situation? What questions would you try to get the learner to answer or what suggestions or options would you encourage the learner to consider?'

We have found that, almost without exception, learners 'transfer' their behaviour, often in quite an assertive manner, and recommend a course of questioning or suggested options that force the issues to be confronted in a positive way. In the process of 'transferring' their behaviour, they often very quickly recognize the reality of their previous reactions and find it easier to resume the session in a new and more positive frame of mind. There is also a tendency to justify this behaviour change by using phrases like, 'Of course, the reason that I didn't decide that in the first place is...'. At that point, it becomes easier to probe further into their real reluctance.

The transfer technique enables the coach-mentor to help learners free themselves from some of the in-built assumptions that are limiting their freedom to think differently. In this sense, the technique gets close to what Kline calls the 'incisive question' in her book *Time to Think* (1999). She writes: 'Over the years I have collected Incisive Questions that made a difference to people's lives and organizations.' Below are some samples. Note that the first part of the question asserts a positive assumption; the second part directs the thinker's attention back to his or her issue or goal:

- If you were to become the chief executive, what problems would you solve first and how would you go about it?
- If you knew you were vital to this organization's success, how would you approach your work?
- If things could be exactly right for you in this situation, how would they have to change?
- If you were not to hold back in your life, what would you be doing?
- If a doctor told you that your life depended on changing the way you lived, what would you do first for yourself?

These examples give just a glimpse of the powerful impact the skilful coach-mentor can have in liberating their learners' minds to think in completely new and potentially beneficial ways of the options that really exist for them.

Lack of confidence or self-belief: the 'appreciative inquiry' technique

Appreciative inquiry was originally a theory for organizational development, developed in late 1980s and early 1990s by Cooperrider *et al* (2008). In recent years, with the growth of positive psychology, its potential as a coaching technique has become recognized, particularly where learners tend to see only the negative aspects of themselves or their situation.

When working with disadvantaged communities, Cooperrider and his colleagues noticed that the traditional problem-focused 'tell me what is wrong' approaches seemed to produce problem-centred answers. Therefore, they began to frame their questions differently: 'Tell me what is right.' They found this approach produced more positive and empowered responses, with the community starting to take responsibility for their own development. In this way, the appreciative inquiry technique represents a viable complement to conventional problem-oriented approaches. The different approaches are illustrated in Table 8.1.

Table 8.1 Problem-solving process

Traditional Process	Appreciative Inquiry
• Define the problem • Fix what's broken • Focus on decay	• Search for solutions that already exist • Amplify what is working • Focus on the positives
What problem are you having?	*What is working well around here?*

The concept of appreciative inquiry is based on a set of assumptions described by Hammond in *The Thin Book of Appreciative Inquiry* (2013):

1 In every society, organization or group, something works.

2 What we focus on becomes our reality.

3 Reality is created in the moment, and there are multiple realities.

4 The language we use creates our reality.

5 The act of asking questions of an organization, group or individual influences them in some way.

6 People have more confidence to journey to the unknown future when they carry forward parts of their known past.

7 If we carry forward parts of the past, they should be what are best about the past.

8 It is important to value differences.

From the perspective of a coach-mentor working with someone lacking confidence or self-belief, these assumptions can be liberating:

• People's view of their reality will be shaped by what they persistently talk about.

• By inquiring about the best of the learner's past you can create a more desirable future.

• By asking about positive options and possibilities, a coach-mentor can build confidence.

• A powerful positive image of ourselves will inspire us to action.

From these assumptions an appreciative inquiry technique of sequencing questions has been developed, consisting of four steps in a logical sequence similar to GROW and HELP. These four steps are:

1 Discovery.

2 Dream.

3 Design.

4 Deliver.

The following example illustrates how these steps could be applied to a coach-mentoring session.

1. Discovery: appreciating the best of what is

The purpose of this first step is to encourage learners to recall the conditions that surrounded and supported similar positive experiences in the past. This way you help 'anchor' their vision of a future situation to what has worked for them before:

- Recall positive experiences similar to your current challenge. What kinds of conditions were present during these positive experiences?
- Think back to a recent success. What did you do to make it successful?
- What was it about the environment/the community/the organization/the people that contributed to this good experience? What was your own contribution?
- Tell me about those times when you felt most productive, engaged, energized: how did that make you feel?
- What do you value about yourself as a professional and what you have to offer?
- What is the core factor that gives meaning to your work?

2. Dream: create in your own head the results of what might be

The purpose of the second step is to help learners imagine what their perfect future situation would look like. Having a clear vision of a desirable future will help them focus their development efforts, expand their potential and challenge any barriers:

- Imagine your current situation with everything going as you would wish it to be.
- What would the situation look like if all the factors were in place?

- What would your situation look like if all the factors that are most conducive to your performance were in place for you?
- What would the ideal outcome be for your dilemma?
- If your wishes came true, what would your perfect day be like?
- Imagine that some time has passed. What would your situation look like if everything had gone as planned?

3. Design: co-constructing the ideal

The purpose of the design stage is to help learners take their dream seriously for a moment and to produce imaginative ideas about what would need to happen for them to realize their dream. Thinking about innovative ideas will also help them define the dream in more detail. The coach-mentor should encourage them to be as imaginative and innovative as possible without worrying about being practical:

- Building on your previous positive experiences, how could you realize your dream?
- What ideas could be effective in helping you achieve your positive goal?
- What ideas could have high impact in shifting your current situation toward your ideal?
- Think of three things that would significantly change your situation and contribute to achieving your ideal situation.
- If you had a magic wand, what three changes would you make to improve the enjoyment and pleasure you gain from your work?
- What are the main actions or elements contained in each of the previous ideas?

4. Deliver: realizing the dream by transforming your ideas into practical actions

The purpose of the fourth stage is to help learners decide what actions they will take immediately as practical steps towards their ideal goal, building on their ideas from the design phase. This is an iterative process where learners may need to revisit their earlier reflections. The actions should be realistic and as concrete as possible and only agreed if the learner is really committed:

- What actions are you ready to take to move towards your ideal?
- What will you seek to do?
- How are you going to make this happen?

- When will you make this happen?
- Who do you need to contact?
- Who else needs to be involved?

Imagining a positive future outcome built on past positive experiences is an important technique for countering initial negative images, beliefs and expectations.

Work–life balance: the 'balance wheel' technique

As the name suggests, the balance wheel technique is particularly useful where learners want to work on improving the balance of parts or the whole of their life. The technique can be used in a wide variety of contexts: for example, the wheel of life can be used where they wish to rebalance their whole life; the wheel of work can be used to improve the balance between different aspects of their work.

The technique consists of drawing a large circle and dividing it into eight wedge-shaped segments of equal size. Each of the segments of the wheel represents an important factor to the learner. An example of the wheel of life is illustrated in Figure 8.4 and the wheel of work in Figure 8.5.

Figure 8.4 Wheel of life

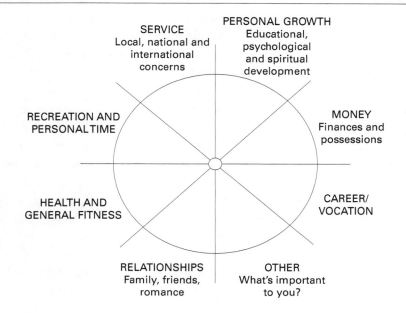

Figure 8.5 Wheel of work

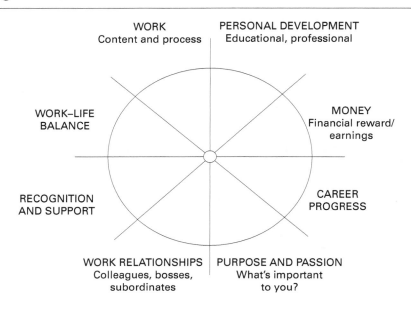

Using the wheels

The example headings in Figures 8.4 and 8.5 are common to nearly everyone in the context of life or work. One or two segments should be left blank for the individual to put in what is important to him or her. The choice of headings for each of these factors should be up to the learner. This has two benefits: labelling some of the segments saves time in creating the tool and helps the learner understand what would be appropriate descriptors for the other headings. Alternatively, the learner could be shown a completed wheel as an example and then given one with no prescribed headings. This would acknowledge the importance of the learner feeling ownership of the headings by being able to choose what is important to him or her. However, this approach will be more time-consuming.

Each segment of the wheel has a scale of 0–10, with 0 at the centre representing total dissatisfaction and 10 at the outside representing total satisfaction with that factor. The learner is invited to shade in each segment to the degree to which he or she is satisfied with that factor of his or her life or work. Note that the important factor is the degree of satisfaction, not the amount of time spent on each factor or topic. The individual may not spend much time or energy on a certain section; he or she may be totally satisfied with that area and would shade it all in. Conversely, he or she may spend all his or her time in one area but be very dissatisfied; in this case he or she would only shade in a small part of the segment.

When the learner has completed the wheel, the relative size of the shaded segments is important to the diagnosis, and represents a new perimeter made up of the heights of all the shaded segments. The coach-mentor may want to ask such questions as: 'If the new perimeter of the circle represents your wheel of life, how smooth would the ride be, if this were a real wheel?' The implication is that significant variations in the size of each segment suggest a corresponding imbalance in their life and work. The joint exploration of what the completed wheel means for the learner should prove beneficial in helping him or her understand his or her situation and how to improve it.

The effectiveness of the technique lies in its powerful visual impact combined with the simplicity of its creation. Its use is easily explained to learners, who choose their own words to describe the segments of their wheel.

Simplicity tips – improve your questioning skills

1 Work hard to build rapport and put the other person at ease by adopting a friendly, supportive, helpful manner.

2 Be prepared to explain clearly why you need to ask questions.

3 Think about some questions in advance. However, do not be constrained by prepared questions. You need to be flexible enough to probe where necessary.

4 Try to ask clear, concise and specific questions but remember that open questions usually provide the most useful information.

5 Always acknowledge answers positively and in an encouraging tone.

6 Give answers real consideration before responding yourself. A pause will show that you have done so.

7 Use silence when appropriate (it may intimidate, so be careful, but it can provide additional, sensitive information as respondents may feel the need to keep talking).

8 Probe, where you need to, for extra information. Use phrases such as, 'Is that all?' or 'Are you sure we have covered everything?'

9 Realize the importance of developing self-awareness by using questions such as, 'How did you feel as you did it?', 'When and where did you think your performance began to improve?' or 'Why do you think you got that response?'

10 Always check your understanding by summarizing and using reflective questions.

Endnotes

Cooperrider, D, Whitney, D and Stavros, J (2008) *Appreciative Inquiry Handbook*, Berrett-Koehler, San Francisco, CA

Downey, M (2014) *Effective Modern Coaching*, LID Publishing, London

Gallwey, W T (1974) *The Inner Game of Tennis*, Random House, New York

Hammond, S (2013) *The Thin Book of Appreciative Enquiry*, Thin Book Publishing, Plano, TX

Kline, N (1999) *Time to Think: Listening to ignite the human mind*, Cassell, London

Whitmore, J ([1992] 2010) *Coaching for Performance*, Nicholas Brealey, London

Situational supervision? 09

Situational supervision

Before 2000, the term 'coaching supervision' hardly existed and was rarely mentioned in any of the coaching manuals. Since then there has been a steadily increasing interest in supervision to the point where every book on coaching, including this one, has to take it into account.

In 2014, the CIPD updated the research into the development of coaching supervision from the original 2006 survey. This study covered more countries and approximately the same number of respondents. The updated findings show a very large increase in the percentage of coaches receiving supervision. In the UK it rose from 44 per cent to 92 per cent, with supervision becoming more widespread across other regions of the world.

In the previous edition of this book, coach supervision was only worth part of the chapter looking at the emerging profession. In this edition, we have given the subject a chapter to itself in recognition of its continued growth. We are going to consider what has led to this growing interest and how it relates to professional development for coaches and mentors. We will introduce a model showing that coach-mentors will need more than one type of supervision at different stages of their personal development. We also hope it will help coaches and mentors consider supervision for themselves and how it might apply to their own development.

Supervision has been an established part of other professions, such as psychotherapy, counselling and nursing, for many years. It is a job requirement for people in these professions to be engaged in supervision on a regular and regulated basis. The National Health Service describes clinical supervision as: 'A formal process of professional support and learning which enables individual practitioners to develop knowledge and competence, assume responsibility for their own practice, and enhance consumer protection and safety of care in complex situations.'

The importance this profession puts on effective clinical supervision is further illustrated by how the Mental Health Nurses Association describes it:

> A dynamic, interpersonally focused experience promotes the development of therapeutic proficiency. One of the primary reasons for all supervision is to ensure that the quality of therapeutic intervention with the client is of a consistently high standard in relation to the client's needs. Consequently, supervision must be acknowledged as a cornerstone of clinical practice.

We believe that it is not a coincidence that the increase in the number of psychotherapists and psychologists entering the coaching profession coincides with an increase in discussions about coaching supervision. As individuals from these professions move into the coaching environment, it is natural that they will want to bring their established and respected practices with them. It could be argued that it is the psychologists and psychotherapists who are driving the move towards making it a professional requirement for coaches to be 'in supervision'.

At the time of writing the previous edition, there was a lively debate among professionals about the use of the word 'supervision' in the context of coaching and mentoring. This was because of its connotations with clinical supervision and line management. In many practitioners' views, supervision is basically a post-qualification or post-basic training requirement that relates to the ongoing professional development and practice of a coach or mentor to ensure that he or she continues to be competent and up to date with current developments and ideas of 'best practice' in the profession. Thus the debate centred on the need to agree definitions, standards and perhaps consider an alternative and more appropriate term than 'supervision'.

That debate now seems to be settled, judging by the fact that several international coaching bodies, including APECS, AC, and EMCC, have published accreditations for coach supervisors. The EMCC have also published an accreditation process for coach supervision training programmes.

Self-regulation

It would appear that the case for supervision is being driven by regulatory pressures from a number of the leading players in the profession. The EMCC, as part of its role in bringing the key influencers of the profession together, has stated in its code of ethics that members are required to: 'Maintain a relationship with a suitably-qualified supervisor who will regularly assess their competence and support their development.'

Most of the major professional bodies mentioned earlier have similar expectations of their members to be in regular supervision. However, there are many individuals in the profession who don't need to be 'told' to have supervision. Many coaches, whether they are members of professional institutes or not, see supervision as an essential part of self-development. They seek it out because they know that continuous professional development makes a significant difference to their practice.

Many organizations employ internal coaches to promote coaching as a driver of cultural change, develop a coaching culture, or provide individual coaching for identified employees. Among these internal coaches there is also the recognition of the need for coaching supervision. In this case, the additional organizational drivers are to increase internal capability, standardize approaches and disseminate best practices across the community.

What is coaching supervision?

There seems to be quite a wide spread of wording when it comes to defining coaching supervision. Most definitions seem to be a variation on Bachkirova *et al* (2005) who describe it in businesslike terms as: 'A formal process of professional support, which ensures continuing development of the coach and effectiveness of his/her coaching practice through interactive reflection, interpretive evaluation and the sharing of expertise.' At its most basic: 'Supervision is a regular, protected time for facilitated, in-depth reflection on coaching practice'(Bond and Holland, 1998).

Whatever actual definition is preferred, there appears to be a common agreement that coaching and mentoring supervision is set up to facilitate the ongoing learning, development and continuous improvement of coaches and mentors. Taking the various definitions into account, we believe the essential elements of effective coaching supervision are:

- *Regular sessions* – how often you should have a supervision session is not clear and there do not appear to be any universal standards. One considered approach is to link supervision frequency to a specified number of coaching hours as with counselling and nursing supervision. However the frequency is worked out, it is clear that for coaching supervision to be effective it needs to be seen as a regular process. The most common frequency seems to be every two or three months but it ranges from monthly to six-monthly. There seems little evidence of frequency linked directly to hours of coaching practice.

- *Reflection on practice* – the main topic of conversation during a supervision session is the supervisee's coaching practice. Past experiences are reviewed to extract the learning from the experience to improve future practice.

- *Alternative perspective* – the role of the supervisor is more participatory than in many coaching relationships. The supervisor is expected to be more of a mentor, bringing and sharing his or her own experiences, knowledge and understanding to enhance the learning.

- *Independent integrity* – the supervisor takes an impartial and external view, acting on behalf of the whole profession and the end client. This enables him or her to hold up the supervisee's behaviour to professional scrutiny, challenge it on occasions and, in some instances, report on trends and key issues to a sponsor or professional body.

- *Learning focus* – the main purpose of coaching supervision seems to be to facilitate the learning and ongoing development of the supervisee. This is done through a combination of reflection and analysis of past experiences, sharing good practices, and teaching new techniques and theories.

Having said there are several common features of coach-mentor supervision, there are several distinct types of supervision depending on the situation.

Formal or informal?

We could argue that if the key role of a coaching supervisor is to facilitate learning and continuous development for the coach and mentor, this is just what an experienced coach does for his or her clients. A coach does not need to be a subject expert to help learners reflect on their situation. Doesn't a coach enable learners to draw significant learning through active listening and probing questioning?

Many of a coach's needs for support can be met through informal peer supervision between equals, either one-to-one or in groups. This form of relationship will satisfy the need to share experiences and ideas and will also help to reflect on incidents and dilemmas from past sessions. If we believe that peer coaching makes the learning experience richer through the expression of a diversity of views, we can accept that informal peer supervision is a very effective and legitimate form of supervision.

While the intentions of both relationships are the same, we believe the main differences between formal coaching supervision and informal peer coaching or 'coaching the coach' are as follows:

- Part of the supervisor's role is that of teacher, so it is expected that the supervisor is more experienced, skilled and/or knowledgeable than the supervisee in specific aspects of coaching and mentoring. The supervisor enhances 'seeing': the seeing into the coaches' practice, the illumination of subtle processes in coaching conversations and of blind spots, deaf spots and dumb spots in themselves and in their thinking.

- Coaches in supervision often refer to the relief of having time and space to think about particular aspects of their work and especially to think/ reflect with a trusted colleague who will microscopically explore practice with them and contribute to their understanding.

- This support enables coaches to contain and resolve some of the more challenging parts of their work, for example:
  - their frustrations with learners;
  - their concern that they are not doing enough;
  - the difficulty of keeping to a coaching contract when the coaching approaches boundaries;
  - the undue influence of the organization (often implicit) or of key stakeholders that might reduce coach effectiveness (power disempowerment);
  - unexpected emotional material either within the coach or in the learner;
  - 'ruptures' in the coaching relationship.

- Therefore, a supervisor needs a good appreciation of philosophy and psychology to provide this 'super-vision' of the coach's practice.

- The supervisor is also expected to represent the profession and uphold the associated ethics, values, standards and policies. The supervisor is therefore effectively playing an independent 'managerial' role. This part of the role provides some level of protection for clients, their purchasing organizations, the provider organizations and the professional bodies.

The expertise and experience needed to effectively carry out these complex roles may be difficult to find in a colleague.

A significant potential weakness of the informal peer supervision is the 'blind leading the blind' or 'we don't know what we don't know'. If the peers in this form of relationship have equal knowledge and experience, where will the learning come from? The quality of the anticipated continuous professional development may suffer without the input from a more skilled and knowledgeable coach-mentoring supervisor.

Another potential weakness is the danger of collusion between peers. Where peers work for the same organization, perhaps in the same department, there is a temptation not to challenge. This may be through wishing to be friends and not upset people, or in support of an internal policy, or in fear of reprisals, or due to other internal politics. In these situations, it is felt that only an external supervisor can provide the required independent and objective challenge.

Many descriptions and definitions, such as this one, specifically refer to development of the coach as one of the main purposes of coaching supervision. People seek out experiences that will help them to grow, develop and change over time. Therefore, the purpose of supervision is to provide a 'safe' and effective way of extracting learning and meaning from critical cognitive conflicts. Safe because the communication between supervisee and supervisor works on the level of professional peers. It is easily understood and accepted by both and less intimidating or partial than advice from a superior.

Having discussed the essential elements of coaching supervision, it is clear that it is not a case of 'one size fits all'. There have been many concepts published describing different ways in which adults learn. It therefore follows that there are different ways in which supervisees learn from supervision. If coaching supervision is a core part of continuous professional development, a supervisee will have different development needs at different stages of their professional development. It therefore follows that they will need different types of support at these different stages from their supervisors.

Situational supervision

This section of the chapter combines changing development needs and corresponding supervisor skills and attributes into a coherent framework. This framework is called the 'Situational Supervision model' based on Blanchard's 'Situational Leadership' four-box model, discussed in Chapter 1. The simple but powerful premise is to substitute the role of the supervisor for that of the leader and expand the framework from two-two to three-three.

The model shows three distinct stages of learning and development – interpersonal, institutional, and interindividual – based on the work of Robert Kegan. Each stage requires a different role for the supervisor: super-coach, peer-mentor and psychologist-coach.

Super-coach supervisor

Many supervisees start in the interpersonal stage of their development as inexperienced coach-mentors. This is demonstrated by their lack of confidence in their own ability. They have low self-esteem in relation to their coachees. They believe there is a 'right' way to coach and want to do it the right way. They tend to see the supervisor as someone who knows the answer and will help them make the correct decisions. This is informational learning, as their primary focus is on the acquisition of more coach-mentor skills and increased knowledge. The supervisee needs advice on the appropriate use of the various tools and processes associated with effective coach-mentoring. Therefore, at this stage of the supervisees' development, the supervisor predominantly requires a thorough knowledge of tools and processes.

Peer-mentor supervisor

At the institutional stage of their development, the supervisees are self-motivated, self-evaluative and able to make their own decisions. They see themselves as co-creators of their environment and their context and demonstrate the attributes of 'self-directed learners'. This order of consciousness is where most supervision relationships seem to spent most of their time. This is characterized by the emergence of a clear independent sense of who they are that is distinct from the co-constructed version built up in the interpersonal stage. This supervision role here is to help the supervisees build confidence to work in a variety of organizations and construct an identity for themselves that will be coherent across different coaching contexts.

Psychologist supervisor

In the interindividual order they have reached the stage in their own development where they are mature enough and confident enough in themselves to question their own values and assumptions, not just as coaches and mentors but also as individuals. The supervisor working at this stage of the model needs to be skilled and experienced in the practical application of a range of psychological concepts and theories. Supervision sessions will be concerned with helping the supervisee understand who they are as a person and their place in the world.

Having said there are three distinct states in the development of a supervisee, research suggests that within each of these development stages there are three incremental levels. These levels are characterized as 'novice', 'developer' and 'practitioner', derived from the skills development model.

The model shows a progression route to develop any skill or capability. This is the well-known model described earlier in Chapter 4. In Figure 9.1, I have added my own descriptions to the model to suit this context:

Figure 9.1 Skills Development Model

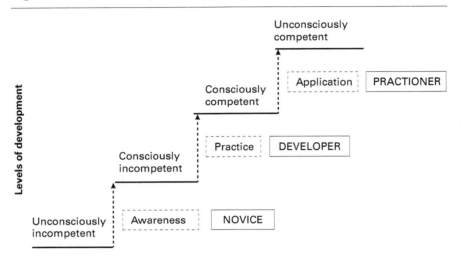

Novice describes someone who doesn't know what they don't know and is said to be 'unconsciously incompetent'. At this lowest level, supervisees would not know what they should be doing and genuinely need to be made aware of what to do. For example, those supervisees in the interpersonal stage, novice level start not knowing which tools to use and not knowing how to coach. This is how the unconsciously incompetent level manifests itself. For those individuals in the institutional stage, this novice level is characterized by working in one coaching context and not having experience of other contexts. The development need at this level is for gaining information and knowledge to raise awareness.

Developer level describes someone who knows what they should be doing but cannot do it well; in other words they are consciously incompetent. At the institutional stage, conscious incompetence comes through exposure to other contexts and realizing what they have to develop in order to work effectively in these unfamiliar contexts. Their need at this level is for practice and reflection on their practice to develop understanding.

The third level is called *Practitioner*, where they are 'consciously competent' because they have the skills and ability to do it effectively and the confidence to put it into practice. The supervision at this level focuses on widening their understanding, broadening the context and challenging them to move outside their comfort zone.

The supervisee is ready to work at the next stage in their development when they reach the unconscious competence level. Once a coach feels they have mastered the use of coaching tools and techniques they seek to broaden the context in which they work. This means they become incompetent again and the next cycle of development begins. Once they are comfortable working in any context they seek to understand themselves better. This is where they seek to identify their personal values and drivers.

The combination of Kegan's top three stages or orders with Maslow's three skill development levels provides the dimensions for the Situational Supervision model. The full logic of this concept is explained by the descriptive paragraphs in each box of the model in Figure 9.2.

Figure 9.2 The Situational Supervision model

ROLE OF SUPERVISOR			
Super-coach	**Peer-mentor**	**Coaching psychologist**	
Develop their own tools and/or the confidence to work without tools	Confidence to work in any context or regardless of the context	Start to define their own psychological model	**Practitioner**
Advice on more advanced tools	Confidence to work outside their familiar contexts	Question their own behaviour and articulate and live by their values	**Developer**
Advice on simple tools. Joint exploration of simple and familiar contexts	Start to consider their own values and behaviours	Start to consider their own values and behaviours	**Novice**
Understand tools	**Understand context**	**Understand themselves**	
NEEDS OF SUPERVISEE			

This model shows how the role of the supervisor changes to match the supervisee's development needs, as expressed in Orders of Consciousness, and their appropriate intervention changes to match the supervisee's skill developmental level. The model specifies the three distinct roles of a coach supervisor.

This Situational Supervision model provides a simple and pragmatic framework that encompasses the whole range of supervision concepts. The implication is that a coach-mentor seeking a suitable supervisor may need to consider which stage of their development, or situation, they are in and therefore what skills and experiences they need from a potential supervisor.

This model helps to explain the various supervisor roles and approaches within the overall umbrella of coach-mentoring supervision and how to relate them to the changing developmental needs of the supervisee. This will enable both the supervisee to more effectively choose an appropriately skilled supervisor and the supervisor to match their style of support and development interventions to the situational needs of each supervisee.

How does supervision add value?

If there is a case to be made for formal coach-mentoring supervision, what are the actual benefits? The best people to answer this important question are coaches and mentors who are receiving supervision for their own benefit. Here are some of the comments from an OCM discussion forum of professional coaches asking that very question:

> Sometimes we need a 'back stop'– a route to discuss those inevitable dilemmas we face where we are not quite sure how to proceed. Good supervision can clarify our thinking and help us to determine a way forward. It can mitigate any feelings of isolation or even helplessness, giving us confidence, fresh perspectives or perhaps just a reality check.

> It is a mechanism for helping us to develop personally our effectiveness as coaches. It should be a sounding board for testing our skills and abilities and enabling us to improve in such respects. I firmly believe that coaches need coaching too, to avoid us slipping into or perpetuating bad habits.

> It's not just about identifying when we are stuck – you could argue that when we are conscious of an issue we are on the way to resolving it. Supervision is also there to help us pay attention to the elements we are not.

> Supervision helps us to work in a professional fashion and keep within professional boundaries. As an emerging profession we need to have good supervision arrangements in place. Each case of bad practice undermines the credibility of coaching and weakens the case for coaching as a valuable learning experience.

The same group of professional coaches was then asked whether supervision should be a mandatory part of accreditation and continued professional practice. Some thought that it should not be compulsory because, in the words of one coach:

> Any good coach will seek some form of supervision even if it's from their peers. Make it mandatory and it may lack value, becoming another tick in the box, which may not be valued by either the coach or the client.

However, most thought supervision should be a mandatory part of being a professional:

> As much as it is for other people professions but it should equally be entered into voluntarily!

> Like having a coach, I don't believe that this is an option if we seek to present ourselves to the world as professional coaches. This is a mandatory expense of being involved in the work that we do, in the same way as we register under the Data Protection Act and have professional indemnity insurance.

Do all coach-mentors need supervision?

If there is a case for practising professional coach-mentors to be in regular supervision, why isn't everyone doing it? In 2006, a survey by the CIPD found that 'while 86 per cent of coaches responding to our survey believe that coaches should have coaching supervision, only 44 per cent actually do so'. This went up to 92 per cent when the survey was repeated in 2014. However, this was a survey of professional coaches belonging to bodies strongly recommending their members should be in supervision and therefore may not be representative of the whole coaching and mentoring community.

It appeared that many practising coaches and line managers who coach their teams as part of their leadership role did not see the need for formal structured supervision. The reasons given tended to fall into the following categories:

- *Cost*: cannot afford to pay someone to supervise them.
- *Quantity*: do not do enough coaching to make it worthwhile.
- *Context*: only coach 'technical' or 'managerial' skills so don't get into problem emotional areas.
- *Competence*: already know enough and do it well enough, so don't need to go deeper. I do my own reflective practice.
- *Peer support*: get support from my peer network when I need it. I discuss issues with my own coach.
- *Availability*: cannot find a suitable supervisor.

There seems to be a subtler reason why coaching supervision is not universal:

- *Requirement*: The most common reason for having supervision is a requirement of a professional body or client organization. Therefore, if it is not an external requirement some don't see the need.

For internal line managers who simply coach their teams as a style of leadership, these views were understandable. Where coaching is seen as only one 'tool' a manager may choose to use with individuals or teams, the need for supervision is difficult to justify. Does a manager need supervision for his or her delegating or other people-handling skills? We would argue that coaching supervision for line managers is an integral part of the role of their own line manager or mentor. If managers at all levels adopt a coaching style as their normal management style, then they will be practising many of the characteristics of coaching supervision within their line role.

Also, there is considerable evidence that managers, particularly senior managers, learn best in small groups where they can share experiences and discuss ideas and dilemmas with peers in a supportive and challenging environment. Often described as 'action learning sets', these small group meetings could also be described as 'peer coaching supervision'. We believe that, as long as these sessions include and stick to a robust and rigorous learning process, they can provide effective coaching supervision in that context.

Effective continuous professional development

So in conclusion, if an organization has established a coaching culture, the need for coaching supervision should be covered by line manager reviews and formally structured action learning or peer coaching sessions. For internal, external and independent coach-mentors, the case for professional coaching and mentoring supervision is becoming clearer and more widespread. For those working in complex, diverse or emotive situations the case is already made by psychologist and author Graham Lee (2007) who summed up the situation admirably when he said:

> Coaches must ensure that their psychological and business skills are kept current through continuing professional development. This typically includes attending conferences, going on courses, reading, and in some cases, making use of a personal coach, counsellor or psychotherapist. However, the most important element of ongoing development for coaches is the use of consultative supervision.

All professions expect their members to undergo a continuous programme of professional development, or CPD. This is to ensure their knowledge and skills are kept up to date so that clients can be reassured of the competence of their coach and mentor and their continuing 'fitness to practise'. All the professional bodies described earlier have a measure of CPD criteria built into their membership requirements through their code of ethics and competence standards.

At this stage in the development of coaching and mentoring, one of the most powerful arguments for formal supervision is that it provides a very effective method of continuous professional development. Therefore, for coaches and mentors who judge themselves to be professionals, we believe they should seriously consider entering a supervision relationship.

Adults grow through transformational learning, which not only increases knowledge, but more importantly leads to deep and pervasive shifts in the learner's perspective and understanding. This transformational learning comes not from what people know but how they know. It relates to expanding and enhancing the way people actually understand the world and their experiences. This means their development processes must match their capability to make meaning from the experience. A very effective way of facilitating this is through supervision.

This suggests that the supervisor needs to be careful not to use an approach that is developmentally too basic or too advanced for the supervisee. They should consider the supervisee as a 'person evolving'. Therefore, the role of supervisor is to ensure that they become a part of the person's progression, trying to join them where they are on their developmental journey.

Endnotes

Bachkirova, T, Stevens, P and Willis, P (2005) Panel discussion on coaching supervision, Oxford Brookes Coaching and Mentoring Society, Oxford

Bond, M and Holland, S (1998) *Skills of Clinical Supervision for Nurses: A practical guide for supervisees, clinical supervisors and managers (Supervision in Context)*, Open University Press, Buckingham

Lee, G (2007) *Leadership Coaching: From personal insight to organizational performance*, CIPD, London

An industry or a maturing profession?

10

This book began by describing what are believed to be the key influencers in the field of coaching and mentoring. In the previous chapters we hope we have made clear that applications and experiences of coaching and mentoring will be different in different international and cultural environments and that we cannot hope to do them all justice in this book. However, we believe there has been a 'convergence' of these key influencers over recent years, resulting in many benefits from learning from each other.

This increasing cooperation and collaboration across the profession is a clear sign of maturity. However, throughout this book we have used the term 'profession' and it is the use of this term that raises the fundamental question we will attempt to answer in this chapter, namely: 'Do coaching and mentoring constitute an industry or a profession, or a subset of other professions?'

In attempting to answer this question, this chapter will examine the growth of professional bodies associated with coaching and mentoring and look at their recent developments. Before we do this, we will identify what we believe are the key requirements for a profession based on the models of other related professions, thus enabling us to map the current and predicted activities of the professional bodies against these key requirements and help provide an answer to the above question.

What makes a profession?

Looking at professions in related fields, they appear to share several common features:

1 Body of academic and research literature.
2 Membership bodies with differing grades or levels and status.

3 Agreed statements of ethics, values and discipline.

4 Accreditation and qualification requirements.

5 Continuing professional development requirements and criteria.

By considering each of these in more detail, it is possible to review what is currently happening in the world of coaching and mentoring and anticipate what might happen in the near future.

1. Body of literature

One of the features of a profession is a significant quantity of published academic and research literature; a profession must carry out and publish regular and rigorous research. A search on Amazon.com at the time the previous edition of this book was published identified nearly 2,500 books on coaching and mentoring; now there are six times as many at nearly 15,000. Many of the coaching publications are by practising coaches sharing tips, techniques and their best practices in how to coach. Since our previous edition, there has been substantial growth in the amount of evaluative research produced by universities in various countries. These act as a balance to those published by coaching organizations that wish to prove that their coaching has been beneficial to the organization. Understandably, there may be some concerns about the independence and objectiveness of the studies done by organizations with a vested interest in showing coaching to have been successful. On the other hand, most coaching and mentoring takes place within commercial organizations. Whilst this can generate an understandable reluctance by some to publish details of what goes on within their organizations, there has been a noticeable increase is such case studies.

However, there are a significant number of journals containing academic research, independent evaluations and practical case studies of coaching and mentoring. Here are just a few:

Coaching: An International Journal of Theory, Research and Practice

Journal of Evidence Based Coaching and Mentoring

International Journal of Coaching in Organizations

International Journal of Mentoring and Coaching

Research Papers and the Coaching at Work Journal

The Coaching Psychologist

International Coaching Psychology Review

Since the previous edition there has continued to be a steady growth in the body of published literature across all aspects of the field. This growth is in both quality and quantity, including a significant amount of research literature. Interestingly, there is still more research published about mentoring than there is about coaching. This is due to a number of factors:

- Formal mentoring programmes have been in place for a number of years.

- They are usually company sponsored and have administrative resources allocated, which makes the capturing and dissemination of the data a requirement and therefore easier.

- They are often set up with specific and common goals to be achieved and the achievement of these goals is closely monitored and published.

- Coaching programmes in contrast tend to be more individual and/or low key, making large-scale research more difficult, although the growing need to prove value for money or return on investment has increased the number of coaching case studies published.

2. Membership bodies, grades, levels and status

To be defined as a profession requires there to be one or more professional bodies to which members belong. These bodies should ideally set differing grades, levels and requirements for membership, monitor and maintain quality of practice, and provide forums for sharing good practices.

In recent years, a considerable number of professional bodies associated with coaching and mentoring have become prominent throughout the world. This proliferation can lead to some confusion for coaches and mentors seeking to join an appropriate body. Considering those predominantly in the UK, whilst they are in many ways very similar, they tend to fall into one of three categories.

Category A

This covers a much wider remit and contains special interest groups. For example:

- British Association for Counselling and Psychotherapy (BACP) – has a Coaching Division.

- British Psychological Society (BPS) – has a Special Group in Coaching Psychology and is part of the International Congress of Coaching Psychology.

- Chartered Institute of Personnel and Development (CIPD) – runs a number of courses on coaching and mentoring as well as including coaching and mentoring in its standard professional qualifications.

Category B

This category contains other professional bodies that exclusively support coaching and mentoring in various contexts, such as:

- Association for Coaching (AC) – a powerful, marketing-led organization focusing mainly on the promotion of the services and development of individual coaches and the status of the AC as a professional body.
- European Mentoring and Coaching Council (EMCC) – individual training, academic institutions and corporate members focus mainly on the quality and standards of coaching and mentoring across Europe.
- Association of Professional Executive Coaches and Supervisors (APECS) – a breakaway group from the EMCC that emphasizes the primacy of a psychotherapeutic approach to senior executive coaching, including a strict supervision regime for professional coaches.
- The International Coach Federation in the UK (ICF) – originally a US-based organization focusing on the promotion and credibility of individual coaches, but now with a large international membership structure.
- The World Association of Business Coaches (WABC) – a Canadian- and US-based organization that promotes a distinctive business focus for coaching in comparison to a more holistic approach, such as that of the ICF.

All these professional bodies have different roles and purposes and therefore appeal to different groups of coaches and mentors.

Category C

In the UK, the government plays a significant role through the Quality and Curriculum Authority (QCA), which sets the standards for all academic and vocational qualifications. Academic institutions offer a range of qualifications but, in the vocational arena, the various awarding bodies apply National Occupational Standards (NOS) frameworks.

NOS frameworks describe what people need to do, know and understand in their job to carry out their role in a consistent and competent way. They are widely used as building blocks for UK vocational qualifications and business improvement tools. The standards are developed by groups of employers for their employees through a Sector Skills Council (SSC) or Standards Setting Body (SSB) and the qualifications are often termed National Vocational Qualifications or NVQs. The SSB responsible for the Coaching and Mentoring National Occupational Standards is known as ENTO.

As well as membership bodies, a requirement to be considered a profession is the identification of different levels or grades of practitioner. A review of the current professional bodies shows that they all have a number of membership grades to identify levels of coaching and mentoring. These levels typically are:

- Affiliate – for those interested but not considered as competent.
- Associate – for those learning or just starting to develop their competence.
- Member – for those considered as competent and experienced.
- Fellow – for those who have made a significant contribution or are very competent and very experienced.

The exact descriptions tend to vary, but the above list covers the concept and is transferable across most professions. The requirements for different levels of membership are usually a combination of experience, often expressed as a number of years' proven practice, plus qualification training and ongoing professional education attainment.

3. Agreed statements of ethics, values and discipline

All professions produce a statement of ethics and values that all members of that profession agree to abide by in their practice. These statements or codes are published by the professional bodies and adhering to the relevant code is a condition of membership. But is there an agreed code of ethics and values for coaches?

At the time of writing the answer would have to be that there is not a single code that everyone supports. However, there are a number of coaching bodies, each producing their codes of ethics. Although these codes are not identical they do contain many similar statements and cover the same areas. They all seek to champion coaching excellence and to advance its professional practice.

The common themes the various codes define and describe include:

- *Competence* – training, continuing professional development, supervision and experience.

- *Context* – the relationships, expectations and contracting.
- *Boundary management* – referrals and conflicts of interest.
- *Integrity* – confidentiality, disclosures and the law.
- *Professionalism* – protecting the client, openness and exploitation.
- *Breaches of the code* – the complaints procedure.

The main professional bodies globally are the European Mentoring and Coaching Council (EMCC), the Association for Coaching (AC), and the International Coaching Federation (ICF). They have shared aims and have been collaborating closely in recent years.

A tangible sign of the increasing collaboration between these bodies was the creation of the **UK Coaching Bodies Roundtable** in 2005. The term 'Roundtable' was agreed as a compromise to protect the aspirations of some of the bodies who feared domination by other bodies. The objective of the Roundtable was to work together to maintain the principles on which the various bodies agreed and through which they would operate. Specifically:

- to cooperate to enhance the reputation of the coaching industry;
- to issue joint statements on issues of shared concern;
- to discuss the areas where collaboration might be of benefit.

The first area where this collaboration saw tangible progress was in 2007 with the publication of a unanimously agreed 'statement of shared professional values'.

This published statement was followed by the establishment of a joint project in 2008. This involves all bodies agreeing on definitions, descriptions and standards for coaching supervision.

These lead bodies have continued to work together and in 2012 formalized and launched the **Global Coaching and Mentoring Alliance** designed to advance the professional coaching and mentoring industry. As a demonstration of their ever-closer cooperation they published a formal agreement which stated:

> As a collective of global professional coaching and mentoring bodies we seek to build alliances, a cooperative spirit, purpose and initiatives where we can partner to make a difference to the emerging profession and society as a whole.

As part of this work, in 2015 the alliance reviewed and confirmed the alignment of a global set of common coaching and mentoring competences. Then in 2016, the AC and EMCC jointly published a Global Code of Ethics for Coaches and Mentors, which states:

As membership bodies, we are committed to maintaining and promoting excellent practice in coaching and mentoring. All our members, as part of their continuing membership, agree to adhere to the elements and principles of this code of ethics. This code of ethics aligns with the content and requirements set out in the Professional Charter for Coaching and Mentoring. The Charter, which was drafted in accordance with European law, is registered on the dedicated European Union database, which lists self-regulation initiatives in Europe. This code of ethics sets the expectation of best practice in coaching and mentoring and promotes the development of coaching and mentoring excellence. Its purpose is to:

- Provide appropriate guidelines, accountability and enforceable standards of conduct for all our members.

- Set out how our members are expected to act, behave and perform when working with clients.

- In conjunction with our respective bodies' competences, guide our members' development and growth in the profession.

- Serve as a guide for those individuals who do not necessarily identify themselves as a professional coach or mentor, but nonetheless use coaching or mentoring skills in their work.

Although the industry seems to be dominated by these inclusive professional bodies there are many more which support specific sectors, such as the Association of Professional Executive Coaches and Supervisors (APECS), or individual countries. So although there is not quite a single code of ethics and values, there is sufficient commonality combined with specialist alternatives to enable any aspiring professional coach or mentor to find a code that matches his or her own values and philosophy.

4. Accreditation and qualification requirements

Accreditation, certification and qualification are common terms used within all professions and coaching and mentoring are no exception. These terms are often used interchangeably and incorrectly. Before considering coaching and mentoring specifically this section will try to clear up this confusion and clarify the meaning of each term.

Accreditation is the process by which a formal, third-party authoritative body gives recognition of an organization's competence to perform a specific task or tasks. Accreditation is the confirmation that such an organization, or body, has the appropriate quality management systems and is competent to effectively assess against the appropriate requirements in a fair and efficient manner. Such accreditation would normally involve an auditing process by an impartial and independent 'accreditation body'. Once a body is 'accredited' they can then 'certify' others.

Certification is the verification that an individual has adequate credentials to practise specified activities. This is usually provided by an external review, assessment or audit. An independent 'certified' body provides certification via some form of written assurance to confirm the service or product meets specific standard requirements. The certification verifies that the individual has achieved a specified level of compliance and competence within a specific professional area.

Qualifications generally refer to someone passing an examination or assessment which confers status as a recognized practitioner of a profession or specialized activity. The successful achievement of a qualification gives a reliable indication the individual can demonstrate the required minimum standard of knowledge, experience and understanding of the subject being assessed at a specific level of capability. Qualifications often consist of several levels of attainment grouped together for a specific subject, each level indicating a higher requirement of knowledge, expertise or experience.

Accredited qualifications, also called regulated qualifications, are those that are reviewed, recognized and monitored by the relevant regulatory body in order to ensure they meet specific criteria and quality standards. This gives a guarantee that the qualification is of appropriate quality and conforms to the requirements of the relevant profession.

Most professions have a qualification requirement before an individual can achieve full membership of the profession. In the UK, that qualification must be recognized by the government's QCA as well as the profession's membership bodies.

This has posed a problem for some of the emerging professional bodies, which have opted for a process of self-certification of experience (or accreditation) without direct links into the recognized governmental structures and with varying levels of rigour in their training requirements in their 'credentialling' process. In part, this slightly odd term 'credentialling' has been imported from the United States by the ICF, which based its process largely on the US experience. This has led to confusion because most Europeans tend to see accreditation as a post-qualification process to confirm ongoing 'fitness to practise' whereas the ICF process, although very rigorous, can be seen as an alternative to a basic qualification requirement. As the profession has matured, agreements have been reached around applying the concept of 'equivalence', which recognizes identical or very similar practices using different words and sometimes differing processes.

Although most of the bodies have a structured approach, the EMCC approach is described in detail. EMCC initially carried out a three-year worldwide research project to survey all published competency frameworks as the basis for developing its own. The EMCC then conducted a further two-year consultation period across the coaching and mentoring community. This led to a reduction in the number of levels and a simplification of the language used to make it more easily understood and applied to the variety of contexts in which coaching and mentoring apply. The published competence framework and associated set of competence statements suggested four levels of capability:

Foundation Level	Equivalent to NVQ 4
Practitioner Level	Equivalent to Postgraduate Certificate
Senior Practitioner Level	Equivalent to Postgraduate Diploma
Master Practitioner Level	Equivalent to Master's Degree

This framework has enabled practising coaches or mentors to 'map' their capability against the various competence levels and statements to establish where their level of competence fits against such a universal standard. The competence framework also allows different coaching qualifications and training programmes to be benchmarked against the levels. There is a quality assurance process run across Europe by the EMCC, which has enabled many of the leading training organizations to submit their training programmes to be assessed against any of the four levels.

This carries many benefits relevant to a professional status. It enables potential purchasers of external coaching to compare suppliers on an equal basis. It also helps training organizations to explain which level of capability their qualification equips someone to achieve. This in turn helps someone seeking a qualification or training programme to choose the most appropriate one for his or her current capability and aspirations.

Although there is not one professional 'lead body', this benchmark framework satisfies another requirement of a profession, making it possible to compare different qualifications and coaches and mentors working in different contexts against a common standard. Again, the concept of 'equivalence' will prove to be a unifying instrument to achieve wide acceptance.

Qualifications are available from many suppliers as well as some of the professional bodies that completely or partly cover the competences related to specific levels. This enables anyone to source training or development programmes that will enable them to satisfy the education requirements for all the professional levels. Becoming a qualified coach or mentor does not require an individual to complete a programme of training or development carrying the appropriate accreditation. A process to accredit individuals is widely available that recognizes that there are many individuals who have developed considerable expertise, and have significant experience as practising and successful coaches and mentors, without undergoing a formal qualification or training programme. This individual accreditation process uses the well-established 'Accreditation of Prior Experience and Learning' or APEL process. The availability of this individual accreditation process to complement the formal accreditation programmes means everyone has access to a suitable qualification.

5. Continuous professional development criteria

All professions expect their members to undergo a continuous programme of professional development, or CPD. This is to ensure their knowledge and skills are kept up to date so that clients can be reassured of the competence of their coach and mentor and their continuing 'fitness to practise'. All the professional bodies described earlier have a measure of CPD criteria built into their membership requirements through their code of ethics and the competence standards. This CPD generally includes some form of supervision or structured reflection on learning from working with their clients. This ongoing development of skills and practical experience is seen as essential for the professional coach-mentor.

So once again another requirement of a profession is satisfied. There are a full range of qualifications available and clear statements of the CPD requirements.

So, is it a profession or an industry?

Let us first consider the case against a 'profession'.

It is probable that many coaches and mentors are not currently a member of one of the professional bodies described in this chapter. They may not subscribe to a code of ethics and may not have a formally recognized qualification. There may be those who do not regularly practise CPD or take part in supervision sessions. Some coaches and mentors working in organizations where it is only one part of their role would consider most of this irrelevant or inappropriate to what they do.

There is not a single 'lead body' or dominant professional institute. While there is increasing cooperation between bodies, such as the Global Coaching and Mentoring Alliance, there are differences in their philosophy and approach. Also, there is no government regulation for coaches and mentors; they are not required to be a member of a professional body or to have a qualification to practise. A coach or mentor cannot get 'struck off' or banned from practising by any professional body.

However, huge sums of money are being spent by organizations on buying external coaching, and the quantity of people calling themselves coaches or mentors is also significant. So, in terms of quantities and proliferation across both public and private sectors, there is a case to say it is certainly an industry.

A 'profession' or simply 'professional'?

Now let's consider the case for coaching and mentoring being a 'profession'.

First, many people entering the field of coaching and mentoring would consider themselves as professionals moving from other professions. These would include psychotherapists, psychologists, therapists, counsellors, trainers and managers. Therefore, describing the world of coaching and mentoring as an industry containing many professionals would be accurate.

Second, there is an increased expectation for external and internal coaches and mentors to be accredited by a professional body. There is more emphasis on demonstrating commitment via evidence of CPD such as completion of accredited training programmes, ongoing reflective practice and/or supervision. Clients expect their coaches to adhere to a code of ethics and values.

Third, there is a growing consensus and collaboration between professional bodies. Although there is a number of them, there is sufficient commonality between them to satisfy this requirement of a profession.

Historically, most professions have started in a similarly disjointed and piecemeal way. There has been increased momentum in recent years of these discrete components coming closer together both in the UK and across national boundaries. The general acceptance among all stakeholders of common quality standards, codes of ethics and criteria for continuing professional development combined with genuine dialogue and cooperation between several powerful professional bodies are tangible steps towards the establishment of a real 'profession'. Therefore, as described in this chapter, all the elements for a profession are in place.

To answer the question asked in the title of this chapter, it is our belief that the industry of coaching and mentoring has established all the required elements for a distinct profession which is continuing to mature.

PART TWO
How to effectively implement coaching and mentoring in organizations

Why invest in CAM? What and where is the need?

11

ED PARSLOE

I believe that you have to start here – this is the key question that needs addressing for any successful implementation. Investing in coaching and mentoring (CAM) as 'a good thing' or 'nice to have' really is not an option in today's resource-strapped and time-poor organizations. In this chapter I will explore:

- What is great CAM?
- What is the focus of a CAM agenda? Where will it have the biggest impact?
- How do you create buy-in and build a business case?
- What will you measure to demonstrate impact?

What is great CAM?

We can all think of examples of where we have seen good CAM taking place inside organizations. You can probably think of examples inside your organization. For me, good CAM should go beyond personal or individual benefit to have a positive impact on an individual's or team's performance, enabling him/her/them to be more effective in their role, possibly even maximizing their potential.

Good CAM might be formally organized through HR and/or L&D. There might well be effective policies in place and processes for measuring its impact on performance. In some organizations, but sadly not all, there are measures in place to demonstrate return on investment (ROI). This is all good and to be encouraged. It's certainly a million miles better than what we would consider poor coaching investment, whereby CAM is a remedial activity, a last-ditch attempt to solve 'issues' with individuals or is used to prop up rather than address issues of ineffective line or performance management.

But doesn't this rather miss the point? Should we not be demanding more from our investment in CAM? Surely it should seek loftier and more impactful ambitions than at best enabling performance improvements?

In a world where budgets are tight and there are lots of initiatives competing for organisational 'air time', I think it should. I passionately believe that *great* CAM should look beyond performance and seek to impact on both the current organizational strategy *and* the future potential of the organization. This doesn't mean that you jettison performance, quite the opposite; performance improvements are at the heart of great CAM.

Figure 11.1 Great CAM

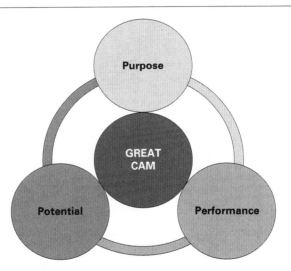

What is different with great CAM is that you align the performance improvements of individuals and teams against what is needed to deliver the strategy of the organization whilst seeking to develop behaviours, skills and mindsets that will help future-proof the organization. Great CAM works with Performance in role, creates change and opens up new possibilities as it delivers against organizational Purpose AND develops Potential in the talent of the organization.

By positioning CAM as a strategic enabler, both inside and outside the business, it becomes easier to demonstrate the impact CAM is having on the business, not only now but in the future too. This not only makes it easier for you to calculate a return on your investment but will also help you gain buy-in from the business for greater CAM investment in the future. CAM will cease to be seen 'as a good thing' or a 'nice to have' delivered by HR or L&D and become a core tool used by the organization to deliver strategically important business goals.

Break-out box – what do we mean by future potential?

We know that good coaching promotes business performance but we argue that great coaching should also help build capability in individuals and teams to support the future potential of the business. But what do we mean by future potential? Future potential is the capacity of an organization to learn and constantly adapt to the rapidly changing, complex and increasingly volatile world in which we operate. And to do so whilst continuing to deliver on the business strategy and purpose. One of the best descriptions of this idea is the concept of 'Organizational Health' provided by the consultancy firm McKinsey (Keller and Price, 2011). They describe organizational health as:

The ability of your organization to align, execute, and renew itself faster than your competitors... Organizational health is about adapting to the present and shaping the future faster and better than the competition... Healthy organizations don't merely learn to adjust themselves to their current context or to challenges that lie just ahead; they create a capacity to learn and keep changing over time.

This is where great CAM can really help. There is no better intervention than CAM to support change, build resilience, promote adaptability and encourage innovation. The challenge for organizations is to focus CAM, working out where that investment will have the greatest impact. You must be clear: 'Why are we doing this?' because there are always barriers to investing in great CAM – lack of time, lack of understanding and resistance to change to name a few – but if you can show how CAM will drive performance and build the future potential of your organization, you will win over the doubters.

In summary, great coaching helps leaders to deliver performance, helps achieve the organization's strategy and builds the future potential of individuals and the wider organization. Sometimes all of these can be achieved simultaneously. Sometimes there are trade-offs to be made between them. Great coaching helps leaders to make these trade-offs in a deliberate way, with a clear view on how to mitigate any consequences.

I'd like to share an example of what we mean in a technical engineering company.

This company had already made some investment in CAM, both to support the development of senior leaders through executive coaching and to build some internal coaching capability. Whilst there were some examples of good coaching on an individual (performance) level, by their own admission they were struggling to make the case for wider investment or use of CAM. The highly technical managerial population didn't 'get' coaching or see how it could be used to support them in their highly pressurized and regulated sector.

The key was to look for a strategic link and ways in which they could redeploy the existing coaching pool to support people in the business in an impactful way. It didn't take long to find. The business was about to go through a significant period of upheaval due to enforced regulatory changes. Dozens of new, cross-functional project teams were to be formed and all front-line operational staff were going to be affected. It was clear that a failure to support the operational managers to effectively implement the change and not ensuring new teams were performing to their potential represented a serious strategic risk.

Following some additional training around supporting change, building resilience and team coaching, the internal coaching pool could be redeployed to support these two groups in driving change and performance through the business. This approach would not only address a current strategic challenge, but would also create highly performing teams in strategically important projects and increase the capability of the leadership population to support the future potential of the business.

It is this three-way link between current performance, strategic linkage to purpose and future potential that will help you create buy-in, build a business case and secure funding to invest in great CAM for your organization. However, in order to do this, you may need to start thinking differently and helping others to do so. It may require you to design and deliver CAM services in your organization in a completely different way.

This part of the book seeks to provide a guide to help you to think differently to create a sustainable, effective CAM service that is truly great. The first thing you need to think about is where you are, could be or should be focusing that investment to have the greatest impact. To do this effectively, you must always be asking 'why'. If you can answer the 'why are we doing this' question, it will make answering the 'what' and 'how' much easier.

What is the focus of a CAM agenda and where will it have the greatest impact?

What is currently happening?

Before we answer 'why', it's important to review what is already taking place. You may well already have lots of CAM taking place in your organization. Some of it may well be considered 'good' but it quite possibly lacks a strategic focus, with no mechanisms in place to enable you to assess its value to or impact on the organization's potential and delivery against purpose. It always makes sense to analyse what is currently taking place before embarking on change. Like the example provided above, you may well find pockets of good coaching that could be turned into something more deliberate and strategic. If this is the case, you'll need to ask yourself questions like:

- What CAM is taking place? Who for? Why?
- What value is it adding? How do I know?
- Are there policies or processes in place to ensure quality, consistency and business impact? If so, what are they?
- Are there any links to wider business or departmental strategy?
- Do we use internal or external resources to deliver CAM?
- How much does this cost?
- How is CAM viewed in the business?
- Do leaders and managers use a CAM approach in their work?
- Is there any CAM training? Who for? Why?

Once you have conducted a thorough review of your existing CAM provision you will be in a position to understand how you can transform it.

Link to the existing strategy

This should provide you with answers to the 'why' question. The most important step when seeking to implement great CAM is to look for existing strategic imperatives, both organizationally and within HR, L&D, and/or talent. It's an obvious statement but it will save you a great deal of time and effort in identifying what strategically important areas you should focus on. It will shortcut discussions and easily create buy-in from senior stakeholders if you can demonstrate how your CAM approach will help them achieve the wider business strategy.

In Chapter 13, 'Implementing Coaching and Mentoring', we discuss in detail the sort of questions you will need to ask your senior stakeholders to ensure they understand the potential impact of great CAM, so we won't go into too much detail here.

Needless to say, each business is unique, and the range of possible strategic objectives would be too numerous to list here. Put very simply, you are looking to identify elements of the strategy that directly depend on and/or impact on your staff and then understand how you can best deploy CAM resources to effectively support those individuals.

By way of an example, let's look at a generic model which shows how talent strategy links to the broader organizational strategy. This framework helps demonstrate how you might use CAM effectively in support of the wider organization's goals and priorities. Here is a generic model of a talent strategy.

It is generally accepted that CAM can impact on the development, performance and engagement of your people. So what might great CAM look like if it were linked to a talent strategy? As an organization you could:

- deliver 1:1 coaching to develop leaders in their existing roles so they are more capable and able to implement organizational strategy;
- build the CAM skills of managers across the business to improve engagement of employees, to maximize the retention of key staff and strength of succession planning;
- support leaders transitioning (assigned) into new roles or teams to increase the chance of success in mission-critical appointments or projects.

It should also be noted that increasingly, CAM can impact on the organization's success in recruiting, since organizations that have a CAM culture also tend to have a strong employer brand. This is especially true for the Millennial generation who place great value in working for organizations who can demonstrate that their culture will actively support their development and career.

If you do have a stated strategy in place, you can engage your senior stakeholders in a discussion around where CAM could have the biggest impact for them. We explore how you might do so in more depth in Chapter 13.

Figure 11.2 Talent strategy model

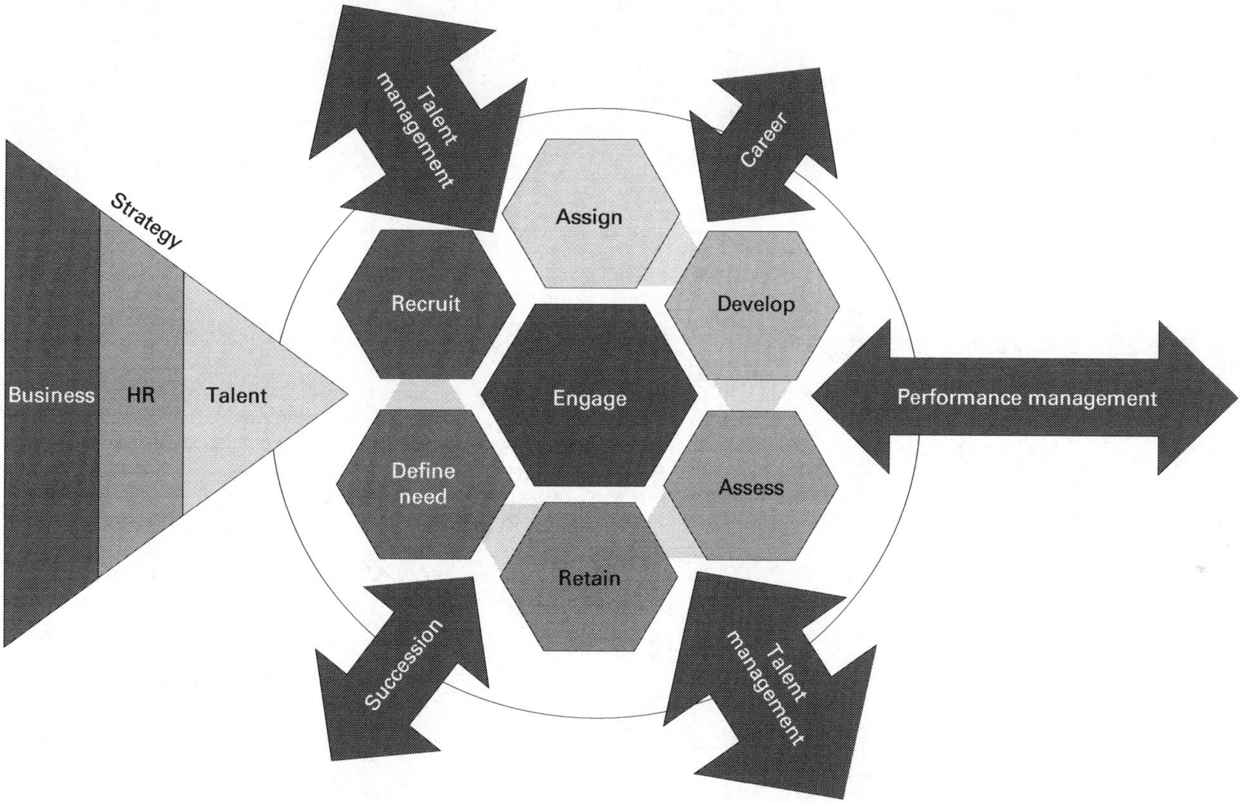

What to do if you don't have a stated talent or L&D strategy and you're starting from scratch

First of all, don't panic. This provides a fantastic opportunity to shape, mould and implement great CAM right from the start. You can set the strategic agenda and help solve a potentially thorny organizational issue. This is a great opportunity for you personally and for the organization. If you're starting from scratch, you will not have to fight against any prejudices that have built up due to previously poorly planned and implemented CAM activities. Have a read of the next section and the simplicity tips in the box for some ideas of how you might go about this.

How do you build a business case and get buy-in?

As we've established, great CAM promotes business performance and also helps build the capability of individuals and teams to grow the future potential of the organization. When you're making a business case, you will need to demonstrate that CAM in all its forms can deliver these benefits in both the short term and the long term. Traditionally, benefits are assessed in financial terms, usually through return on investment (ROI). ROI is important; CAM is intensive and can be a relatively expensive intervention.

However, there are limitations to a strictly financial evaluation of CAM or any other talent intervention. For example, it's not always possible to measure the financial impact of a change in mindset of an individual and/or team on performance now, even less so to understand how these groups contribute to the future potential of the organization. This doesn't mean that financial ROI calculations are redundant, but it does require a broader and more balanced approach to quantifying and measuring benefits. (See later in this chapter for a deeper exploration of what ROI indicators you could measure.)

The drivers for performance and future potential will be different from business to business. So if you're charged with building a business case you will need to really understand your business to make it effectively. Borrowing a few simple models from management consulting or business schools will help here.

Understand your business

You will already have an understanding of the fundamentals: how you make money, what the strategy is, how you are organized. You should already have an understanding of the internal and external pressures you face. If you don't, then using some basic tools like SWOT, PESTLE and Porter's 5 Forces will help you understand the system in which you are operating and some of the pressures which could be affecting individuals and teams. If you don't have the answers to these questions, then you will need to identify people within your organization who can provide you with greater insight.

Understand what future potential means for your organization and find a champion

This is where it starts to get really interesting. An organization's strategy and situation have an enormous impact on what performance and future potential looks like for them. If you have a sound understanding of the business, its strategy and its unique situation, you will find it much easier to identify the risks and opportunities that the organization faces and make the case for CAM interventions to address them. When trying to make the case for coaching, the more specific you can be about the particular opportunities and risks you are trying to address, the more likely you are to be able to identify and engage with a senior stakeholder who really cares about that potential to be your champion and create buy-in for your investment. Table 11.1 lists some aspects of future potential and performance that could be relevant to a large consumer business.

Understand the stakeholders

Having identified the impact you wish to have on performance and potential, you will then need to engage with the main stakeholders to secure their buy-in. As mentioned above, identifying a champion for your CAM activities will have a significant impact on the likeliness of success. But don't ignore other players in the system; engaging with them and understanding their drivers is just as important to the overall success of your plan. For example, it may well be the case that you need to present your case differently to individual stakeholders. In Chapter 13, we discuss in detail the importance of creating senior-level buy-in for the successful long-term implementation of CAM programmes. Furthermore, Chapter 14 is dedicated to understanding the roles of the various stakeholders, with the most important from a strategic perspective being:

- HR director/head of L&D;
- HR business partners;
- the line manager;
- strategic leaders.

Now that you have identified what the focus is and where you can have the biggest impact, you need to understand what you can measure and how to measure it. This is where we return to the broader understanding of the concept of return on investment.

Table 11.1 Aspects of future potential and performance

Example organizational opportunities and risks	Examples of coaching interventions to address them
Opportunity to deliver key multi-disciplinary project	Team coaching intervention to establish shared goals, ways of working and contingency plans to deal with conflict
Upcoming retirement of mission-critical technical staff	Coaching training and individual coaching to promote knowledge sharing and collaborative working between employee groups
Retention issues in mission-critical talent pools	Individual coaching for team leaders to improve leadership capability and engagement
Falling customer satisfaction in major buyers share	Coaching for sales teams around customer understanding and engagement; coach training for sales leaders
Growth – recruitment of new technical professionals requiring great knowledge transfer	Structured mentoring programme, including training and ongoing support for mentors

Break-out box – simple tips for focusing CAM

Simplicity tip 1 – look for a change

CAM is often most effective when it's in service of change. Change comes in all shapes and sizes, from the commercial – 'we need to change the way the sales team interact with our customers' – to the behavioural – 'we want our managers to have more impactful conversations'. Whatever, the change needed in your business will be unique, so don't be afraid to think outside the box. If you can identify a strategically important change that needs to be made in individuals, a team or a department, and work out how best to deploy CAM resources to support it, you'll be well on the way to answering the important 'why' question.

Simplicity tip 2 – look for a champion

We all know that organizational initiatives that have senior-level support are much more likely to be successful. CAM is no different. If you can find a willing and able leader of a team or department who understands CAM and is willing to support your initiative, do everything you can to support them because you're much more likely to succeed with their support. Have a read of Chapter 13 about gaining buy-in and Chapter 14 for some useful tips on what you're looking for.

Simplicity tip 3 – start small, measure effectively

I know you're keen and want to create a big impression – that's great; we want you to as well! However, if your organization is new to CAM then it's going to be a bit of a culture shock and potentially risky, for you and CAM, to embark on a big project. A better tactic would be to look for something more manageable (see above tips) and know that you can have a significant impact on a relatively low investment. It's also really important that you put lots of metrics in place so you can effectively measure the impact and/or change the CAM has helped create. You'll then be in a great position to build a strong business case, supported by evidence, when you ask for more investment in the future.

What will you measure and how will you measure it?

If you aren't linking CAM to strategy and future potential then you need to be asking yourself whether investing in CAM is really the right approach for you. Similarly, if you are not measuring the impact CAM is having on performance, strategy and future potential then you're not delivering great CAM. It can be hard to measure impact but if you have really considered WHY you are investing in CAM and WHAT you hope to achieve then it becomes much easier to demonstrate a return. There are no excuses!

As I've mentioned, measuring strategic impact and changes to future potential requires a broader understanding of what you mean by a return on the investment. Because what is driving the investment in CAM will be unique for each organization, it follows that what you measure will be dependent on the impact you are seeking to make. Here, I am offering some ideas of what a more balanced approach to what and how to measure impact might look like. Chapter 13 explores how to measure the effectiveness of individual CAM assignments.

Measurement costs money and time, and different organizations have different metrics that they measure regularly. Ideally, when seeking a measure of ROI, you want to choose one that already exists.

Metrics to look for in your organization to assess the impact of great CAM:

- **Business process and production metrics** – there are numerous approaches out there (Six Sigma, Lean, Quality) and CAM could well impact on your ability to improve your scores.

- **HR systems data** – many organizations have reliable data on retention, absence, talent management, employee satisfaction surveys, and learning attainment. CAM is a great way to support strategy in these areas and can be relatively easily measured.

- **Target, audit and compliance data** – many of us work in highly regulated environments, so shifts in an organization's ability to meet and exceed these requirements are often highly prized strategic goals.

- **Psychometrics** – if you're seeking to change behaviour in individuals and/or groups, psychometrics are a great mechanism of analysing demonstrating impact.

- **Performance dashboards** – many organizations link and monitor individual KPIs through performance management systems, so these could be a useful source of data to benchmark against.

- **Improvements to compliant ratios** – particularly relevant for many organizations given the recent recession and its impact on the financial sector.

- **Training costs and impact** – using CAM to support 70–20–10 approach can be a highly effective way of improving the 'stickiness' of training. helping to reduce the overall training budget.

- **Internal promotions and talent pool** – some organizations have complex business models and prefer high-quality internal promotions to external appointments, minimizing risk and reducing search agent fees.

- **Industry recognition** – many businesses apply for Investors in People (IIP) awards or other such schemes; CAM is potentially a way to significantly improve scores in this area.

I hope that I have helped you to a better understanding of what great CAM is and what that could mean for your organization. If you want to take this journey, start by thinking about where you can focus your investment in CAM to have the greatest impact on current performance, on delivering organizational purpose in the longer term and the future potential of your business. This will give you ideas of how you might go about building a strong business case and what you intend to measure to demonstrate the impact and return on investment. The remaining chapters of this section, especially 12, 13 and 14, will help you to think about how to successfully bring your ideas into being.

Endnote

Keller, S and Price, C (2011) Organizational health: the ultimate competitive advantage, *McKinsey Quarterly*, June [online] www.mckinsey.com/business-functions/organization/our-insights/organizational-health-the-ultimate-competitive-advantage

Coaching and mentoring: what they are and how they are used in organizations

12

CHARLOTTE BRUCE-FOULDS, GRAHAM CLARK AND KATHERINE RAY

In this chapter, we'll look more closely at what we mean by coaching and mentoring. We'll explore the different forms that coaching and mentoring can take, how organizations are implementing them, and the kinds of issues which coaching and mentoring can address. Finally, we'll explore the topic of a 'coaching culture' – what this means and how it is created. We have drawn from our practical experience of working with our diverse range of clients to provide examples. Much of our work is with major global brands and organizations so the context of our work can be commercially sensitive. To respect confidentiality and client privacy we have removed all names but shared practical examples from real client engagements. Alongside this we have tried to give you an insight into their collective thinking and experience to help you make the right decisions for your organization.

What are coaching and mentoring?

At their heart, coaching and mentoring are ways of having purposeful, skilful conversations that effectively support performance, growth and development.

As John Whitmore (2002) says:

> Coaching is the art of facilitating the performance, learning and development of another.

Eric Parsloe, founder of The OCM, says:

> Mentoring is to support and encourage people to manage their own learning in order that they may maximize their potential, develop their skills, improve their performance and become the person they want to be.

Coaching and mentoring overlap considerably, but there are some key differences.

Similarities between coaching and mentoring:

There are many areas of overlap between coaching and mentoring – and we have listed some below:

- Both involve conversations which raise performance and unlock potential.
- Both rely on the coach-mentor's skills of listening, questioning and feedback.
- Both require the coach-mentor to have a good understanding of people, organizations and principles of learning.
- Both require confidentiality and clear contracting.
- Both require good governance, supervision and effective processes to have the most impact.

Differences between coaching and mentoring

Table 12.1 opposite shows some key differences between coaching and mentoring. These are general principles rather than hard-and-fast rules, but they reflect how coaching and mentoring typically differ.

Table 12.1 Differences between coaching and mentoring

Coaching	Mentoring
Relationship generally has a set duration	Ongoing relationship can last for a long time
Generally more structured in nature; meetings are scheduled on a regular basis	More informal; meetings can take place as and when the mentee needs some advice, guidance and support
Short term (sometimes time-bound) and focused on specific development areas/issues	More long term and takes a broader view of the person
Coaching is generally not performed on the basis that the coach needs to have direct experience of their individual's formal occupational role, unless the coaching is specific and skills-focused	Mentor is usually more experienced and qualified than the mentee, and can pass on knowledge, experience and open doors to otherwise out-of-reach opportunities
Coach can be internal or external to the organization	Mentor is usually (but not always) internal to the organization
Coaching can be performed by the line manager	Mentoring is not performed by the line manager
Focus is generally on specific development areas/issues at work	Focus is on career and personal development
The agenda is focused on achieving specific, immediate goals	Agenda is set by the mentee, with the mentor providing support and guidance to prepare them for future roles

It's important to bear these similarities and differences in mind when considering what the right solution might be for you. Having said this, when The OCM work with our client organizations, we notice that they are sometimes hung up on the labelling of coaching and mentoring and may even refer to 'coaching' when they mean 'mentoring' and vice versa. Coaching has been, and remains, very popular; however, we have seen a resurgence in the use of mentoring over the past few years as organizations' issues or challenges require the use of mentoring rather than coaching. Therefore, it's important to have a clear understanding of what coaching and mentoring mean for your organization and to be clear on how they differ. This will help you to know which one to use to achieve the outcomes you want to see. Some organizations don't even refer to coaching or mentoring; they use phrases such as 'people development' or 'development conversations' instead.

Coaching is becoming increasingly used 'for all' in organizations, whereas mentoring tends to be used to address specific gaps in a talent pipeline, focusing on specific groups with specific needs. For example, mentoring is often used to help graduates with the on-boarding process, to make progress and grow a network. Mentoring is also used successfully with women to help them get promoted and increase an organization's gender balance in senior leadership positions.

The emergence of the coach-mentor

Although it's helpful to look at the similarities and differences between coaching and mentoring for the purposes of clarity, it's also worth reinforcing that there is a lot of overlap. In fact, we find that the most effective approach uses a blend of coaching and mentoring stances, depending on what the client needs – and practitioners who do this are often referred to as coach-mentors.

In a coaching scenario, the coach may choose to be more direct to share his/her expertise, knowledge and experience, if the time is right. Similarly, in a mentoring relationship, mentors should not feel obliged always to offer their advice – instead they can use great facilitative questions to surface greater insight from the mentee. A great coach-mentor has a range of styles and stances in his/her toolkit which they adopt depending on the situation. We will revisit the role of the coach-mentor in Chapter 14.

How organizations implement coaching and mentoring

Coaching and mentoring are becoming almost ubiquitous as part of organizations' learning and development strategies. Extracts from General Findings in the 2015 CIPD Learning and Development Survey show the following:

- Coaching and mentoring are used by three-quarters of all organizations and a further 13 per cent expect to use it next year.

- Most expect to increase their use of coaching.
- Coaching by line managers or peers is more widely used and seen to be more effective than coaching delivered by external practitioners.
- Coaching by line managers is seen to be the number one growth activity in learning and development.
- Coaching by external practitioners is seen by a number of organizations as decreasing.

Continued future growth in coaching and mentoring is predicted, for example by the Bersin by Deloitte *Predictions for 2016* research report published in January 2016, which reported that 'all of our research shows that coaching and mentoring are the most valuable talent practices which you can develop in your company' and that coaching and mentoring are going to grow rapidly.

Figure 12.1 Overview of the typical components of a coach-mentoring programme

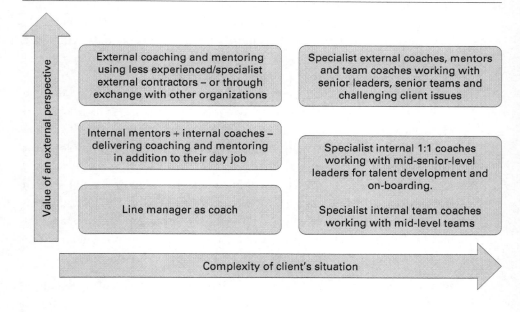

Figure 12.1 shows the likely components of a coach-mentoring or CAM programme. A programme will typically make use of any or all of these. There are two key factors at play here: first, the complexity of the client's situation, and second, the value that an external perspective is likely to bring. A complex client situation would be one that is highly uncertain,

complex, changing, where the stakes could be high, and where many factors are in play. In some cases, it may be very difficult for the client to specify what his/her ideal goals or outcomes are. A simpler client situation would be one with relatively clearly defined goals where the client is operating in a more straightforward situation and where the issues are important but not high risk.

The solutions on the right of the diagram are more time and/or cost intensive than the solutions on the left, in line with the skill levels needed to add value in highly complex situations where the stakes are often high.

Over the next few pages, we present an overview of the different components, including a brief description of each, as well as some advantages and disadvantages. It is worth bearing Figure 12.1 in mind when reviewing the different approaches and considering when each approach is likely to be most appropriate.

Line manager as coach: development programmes where line managers are given coaching/mentoring skills to enhance their impact as leaders. They are not becoming coaches per se; rather, they adopt techniques drawn from coaching and mentoring to complement their existing leadership approach. This then enables them to have more effective conversations with their teams and peers. They learn to 'ask, not tell' and learn the fundamental coaching skills of listening, questioning and feedback.

Advantages: clear link between the development programme and the ability to apply the learning 'on the job'; line managers can have an immediate impact on performance and motivation; side benefits from the greater empathy and listening skills managers require from the development programme.

Disadvantages: variable ability of line managers to apply the skills (often the least capable line managers – who most need to apply coaching and mentoring – are the ones who are most resistant to using it); line managers may feel disinclined to focus on people's longer-term development since this may mean losing team members to other parts of the organization.

Internal coaching using part-time, non-specialist coaches: using a cohort of internal coaches to build the capability of the organization, realize its potential and enhance performance. Most internal coaches are drawn from HR and the line and perform their coaching role in addition to their day job. To illustrate, we have examples from the utilities and academia where internal coaches have been used to support broader leadership development programmes providing coach-mentoring support to help programme participants embed the learning and get the most from the programme.

Alternatively, we have an example from retail where internal coaches provided support for new line managers and mission-critical talent pools of junior/mid-level staff, and coach-mentoring support for those who needed it.

As described above, each organization will have its own driver for wanting to develop a non-specialist internal coaching pool. These are as varied as simply wanting to reduce costs on the use of external one-to-one coaching to having a complex business model and rapidly evolving culture that requires specialist knowledge or skills not easily sourced externally. The important consideration is to establish what driver is going to generate the greatest senior level buy-in and build your business case around it. See Chapter 11 for tips on how to do this.

Advantages: less cost than when using external coaches; coaches will be familiar with the organizational context, culture and strategy; when supported systematically, an internal coaching programme can be a key pillar which supports a 'coaching culture' over time.

Disadvantages: requires good selection of the right internal coaches; requires internal coaches to take time out of their day job, with a risk of tension between both sets of responsibilities; the programme requires ongoing supervision and monitoring to ensure its effectiveness.

Internal mentoring: mentoring relationships and conversations will have a focus on knowledge transfer and forming intergenerational and cross-functional relationships within the business. Mentors come from within the organization and are typically (but not always) more senior than those whom they mentor.

Advantages: builds intergenerational relationships and organizational networks; facilitates knowledge transfer; enhances mentees' feeling of being connected to – and valued by – the wider organization.

Disadvantages: risk of variable skill levels of mentors; risk of poor practice (people stuck in 'tell' mode); requires investment of time from senior leaders; can easily be put 'on the back burner' unless people take it seriously; requires senior-level sponsorship so that the mentoring programme works systematically/strategically and not sporadically. Getting the best from mentoring requires effective selection and training of mentors, as well as ongoing continuous professional development.

Internal coaching using specialist coaches: a pool of specialized coaches who work within the organization to deliver coaching to individuals and/or teams. These will be highly qualified professionals who either coach full-time, or who also deliver related work such as leadership development, competency-based assessment and group facilitation.

Advantages: less cost than when using external coaches; coaches will be familiar with the organizational context, culture and strategy; when supported systematically, an internal coaching programme can be a key pillar which supports a 'coaching culture' over time; greater skill levels than non-specialized, part-time internal coaches.

Disadvantages: maintaining this pool of coaches can be resource-intensive, both in terms of time required and cost of qualifications, supervision and continuous professional development; can be impractical for small/medium-sized business; coaches may not be able to maintain an impartial view of the organization and the client's situation in the way that an external coach can; clients may be less inclined to be challenged by internal coaches or to listen to them.

External 1:1 coaching: use of external coaches to address individual and organizational issues, enhance performance and release potential. Examples are numerous here, from FMCG clients using external coaches to provide transition coaching to newly appointed senior leaders to minimize the risk and ensure a successful transition to a manufacturing client involved in multiple mergers and acquisitions using external coaches to support senior leaders through change.

As accurately described in Hawkins' (2012) evolution of a coaching culture model (Figure 12.2), we cannot think of a client engagement where the development of internal coaching capability was not preceded by the experience of using external coach-mentors, particularly for senior leaders. If your senior leaders haven't had this experience, the chances are you're not yet ready to develop an internal resource and the investment is better placed elsewhere.

Advantages: external coaches are specialists, so quality of coaching is likely to be higher; seasoned external coaches can deal with challenging senior clients, and challenging complex situations; external coaches can 'role-model' what high-quality coaching looks like, especially useful if the organization is new to coaching.

Disadvantages: likely to be a higher-cost option than using internal coaches; it is critical that you ensure that coaches understand the unique culture and strategy of the business so that they are effective.

External team coaching: use of external coaches to coach teams to improve their effectiveness.

Advantages: potential impact of team coaching is huge – including better results for the team and improved behaviours between team members;

external team coaches can 'role-model' coaching behaviours for the team, and enlightened team members will adopt these behaviours and use them with one another, and with their direct reports in turn.

Disadvantages: team coaching needs multiple sessions to be truly effective and can be quite expensive; good team coaching is demanding so selection of the right team coach is paramount – in terms of their skills and experience as well as their fit with the team leader and the wider team.

In Chapter 16, Jackie Elliott shares experience of acting as an internal/external team coach in T-systems.

External 1:1 mentoring: use of external mentors tends to be quite sparing. They are typically used for very senior-level leaders who need the benefit of a highly experienced business professional. The relationship will help them develop specific business skills as well as provide more general development support.

Advantages: a well-chosen external mentor can use his/her business experience to accelerate a mentee's development of specific skills – such as setting strategy, transitioning to an executive team-level role, operating as a woman at senior management level, etc; can be effective where no one within the organization is able to help someone develop particular business skills, or act as an internal role model; accelerates a mentee's development and builds their confidence through working with an external role model; provides a safe space for conversations with a fellow senior-level professional which potentially could not be had internally.

Disadvantages: external mentors are frequently expensive; many external mentors lack a 'coaching' approach, meaning some are prone to 'telling' rather than coaching; risk of the external mentor being unfamiliar with the specific culture and situation of the business.

As we'll see later in the chapter, the right blend of coaching and mentoring approaches is likely to change over time – and (as we'll see in Chapter 13) requires clear links to the overall organization's strategy, as well as a clear three- to five-year plan for the coaching and mentoring implementation.

What topics do organizations use coaching and mentoring for?

Clearly, the range of topics covered by coaching and mentoring is huge. Each individual coach-mentoring relationship will cover several topics in itself. Nevertheless, it's worth considering the most common areas that coaching and mentoring address.

For the purposes of clarity, we've grouped coaching themes into broad areas. In practice, though, as a coaching relationship unfolds, the topics covered may encompass more than one of the areas we've listed below, or may change over time as the client progresses towards their goals. For example, a coaching assignment which starts out being about a performance opportunity may evolve into a behaviour change agenda as the client and coach discover more about the client, the situation and the client's habitual approach.

Transition coaching

In transition coaching the coach-mentor and client work to ensure a smooth transition to a new role. Usually this is an upward move, but sometimes a lateral one. The coaching may take place before the move is due to happen, or may commence after the client is in role. The coach-mentor and client work to understand and shape the client's objectives for the role and to understand the changes that the client will need to put in place. The coach-mentor and client will often work on a 100-day plan with objectives in terms of financial and operational goals, the team, customers and internal and external stakeholders. In addition, change often takes place within the client themselves – larger roles often require a different self-image, and may involve giving up aspects of work that the client previously found energizing.

Transformational coaching

In transformational coaching, the emphasis is on helping the client to effect significant change, within the client themselves and in the client's work environment. Often this change is difficult and there are significant barriers. The goal is often unclear, at least at first, and the situation in which the client is operating may be volatile, uncertain, complex and ambiguous (VUCA). The personal change may require some quite deep-level transformation, breaking 'habits of a lifetime'. Transformational coaching usually requires the coach-mentor to use a systems-thinking approach and also requires political savvy, as well as considerable business acumen. The coach-mentor needs to challenge the client as well as support them, even if challenging seems like a difficult option – and the stakes are often high.

Performance coaching

Performance coaching is centred on clear goals and is focused on helping the individual to find solutions to challenges and to learn and develop from the process. It can be remedial, in as much as it can address performance issues, but equally it can be about building on performance standards that are already good. The coach's job is to help the client clarify their goals, focus on clear actions that they will take and then to review the actions during subsequent coaching sessions. The coach-mentor will also help facilitate the client's learning so that over time they are able to find the best solutions to goals themselves.

Leadership coaching

There is often an overlap between transitional coaching and leadership coaching. In leadership coaching, the coach-mentor helps the client to have a more positive impact on their direct reports and the wider organization. To be effective, the coach-mentor needs to have a strong, practical understanding of the principles of leadership, and ideally needs to have held significant leadership positions themselves during their career. Leadership coaching will often focus on how to create an effective team climate, how to enhance one's impact as a leader, and how to present oneself in a way which inspires trust, loyalty and high performance.

Behaviour change

Coaching for behaviour change involves working with an individual to address a particular deep-seated aspect of a client's behaviour that is having an adverse impact on themselves and/or the people around them. Coaches need a sound understanding of personality, behaviour and the process of facilitating (sometimes painful) change in others. Coaches often use gestalt or cognitive behavioural approaches. Psychometric instruments, 360 surveys and competency-based interviews can also be helpful.

Coaching for resilience

Coaching for resilience helps the client to deal with challenge, adversity and change – and over time to thrive during such circumstances. The coach-mentor will work to improve the client's level of self-awareness to understand their emotional responses to difficult situations and the accompanying thought processes. The coach-mentor will then help the client develop coping strategies to enable them to manage their emotional responses and their associated behaviours. The coach-mentor can also help the client develop the ability to see the opportunities which difficult situations sometimes provide, and to capitalize on the up-side of adversity.

Team coaching

A coach-mentor works with a team to improve their ability to deliver results sustainably. The coach-mentoring will focus on clarity of team goals, clarity of roles within the team, clear processes for decision making and resolving difficulty, and strong, trusting personal relationships between team members. The coach-mentor will provide feedback to the team, guidance and challenge. Crucially, the coach-mentor builds the ability for the team to coach itself over time, so that it grows its ability to work effectively even after the formal coach-mentoring has finished. We will cover team coaching in more detail in Chapter 16.

A coaching culture – what is it and how can I create it?

What is a coaching culture?

In an organization with a coaching culture, the majority of staff will habitually use a coaching and mentoring approach in their daily life – with one another, and with external stakeholders and customers. A true coaching culture is just 'part of the way we do things round here'. Importantly, a coaching culture is still focused on delivering results and improving performance but also on maximizing people's potential for making each other (and the wider organization) stronger and more capable. It is NOT about having coaching conversations for their own sake, or as a diversion from other activities.

Each client is unique and will start from a different place. One financial services client took a top-down approach working with the most senior partners to gradually shift the style of conversations in the workplace and, over time, with their clients. An engineering company with an emphasis on project work took the opposite approach by developing the coaching skills of project leaders to have the greatest impact, gradually shifting the culture as these skills permeated the organization.

The overwhelming feeling is that building a coaching culture is strongly desirable, indeed many of our client engagements start with that simple premise. However, as you'll discover further down, it's not that simple and it takes time. To be successful you need a strong vision, senior level buy-in and, above all, patience. But stick with it; the potential benefits are definitely worth the investment. Keep reading to learn from our collective experience.

If you could be a 'fly on the wall' in an organization with a coaching culture, here's what you might see:

- Managers looking for opportunities to help others learn.

- Employees routinely asking one another open questions.

- Employees at all levels having open, honest and supportive conversations with one another.

- People routinely giving one another feedback, both supportive and developmental.

- Managers coaching team members as an opportunity for development rather than only as a remedial measure.

- Coaching and mentoring relationships forming spontaneously.

- Senior leaders expressing a clear vision that coaching and mentoring are at the heart of how we operate.

- Teams working with clear goals, roles, processes and relationships.

- Compared with other similarly sized organisations, fewer people will be 'playing politics'.

- Leaders at all levels maintaining a pragmatic focus on delivering results whilst helping to build the long-term health of the business.

Many organizations aspire to develop and sustain a coaching culture. There are many potential benefits for individuals, teams and organizations as a whole.

Like many things in coach-mentoring, a coaching culture is a relatively simple idea which is challenging to put into practice. *Just because it's simple doesn't make it easy* is a bit of a catchphrase for us! Developing and sustaining a coaching culture requires concerted effort over time, driven by visible support and a clear vision from senior leaders. Moreover, they require senior leaders voluntarily to cede a certain amount of power and control to leaders and employees at lower levels in the organization, and to do this for a sustained period of time.

A coaching culture isn't Utopia. Adopting a coaching approach simply isn't appropriate in all situations. Organizations need to deliver results and there are times that demand 100 per cent focus on immediate delivery – where coaching isn't the right thing to do. Another oft-used phrase is: 'You don't coach someone out of a burning building.' Perhaps the key hallmark of a coaching culture is that leaders have a good sense of when to coach others and when not to. Leaders balance the need to deliver results now with the need to build a healthy business that can deliver results for the future as well. A healthy coaching culture is a challenging but stimulating place to work – it's not a soft option. The key is that leaders get the best from their people over a sustained period without 'sweating the assets' to an unhealthy extent.

It's important to note that a coaching culture in one organization will look and feel quite different from a coaching culture in another. Organizations will have their own heritage, history, strategies, business and operating models – and all of these will have an impact on what a coaching culture will look like.

How to create a 'coaching culture'

Chapter 13 includes some very practical steps that you can take to put in place a fit-for-purpose coaching and mentoring programme – and over time these will help develop a 'coaching culture'. As we'll explore, the most important enabler of any coaching/mentoring programme is consistent sponsorship and support from the organization's leadership team. It's critical to have a clear, enduring vision and purpose for the programme as well as clear and measurable goals. Without this, a coaching culture simply will not emerge, even if the aims of the programme are laudable and the project management is rigorous and well-structured.

We will now look at how a coaching culture typically develops, using a framework originally developed by Peter Hawkins. Chapter 13 then explores the practicalities in more detail.

Peter Hawkins's model shows how a coaching culture evolves, and for a full treatment of this topic we recommend his book, *Creating a Coaching Culture*. For the purposes of this chapter, we have included an overview of the different stages through which an organization passes on the journey to a true coaching and mentoring culture. See Figure 12.2 opposite.

Figure 12.2 The evolution of a coaching culture – from Hawkins (2012)

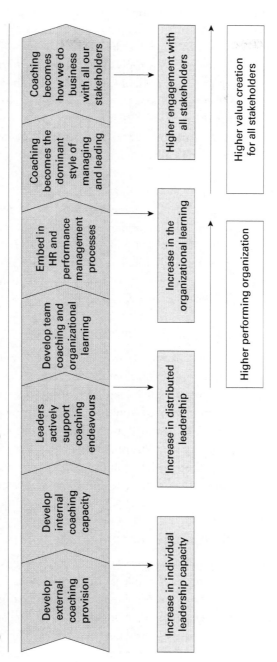

1. Develop external coaching provision

Perhaps the simplest way to consider developing a coaching culture within the management population – in keeping with The OCM's philosophy of pragmatic simplicity – is to consider the idea of encouraging managers to 'ask, not tell'. But many leaders simply don't know how to do this and no matter how strong the encouragement, many will default to a highly directive leadership style. External coaches are often able to help managers make the first steps towards the necessary change.

With this in mind, securing the support of external coaches has two main aims. Firstly, and more tactically, external coaches help leaders to address their key challenges, which will directly benefit them and indirectly benefit the wider organization. Secondly, and more long-term, external coaches help leaders to develop greater self-awareness and a different way of thinking about their own intentions and impact as leaders. External coaches 'role-model' a different way of thinking, behaving and solving problems which directly benefits the individual leader in their day-to-day work. It creates credibility for the approach and may lead to leaders proactively seeking to learn and develop their own coaching style.

2. Develop internal coaching capability

Growing and training a cohort of internal coaches opens up access to coaching to a larger section of the population. As with external coaching, this not only helps coachees to solve their own business issues – it also helps them to develop a different way of thinking about their own intentions and impact. In addition, as we'll explore in Chapter 13, most internal coaches will be delivering coaching in addition to their 'day job'. This means that they will be likely to be role-modelling a coaching approach in their regular day job and over time this will start to have an impact on the pervading culture.

3. Leaders actively support coaching endeavours

Any culture change requires culture 'champions'. In the development of a coaching culture, senior leaders play a huge role by articulating a vision for coaching and by actively supporting it. They also change the leadership culture by coaching their own team members and – crucially – also by encouraging their direct reports to coach their teams. This way role-modelling from the top is propagated down through the organization.

4. Develop team coaching and organizational learning

As we'll explore in Chapter 16, team coaching is an enormously powerful way of increasing the effectiveness of teams and giving them the tools that they need to remain effective even after the support from the team coach has ended. Team coaching often requires support from an external coach as the skills required are quite specialized – but over time, specialized internal coaches can become team coaches. Team coaching is an important part of building a coaching culture because it's about how peers relate to one another when making decisions. Effective team coaching engenders a strong sense of collective ownership of team goals, and requires team members to advise, guide, support, challenge and coach each other in an open way – which are all hallmarks of a coaching culture.

Organizational learning is the means by which an organization creates, shapes, shares and applies knowledge, both internally and with key external stakeholders and partners. There are 'hard' aspects to organizational learning – including systems, processes and formal training which are put in place to share knowledge, as well as 'soft' aspects, which include coaching and mentoring conversations and the deliberate sharing of knowledge in the course of daily work. Coaching and mentoring have an enormous part to play in developing people's ability to share knowledge and in helping them to do so consistently.

5. Embed in HR and performance management processes

For a coaching culture to be sustained, coaching and mentoring must become part of the regular HR talent and performance management processes. As we'll discuss in Chapter 13, deliberate management of ongoing coaching and mentoring by HR can ensure that they are used strategically as part of the growth and development of talent. Similarly, other HR activities such as selection and development (facilitated by competency models), leadership development programmes, and performance management need to emphasize the imperative that leaders habitually adopt a coaching and mentoring approach.

6. Coaching becomes the dominant style of management and leading

This is a natural consequence of putting in place systems, processes and resources to encourage and reward coaching and mentoring, and of attracting, selecting, developing and deploying leaders who habitually use a coaching leadership approach.

7. Coaching becomes how we do business with all our stakeholders

When coaching and mentoring are ingrained into the leadership culture, this way of relating to one another internally will also be reflected in dealings with external stakeholders. Many of the necessary skills for effective sales, relationship management and stakeholder engagement are also core to coaching and mentoring, and include listening, questioning, feedback, systems thinking, empathy and business acumen.

Like any programme aimed at creating and sustaining a defined culture, developing a coaching and mentoring culture requires a judicious combination of 'Drivers' of change and 'Releasers' of change. Drivers of change include policies, procedures, systems, processes, training and incentives. Releasers include a clearly articulated vision from senior leaders (supported by their actions and communication), the actions of line managers, and ongoing consultation with and feedback from employees.

In this chapter we've defined coaching and mentoring and we've explored the similarities and differences between them. We've introduced the concept of the coach-mentor and we've looked at the different forms that coaching and mentoring can take, using internal resources and external support. We've explored the issues coaching and mentoring can address and we've described how organizations can develop a coaching culture. In Chapter 13, we'll look at the steps you can use to develop a fit-for-purpose coaching programme which, over time, can lead to the development of a coaching culture.

Endnotes

Bersin by Deloitte (2016) 10 predictions to guide your talent strategy in 2016 [online] http://marketing.bersin.com/predictions-for-2016.html

CIPD (2015) Learning and Development Survey, CIPD [online] http://www.cipd.co.uk/hr-resources/survey-reports/learning-development-2015.aspx

Hawkins, P (2012) *Creating a Coaching Culture*, Open University Press/McGraw Hill

Whitmore, J (2002) *Coaching for Performance*, 3rd edn, Nicholas Brealey, London, p 21

Implementing coaching and mentoring

13

GRAHAM CLARK

In Chapters 11 and 12, we discussed the importance of addressing the important strategic questions, and of understanding the range of possible coaching and mentoring approaches that could potentially help your organization. This chapter explores how to implement your chosen coaching and mentoring strategy – and I'll consider some key success factors to ensure a successful implementation.

From our expertise and from our experience of working with our clients, there are three critical areas of focus which drive success in coaching and mentoring implementations:

1 Initiation – why are we doing this? How does it link and connect to the business and people strategy?

2 Design/creation – how are we going to do this? What do we want coaching and/or mentoring to achieve? What blend of approaches will we use?

3 Evaluation/impact review and learning – what are we measuring, what has changed and what has the impact of doing coaching and/or mentoring been? What are we learning and how do we implement that learning?

Initiation

As outlined in Chapter 11, rule number one when implementing a strategic coaching and mentoring programme is to link it back to the talent/HR strategy, as well as to the organization's strategy.

There are some important tactical processes to be implemented to ensure that the coaching and mentoring programme runs smoothly. But without the link to strategy, the programme is likely be seen as another well-meaning HR programme of peripheral importance. I will explore both how to ensure that the CAM (coaching and mentoring) programme links to strategy, and some practical steps for implementing it.

Focus and linkage

The most important question when implementing a CAM programme is 'Why are we doing this?' As described in the previous chapter, there are variations on this question – some will resonate more with your employees and stakeholders than others.

In many ways, CAM capacity is a strategic driver for success in organizations per se, but for most organizations any CAM initiative or investment needs to be clearly linked to performance, and is generally seen as one of the many strategies used by the organization to develop and engage talent resources to deliver performance.

'Ninety per cent of strategy is execution. Ninety per cent of execution is people' (Gary Burnison, CEO, Korn Ferry).

When developing support with senior stakeholders, it's important to make this potential impact clear. Crucially, senior stakeholders within the organization should be consulted in helping you to define what the programme is for, the anticipated benefits and key measures of success (and unless you are personally in a senior position with control over substantive budgets, finding a senior sponsor who has real buy-in to both the goal and CAM is key to long-term success).

Here are some questions that you can ask your senior stakeholders when designing the programme, or when ensuring an existing programme is fit for purpose.

- What do you want your people to be doing differently so that they can better deliver the strategy?
- What capabilities do your people need that they don't already possess?
- What is the potential within your business that you would like to unlock? What is getting in the way?
- What part might coaching and mentoring play in helping people to have better conversations and make better collective decisions within the business?

- How might coaching and mentoring progress people through the organization, in a way that isn't happening now?

- What sorts of measures would you like to see to give you confidence that the programme is adding value?

- What might some of the other benefits be? For example, could coaching help people to work across silos?

Figure 13.1 Coaching can – and should – impact on the organization at a strategic level

After your conversations with key stakeholders you need to make sure you have specific and concrete answers to these questions. For each question it's important to document what the organization's aspiration is, and to give tangible examples of what you might see people doing differently. And then to link this back to the organization's strategic objectives *as well as* the HR strategy, talent strategy and L&D strategy.

For example:

> Our mentoring programme will help us to move talent more quickly through the business and also fill more internal vacancies (measured through our HR database). It will also ensure that people work across silos more, measured through two questions on our annual employee survey.

Communication and buy-in with stakeholders

As described above, consulting stakeholders is an important first step. It will create interest and buy-in and will ensure that the programme addresses what senior people are most concerned about.

It is important that after the initial consultation you communicate clearly a set of key success factors that the programme will need to deliver – linking these back to the findings from the initial consultation.

It is critical that these success factors are clear and that they have measures attached to each. Where possible these should link back to the strategic objectives for the overall business – where that isn't possible they should link to the L&D strategy or HR/talent strategy.

An example key success factor:

In Year 1 we will train a cohort of 20 internal coaches using a formal training course. The course will accredit these coaches at foundation level. These coaches will each undertake two coaching assignments in the engineering talent pool, to be commenced by the beginning of Q3. In the short term this will help our engineers manage the current pressures which the engineering function is facing; in the longer term this will help ensure we build the leadership capability that is needed within the next generation of engineers.

Importance of sponsorship within the organization

Clearly, when creating a coaching and mentoring programme we want it to have a lasting, positive impact on the individuals and teams who are coached – and on the wider organization. For this to happen, the programme needs sustained support and funding over a period of years. This, in turn, requires support and sponsorship at senior levels in the organization – not just within HR but as widely as possible. Too many programmes start out well, with good intentions from senior people in the organization. But changes happen within the organizational structure; people change roles and pressures on organizations can erode the organization's commitment to the programme over time.

For this reason it's critical to have a very senior-level sponsor within the business who is prepared to provide long-term support and overall sponsorship to the programme. Ideally, this is the chief executive or COO, or another member of the leadership team. This sponsor should be in addition to the chief HR officer/group HRD.

The sponsor should ideally be someone who has had positive personal experiences with coaching and/or mentoring – typically someone who has seen coaching and/or mentoring as being instrumental in his/her success to date. This means that even when there are pressures to reduce support for the programme, there is still a pull from the top to ensure that the programme endures and thrives.

For example, the project team of a mentoring programme for a Fortune 500 company enlisted the support of the group CEO. He had been mentored earlier in his career, and put his weight behind the mentoring programme. This led to a very significant uptake in the business which would not otherwise have happened – and ensured that the programme retained senior executive team support over a five-year period.

Design/creation

Choosing who the coaching is for and the right tools for the right purpose

As we discussed in Chapter 12, the coaching /mentoring programme will be likely to incorporate a blend of approaches which – together – will deliver the key success factors.

A great coaching programme builds capability within the organization over time, so that line managers, internal coaches and mentors increasingly provide support to employees. Reliance on external providers reduces as the programme progresses and the organization's culture may evolve towards a true coaching culture.

With this in mind, the blend of approaches is likely to change over time. It is helpful to have a plan of what the programme is likely to look like in Year 1 and in Year 5, as well as in the intermediate years. In the plan, define the following for each year:

- Who is the coaching for? What levels of the organization will potentially have access to coaching?

- Do you want to focus the coaching in particular on priority talent pools (eg high potentials or mission-critical functions) or regions (fast growth, priority markets, etc)?

- How many coaching clients are you anticipating for each year (by region, function, etc)?

- What is your likely annual budget for the programme (for as many years out as it's possible to predict)?

- What is the current level of line manager capability in using a coaching approach?
- How accustomed is the organization to coaching (from both internal and external coaches)?

Once you have answered these questions, the blend of approaches depends largely on where you are starting from. If your organization is relatively new to coaching and mentoring, you are likely to rely on external coaches and mentors more heavily initially. These external mentors and coaches can establish credibility for coach-mentoring as a concept and create a 'pull' within the organization. They can also help to create real champions for CAM in senior leaders.

As with any programme, it's important to have a clear end purpose, to plan the overall 'architecture', and to have a good project plan. Advice on creating a project plan is beyond the scope of this book, but many useful templates are available online if you don't have standard templates available in your organization. But you don't have to get the programme or the plan absolutely right on Day 1. You can build iteratively, working overtime to select the right blend of approaches as you find out what works and what doesn't in your organization. As things change, it's important to keep steering towards the original aims of the programme, focused on what needs to be different and how the programme will help deliver these changes

For a full discussion of the range of coaching and mentoring options, please see Chapter 12.

Setting up your project team

Now you have determined the right mix of coaching approaches it's important to set up clear roles and responsibilities to manage and support the programme. This feeds into your project plan.

Chapter 14 looks at organizational roles and responsibilities in coaching. For the purposes of planning, in this chapter I have listed a summary of the roles you might require during the implementation. Clearly the size of the team – and therefore the specific accountabilities that individuals need to hold – will vary depending on the size and scale of the programme and the organizational structure it is working in. The project process needs to be fit for purpose: neither too light a touch (risking standards and service) nor too onerous (taking up too many resources and too much time).

Project sponsor – senior-level line sponsor for the programme. Responsible for championing the programme with senior colleagues, sponsoring group-wide communications about the programme and challenging the programme team to high standards of delivery, ensuring links to the organization's strategic needs. Often a senior HR leader – but can be (very successfully) from a different function.

Project director – overall responsibility for operational delivery of the programme. Responsible for the programme's overall architecture, for creating and maintaining a three- to five-year plan and for holding team members to account to their individual objectives. Responsible for crafting communication materials and overseeing the 'user-facing' aspects of the programme. Overall responsibility for ensuring the programme delivers safe, high-quality, fit-for-purpose coaching and mentoring which help individuals and the wider organization. Often a senior HR leader, but may be a coaching and mentoring or L&D specialist.

Project manager – overall responsibility for day-to-day running of the programme. Duties may include responding to requests for coaching/mentoring and guiding users to the best solution for them based on their needs and the coaching/mentoring resources available. Likely to be responsible for the design and maintenance of intranet resources, as well as systems for monitoring and managing the delivery of coaching and mentoring.

Coordinators – responsible for parts of the programme as required (for example coordination of the mentoring programme or coordination of the internal coaching programme). The scope and number of these roles will depend on the size and scale of the programme.

Once you have listed out the accountabilities and assigned them to different roles, I recommend producing a RACI chart to check that all key deliverables for the programme are covered. RACI is a simple, well-established method for assigning tasks to project team members, and several sets of guidelines for using it are available online.

Following this, it will be important to organize regular project meetings to ensure everyone is focused on the right objectives and to address any issues and celebrate successes as the programme evolves.

It is worth noting that technology-based solutions can help reduce the workload involved in managing coaching and mentoring programmes. Using existing learning management systems can help, as can investing in a third-party solution such as Coaching Director or Insala – online platforms with a range of features to make managing coaching and mentoring much easier and less labour-intensive. Targeted use of technology can improve the efficiency of operationalizing the programme and can make it easier to monitor its impact.

Effective processes

Once you have determined the needs for the programme and the mix of coaching approaches you'll need, and have assigned roles to manage the programme, it's time to plan and put in place the processes that will make sure that the programme delivers on your aspirations. This is not an exhaustive list, but it covers the essential processes that most programmes will need.

Setting standards

Standards in coaching focus on the levels of capability of coaches, their adherence to best practice and ethical standards and compliance with your programme's internal processes. It's important to have a clear definition of the programme's aims and objectives, as well as the standards that all practitioners must adhere to.

It is a good idea to document the standards to which you expect all coaches and mentors to adhere. The EMCC has documented a clear and concise set of standards in its Global Code of Ethics, available on the EMCC website. You can adapt this to ensure that it is fit for purpose in your organization.

Any set of standards that you create needs to cover the following as a minimum:

- ethical standards;
- focus on your organization's needs;
- boundaries and appropriate conduct;
- integrity;
- managing conflicts of interest;
- confidentiality;
- 'safe practice';
- supervision;
- your expectations around compliance with internal processes.

Selecting the right coaches and mentors

The successful implementation of any programme depends in large part on the capability and commitment of the coaches and mentors. So it's important to make sure that you attract and select the right people to deliver for you – both internal coaches/mentors and external providers.

Selection of internal coaches and mentors

Internal coaches and mentors are likely to be selected on the basis of a range of criteria which are likely to include:

- their level in the organization (you can specify a minimum grade/position);
- their experience of line management;
- their willingness to commit time and effort to CAM;
- their intention to become a coach or mentor;
- current level of understanding and competence in coaching and mentoring.

Figure 13.2 is a simple process for selection of internal coaches or mentors before an investment in their training:

Figure 13.2 A simple process for selection of internal coaches or mentors before an investment in their training

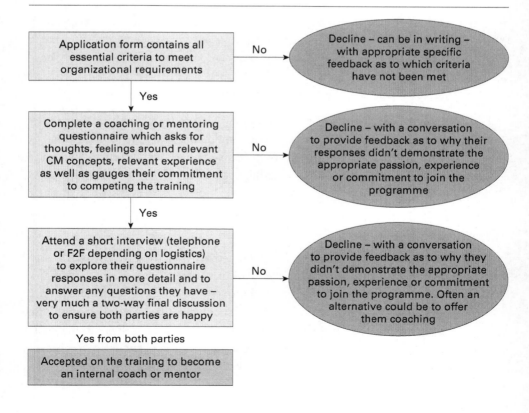

Selection of external coaches

There are many external coaches in the marketplace and the majority will be well qualified and will have the intention to add value. The market consists of many independent coaches and a range of larger coaching firms or consultancies. Independent coaches are likely to work out as less expensive, which is a major advantage. On the other hand, there is more variability in quality amongst independent coaches, compared with coaching firms. In addition, it is often more time-consuming for an organization to manage a cohort which consists of independent coaches than it is to work with a small number of coaching firms/consultancies. The right mix depends on a pragmatic view of what is right for your organization in terms of time required to manage the coaching pool, its cost, and the quality of delivery.

Whether you are working with independent coaches, coaching firms or a combination of the two, it's important to have clear selection criteria for coaches and to have a structured selection process. There is a balance to be struck between the level of rigour in the selection process and the amount of time and effort needed. Bear in mind that if your selection process is too time-consuming, some of the best coaches and firms may not wish to bid for the work!

The most usual process is a CV sift and then a structured assessment process. This could be through telephone interview, development centre, psychometrics, observed coaching practice or some combination of these measures.

Here are some of the criteria you can use when selecting coaches:

- Qualifications – what is the minimum level of coaching qualification or accreditation that you require? You should almost always look for coaches with recognized qualifications unless someone has a very strong track record in a specific skill or capability which is critical for your business.

- Experience – look for evidence that coaches have worked in a range of organizations, and for the ability to adapt to different coaching clients and situations.

- Business acumen – it is important that coaches are grounded and understand the realities of the working environment. Even if they are experts in a range of coaching techniques and can use sometimes esoteric coaching methods to good effect, they still need to understand the fundamentals of your business and to understand and adhere to the goals and purpose of your coaching programme. This is particularly important when working with senior members of your organization.

- Ability to stand on own expertise – coaches need to be confident in their ability to add value and to support and challenge clients appropriately, even when faced with occasional resistance or scepticism from clients. They need to do this in an empathetic, authentic and open way.

- Language and cultural experience – you may require coaches with particular language skills, cultural experience or subject matter expertise. These need to be factored into the selection criteria.

- Coaching competencies – in addition to the criteria above, you should ensure that coaches adhere to the coaching competencies specified by a recognized body. For example, here is a summary of the EMCC competencies for coaches. More details are available on the EMCC's website:

  1 Understanding self.

  2 Commitment to self-development.

  3 Managing the contract.

  4 Building the relationship.

  5 Enabling insight and learning.

  6 Outcome and action orientation.

  7 Use of models and techniques.

  8 Evaluation.

Of these, perhaps the most important is a commitment to self-development. Our own experience in recruiting and managing coaches has led us to the realization that regular reflective practice is a leading indicator for a skilful, resilient coach-mentor.

Size of your coaching and mentoring pool

It's also important to consider how many internal and external coaches and mentors you need. You need a sufficiently large pool to cover the anticipated demand, with a bit of contingency to account for extra demand from the business, and attrition from your coaching pool. However, it's a waste of resources to maintain a pool which is much larger than required.

In general, an external coach should have a maximum of four to five ongoing client engagements within the business. An internal coach or mentor will probably have a maximum of three, and more usually two.

You can use these figures to calculate the size of the pool required based on your anticipated demand and the blend of different coaching/mentoring approaches that you require.

Matching

A good match between the coach-mentor and the client leads to better results more quickly. Matching often includes a check on 'chemistry' which checks that there is sufficient trust and empathy to allow coaching to get off to a quick start.

It is important to make sure that the coach/mentor has the necessary background and experience to be able to add value to the client. To do this effectively the prospective client needs a good understanding of his/her goals for the coaching and it's often useful if the line manager has had some input into goals at this stage.

Here are some of the factors to consider in the matching process – some will be more important than others, depending on the prospective client's goals and needs.

- industry experience and understanding;
- knowledge of your organization/similar organizations and the competitive landscape;
- cultural awareness and understanding including experience of working with under-represented groups;
- personal experience of business leadership;
- experience as a coach-mentor of working with similar clients;
- experience in helping deliver behavioural change;
- understanding of psychology/use of psychometrics;
- life experience which enables the coach/mentor to bring a radically different perspective;
- fluency in a range of languages;
- capacity of the coach/mentor (are they available to take on the assignment?);
- cost of the coach/mentor (if using external providers).

Giving the client the right level of control of the matching process

For coach-mentoring to be successful, the client needs to come to it with a sense of control. If they feel compelled to it, and have no choice over how they work and with whom, they are less likely to engage.

For many organizations, it is important to give individual clients a chance to select their coach-mentor from a preselected group of coaches/mentors who are available to deliver the work, and who have the right range of skills, knowledge, experiences, competencies and – for external coaches and mentors – who will work for the right cost.

Option 1 – self service

In this option, prospective clients can choose their own shortlist from a list of potential coaches or mentors – often available on an intranet page.

Advantages:

- A simple approach which requires minimal effort to manage and therefore has little ongoing direct cost.

Disadvantages:

- Relies on the client having a clear understanding of what kind of person will help them most.
- Hard to monitor and track progress on the matching process.
- Very difficult to ensure the selection of coaches/mentors who are available and who will work for an appropriate rate (with risks of under-/overuse of certain coaches/mentors and of uncontrolled costs for the work).

Option 2 – systems

In this option, the organization uses a platform such as Coaching Director or Insala to aid the matching process. These build on the self-service option and enable the prospective client to select from a list which is tailored to meet the needs of the client. The system only shows CVs of suitable and available coaches and mentors, from which the client selects a shortlist.

Advantages:

- The list of available coaches and mentors can be tailored based on the client's needs and level of seniority, and the cost and availability of coaches and mentors.
- Offers the ability to track the matching process and to report on the levels of utilization of different coaches and mentors (enabling you to utilize your pool more effectively).

Disadvantages:

- Requires investment in the system and requires some support (usually from HR) to manage user issues and ensure the databases in the software are kept updated.

Option 3 – fully managed

In this option, the matching process is managed by a team (usually within HR) who will create the shortlist based on the client's needs, seniority and on the availability of coaches and mentors. A representative from the team will have a conversation with the prospective client and (usually) his/her line manager to understand the goals for the coaching/mentoring and then determine the kind of coach/mentor who is most suitable. Often they will make use of software (as described in Option 2 above) or an organization's learning management system to aid the process.

Advantages:

- Offers the ability to deliver the best-quality matching, particularly if the prospective client is well known to the team delivering the matching.
- Offers the ability to track the matching process and to utilize your pool effectively.

Disadvantages:

- Cost-intensive.
- Relies on the capability and capacity of the team delivering the matching – generally they will be delivering this role alongside a list of other accountabilities.

Option 4 – managed by an external provider

In this option, the process is outsourced to an external provider. The provider is likely to use a combination of an online platform (described in Option 2) and phone calls with the client and his/her line manager (described in Option 3) to determine the client's need and to enable a good shortlist to be provided.

Advantages:

- Offers the ability to deliver high-quality matching.
- Offers the ability to track the matching process and to utilize the pool effectively.
- Requires few resources from your organization to manage the process.

Disadvantages:

- Very cost-intensive.
- Relies on a good relationship with the supplier to provide useful reporting and consistent management of the process.

- Requires effort to ensure that the external provider fully understands the organizational context to ensure a good match.

Clear contracting/setting expectations with individuals and the organization

It is vital that there is a clear contracting process between coaches and individual coaching clients (and similarly between team coaches and the teams they are coaching). It is almost always a good idea to document what has been agreed as this gives the process a mutually agreed anchor point.

Well-trained coaches will often manage the contracting between themselves and the coaching client but may struggle to engage the other stakeholders within the organization – predominantly an individual's line manager and the HR sponsor of the coaching process. I and The OCM strongly believe that three- or four-way contracting, and debriefing, is key to great CAM and should be set as an expectation as you set up your CAM process and engagements.

In general, a good contract should be shared by all parties and cover the following:

- Goals or purpose of coach-mentoring – what will be different. There may be shared goals and some which are confidential to the client and coach/mentor, but these private goals must not run counter to the shared goals.

- Measures – both hard and soft that will show progress towards goals and purpose.

- Process – the number of coaching hours and/or period of time that the coach-mentor and client will work together, how and where they might meet.

- Expectations – how will the coach-mentor and client work together, what are they each responsible and accountable for in the relationship?

- Confidentiality – what is confidential to whom and how those boundaries will be maintained.

- Tools or psychometrics that might be used – particularly if this might increase the cost of the coach-mentoring.

- Reporting – feedback and information that give a check that the relationship is progressing as required.

- Organizational learning and supervision – clarifying how the coach-mentor is supported by a supervisor and the extent to which organizational themes arising from supervision and reflection can/will be shared and with whom.

- Changes – as the coach-mentoring progresses over time there may be changes to the client's situation – how will we respond to those and re-contract the coaching?

- Problem resolution – what will happen if an issue arises in the coach-mentoring relationship? For example, where might the client go confidentially to explore any concerns they have? And to whom might a coach-mentor turn in confidence if they become concerned about the client's wellbeing?

- Exiting – how will the end of the relationship be managed? How will impact be measured and discussed?

- For external coaches in particular, set clear commercial agreements including expectations around cancellation terms which cover changes to scheduled meetings. For many organizations these may be covered in a separate commercial contract, but should be referred to in the coaching contract.

Contracting for internal coaches and mentors

The organization will also have expectations of those who work as internal coaches and mentors. It is important to make these clear to mentors and coaches, to ensure they practise safely and deliver results. As a minimum, here are some principles which internal coaches should sign up to.

As an internal coach/mentor I will:

- make time for the mentoring sessions;
- offer challenge, stretch, guide (not tell);
- show willingness to learn;
- show enthusiasm, openness and honesty;
- encourage, support, empathise and celebrate successes;
- maintain confidentiality.

Role of line managers

Line managers have an important role to play in ensuring that coaching and mentoring are as beneficial as possible for their direct reports. When coaching and mentoring work well, there is clear alignment between the line manager's priorities, the coachee/mentee's development goals and the content of the coaching. Line managers should be informed about the overall coaching/mentoring goals and I recommend that they receive general updates every two to three months. Line managers should also maintain a supportive, two-way conversation with direct reports around the goals and priorities of the team, how these might be changing over time, and the link between the team's needs and the individual's development needs. The roles and responsibilities of line managers will be discussed in more detail in Chapter 14.

Evaluation/impact review and learning

Measuring

I will explore how to measure the effectiveness of the coaching/mentoring looking at this from the perspective of individual coaching/mentoring assignments, as well as the wider impact of the programme on the business, building on some of the ideas concerning ROI that were mentioned in Chapter 11.

Measuring the effectiveness of individual coaching/ mentoring assignments

At the end of a coaching assignment, a feedback questionnaire is often the easiest way to measure how effective a coaching/mentoring assignment has been. This gives the client the opportunity to reflect on and describe how he/she benefited from it, and what might have helped him/her to benefit from it even more.

This will of course be in addition to the conversations that the coach/mentor will have had throughout the engagement to ensure that the coaching/mentoring has remained effective as it has progressed.

There are several coaching questionnaires available to download from the Internet – here is an example of the kinds of themes they explore:

Processes – adherence to processes, timekeeping, and keeping track of progress.

Skills – use of listening, questioning and feedback.

Rapport – showing empathy, support and appropriate challenge.

Benefits – the extent to which the client achieved his/her goals, felt energized and engaged in the coaching, and experienced learning and personal change.

Business impact – how much the coaching/mentoring was linked to the wider organization's strategy and objectives.

Over time, you can build up a database of questionnaire responses to monitor individual coaches' and mentors' effectiveness, as well as patterns across the programme as a whole.

Measuring the impact on the wider organization

The measures that you use for the wider organization should naturally be closely related to the overall key success factors for the programme (see the 'Focus and linkage' section at the beginning of this chapter and Chapter 11 for ideas on other metrics that might be used for measuring ROI). Where possible, I encourage you to develop a broad set of measures as described in Chapter 11, including performance, strategy and future potential.

It's important to be pragmatic about what you measure, however – measurement should not be an end in itself. Instead, you need to be sure that key stakeholders will find the measures useful and that you can use these measures to help make the programme more effective. Measurement takes time so it's important to get a good return for that investment. Where possible, use measures which already exist. These might include staff retention, scores on employee engagement surveys, customer satisfaction measures, etc.

Measures will be vital in communication to stakeholders and to the wider employee population. If the measures tell a positive story, you can use them to generate more enthusiasm and interest in the programme. If they are mixed or less positive, it gives you a framework to explain what you're learning, and how you're adapting the programme so that it delivers more value in future.

Compelling measures of benefit can be very simple. A utilities company measured the benefit in cost savings of replacing external coaches with internal coaches on their Management Development programme, calculating that the investment in developing internal coaches had saved them many tens of thousands of pounds without diminution of benefit to individual clients. But you also need to be open to recognizing the 'unexpected benefits'. After investing in training for senior leaders in coaching, the client recognized that applying an 'ask, not tell' coaching approach could help them differentiate themselves in the market and their coach-mentoring programme was the early catalyst to a change in how they did business.

Learning

The implementation team need to make a concerted effort to learn and develop as they progress with the programme. This will help them to best serve the organization's interests as the programme evolves.

To do this, we recommend drawing on a model which is fundamental to both coaching and mentoring: the Learning Cycle. This is a simple but powerful representation of how individuals and groups learn – and in order to learn most effectively, it is necessary to pass through the sequence of steps the cycle describes.

1 Experience/do something. We take action, or something happens to us which may be positive or less positive.

2 Reflection and reviewing the event – taking time to reflect on what happened and how we feel about it.

3 Draw conclusions – taking time to understand what were the causes and how they fit into the wider system, and what can be learned from the experience.

4 Plan new experiences – with the learning in mind, this step involves making a plan for what we'll do next.

Figure 13.3 The Learning Cycle – based on Kolb (1984)

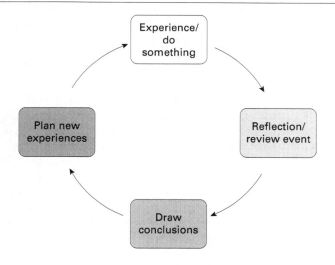

A certain amount of discipline and organization is required to make sure that the team takes time to go through these steps, rather than responding to opportunities and problems in an overly reactive way. Doing so will help the team to fine-tune their approach and ensure that the programme remains fit for purpose, evolving as the organization's needs evolve.

What derailers might you face and how can you address them?

As with any programme, the best advice is to expect the best but prepare for the worst! For the programme to deliver a positive impact over time, it needs to be able to cope with challenges and organizational changes.

Any programme is likely to face most, if not all, of the problems below at some point. We have suggested some simple solutions which either prevent or address each issue – these are a starting point for your discussions rather than the definitive answer.

Table 13.1 Potential problems and solutions

Problem	Solution
Programme is seen as heavy handed and requires considerable expenditure and manpower to maintain	Programme needs to be fit for purpose, not 'best in class'. Ensure a plan to transition to greater focus on internal coaching/mentoring over time. Ensure clear metrics for gauging return on investment. Use technology to facilitate the management of the programme wherever possible.
Programme is not well known within the organization/line managers don't promote the programme	Ensure regular communication to the employee population, using senior sponsors where possible. Ensure material is available on the intranet. Consider using the performance management process to incentivize coaching (in some circumstances). Consult line managers to understand concerns/barriers to use.
Budget becomes reduced over time	This is very common – you should plan that this will happen. Plan to transition to a greater use of internal coaches over time.
Reputational damage because of 'bad news stories' where it hasn't worked	Ensure regular communication to sponsors and the wider employee population of stories of positive outcomes. Emphasize the return on investment where possible.

Table 13.1 *continued*

Problem	Solution
People leave after having been coached/mentored – and the programme is blamed	Ensure that sponsors and line managers are aware that a small number of people may leave after having been coached/mentored. Show the benefits of having people who are clear about what they need from work rather than people who stay but are disengaged.
Programme is seen as a 'nice to have', not a strategic tool	Ensure the programme continues to have clear links to the organization's strategic priorities. Ensure regular measurement of the programme's effectiveness against a set of agreed measures. Communicate the results of these measurements regularly to key stakeholders via the programme's sponsor.
Oversubscription	Potentially a good problem to have but can overwhelm the programme. Manage expectations around who can access coaching and how they 'qualify' for access to it.
Internal coaches who develop a poor reputation	Strong selection processes; focus on continuous professional development; feedback process for post-coaching evaluation.
Programme loses link with the strategic issues over time	Conduct annual audits of the programme to ensure links with the strategy – especially during times of change in the organization. Seek support from the programme's senior sponsor(s) where possible to help with this.

Checklist for successful implementation

As a final thought for this chapter, here is a summary of some key elements of a successful implementation. We've turned it into a checklist to help you prioritize. You can use this both when implementing coaching and mentoring for the first time, and when auditing an existing coaching and mentoring programme:

- Have you clearly documented the links between the purpose of the programme with one or more overall business objectives?
- Have you clearly documented the links between the purpose of the programme and the L&D/talent strategy?
- Do you have an overall programme sponsor who sits on the senior executive team?

- Do you have a clear project team with assigned responsibilities?
- Do you have a communication strategy for the programme?
- Do you have a list of measurable key success factors for the programme overall?
- Are you committed to measuring these key success factors over time to test how well the programme is performing?
- Do you have clear standards in place for internal and external coaches in terms of training/qualifications and continuous professional development?
- Have you created a risk register to document what might derail the programme?
- If you are planning to help managers to use a coaching approach, have you conducted a full training needs analysis to understand what they need to be doing differently?
- Do you have a clear view of the mix of external coaching, internal coaching and mentoring that you would like to see in the programme – and how you would like this to change over time?
- Have you created clear processes for:
  - matching clients with coaches/mentors?
  - contracting – clear guidelines for how to contract and essential elements of the contracts themselves?
  - monitoring – how you will measure the impact of the programme over time?
  - exiting – how people should exit coaching mentoring relationships?
  - links with line management – how line managers are expected to benefit from and lend their support to coaching and mentoring?
  - CPD – how your coaches and mentors will ensure they practise safely and have a positive impact?

Endnote

Kolb, D A (1984) *Experiential Learning: Experience as the source of learning and development*, Prentice-Hall, Englewood, NJ

Roles and responsibilities in coaching and mentoring

14

KATHERINE RAY

In the previous chapters we have looked at how coaching and mentoring are invaluable tools which help organizations deliver their strategy if used well. We've looked at the different forms CAM can take – and the broad range of different issues they can address in an organization. We've also looked at how CAM typically evolves, initially making significant use of external providers, to a situation where, over time, most of the coaching and mentoring are conducted by line managers and an internal coaching cadre.

Once an organization has a clear roadmap for a CAM implementation, the hard work really begins. In Chapter 13, we explored the importance of a clear plan as well as clear roles and responsibilities. In this chapter we'll explore the roles in greater depth, focusing in particular on the roles and responsibilities of HR and the line – and the value that both can add when working together towards a shared agenda. HR are often seen as the drivers and owners of CAM programmes, but as we'll show, it's more effective when they work in concert with the line and senior leaders in a joined-up way.

In this chapter, I explore the various roles and responsibilities individuals play when implementing and doing coaching and mentoring in organizations. I will look at the following areas:

- Whose role and responsibility are coaching and mentoring in an organization?
- The different organizational roles and responsibilities of those involved in coaching and mentoring within any organization including:

- HR director/head of L&D;
- HR business partners;
- the line manager;
- strategic leaders;
- the client;
- the supervisor.
- The role and concept of the coach-mentor.

Whose role and responsibility are coaching and mentoring in organizations?

When organizations approach us to talk about helping them implement coaching and/or mentoring it is almost always someone from HR or Learning and Development (L&D) who we have the initial conversations with. This makes sense given that HR's role and responsibility are the development of people and organizational capability. Their role should be to understand where the capability of the organization and its people connects to the business strategy and to determine what future development is needed to build the skills, competencies and behaviours that will enable the organization to grow and achieve its business goals. HR will almost certainly have more expertise and experience in coaching and/or mentoring than other functions in their organization, and so they are best positioned to advise and influence the business to invest in coaching and/or mentoring appropriately.

Increasingly, some organizations have specific roles such as 'coaching lead' with a focus on coaching; individuals who are qualified internal coaches and are responsible for managing any external coaching requirements and building internal coaching within the organization.

We know from many publications and research that 'talent' still remains one of the top concerns of many CEOs; without the right people they know they can't deliver their business strategy. Research from 'What CEOs want from HR' published by Henley Business School (Holley, 2014) tells us that apart from getting the basics right, the expectations CEOs have of HR 'revolve around the employee lifecycle, performance, culture and organizational development – creating a culture where people are developed'.

From our expertise and from our experience of working with our clients, there are three critical phases of implementing any coaching and mentoring which HR and/or L&D need to own:

1 The initiation phase – why are we doing this? How does it link and connect to the business and people strategies?

2 Design/creation phase – how are we going to do this? What do we want coaching and/or mentoring to achieve?

3 Evaluation/impact review and learning – what are we measuring, what has changed and what has the impact of doing coaching and/or mentoring been? What are we learning and how do we implement that learning?

From our experience, in order for any coaching and mentoring to be successful (and by successful we mean producing tangible business impact and results) there are a number of different roles that play an important role in the success of any coaching and/or mentoring activities. This means that whilst HR and L&D may be the initiators and owners, they are not solely responsible for the success of coaching and mentoring. There are others who can play their part.

For more information about implementing coaching and mentoring, please refer to Chapter 13.

HR director/head of learning and development/the coaching and mentoring lead – strategic catalysts

The role of HR is crucial in getting any coaching and mentoring activities off the ground. We have stated that in most organizations HR manage the investment in development and so act as a 'gatekeeper' for all coaching and mentoring activities (internal and/or external) and are accountable for ensuring they are embedded within the organization. They are the people within any organization who have the knowledge and experience of coaching and mentoring. But where an organization is large enough to have separate HR and L&D functions, what are the differences between them and does it make a difference who owns them?

The CIPD Annual Learning and Development Survey 2015 found that 'L&D is usually incorporated within the HR function – in over two-fifths of organizations L&D is a specialist function/role within the HR department and in one-fifth it is part of generalist HR activities'. This enables alignment between the L&D strategy and business strategy, as they found that 'in a quarter of organizations, the L&D strategy is extremely aligned with the needs of the business with a further two-fifths reporting that they are broadly aligned'. This fact alone demonstrates that HR or L&D have a critical role in ensuring that the people strategy is represented in the business strategy. Their role simply is to be the catalyst for bringing the people strategy to life.

The survey also found that 'the number of people employed in the L&D function increases with the size of the organization' and we see this when working with a range of different companies. The bigger companies tend to have a specific L&D function that sits within the HR function, whereas with smaller companies, the role and responsibility for L&D tend to sit within the role of the HR director or head of HR. These organizations tend to have a role specifically focusing on coaching and/or mentoring as well.

Does it make a difference whether the responsibility for coaching and/or mentoring sits under HR or L&D?

I would argue not, as what's important are the knowledge and experience of the HR professional (whether in HR or L&D) who is responsible for implementing coaching and/or mentoring. What is important is that there is alignment between the people strategy and the business strategy to provide clarity on what coaching and/or mentoring are trying to achieve. This is particularly important in the initiation phase and it is one of the first questions we ask our clients – what are you trying to achieve by investing in coaching and/or mentoring?

HR and/or L&D play a vital role in educating the business around the use of coaching and mentoring and influencing decision makers to invest in them appropriately. Their influence comes from being seen as credible business partners who have expertise in this area. It's a great opportunity for leaders within any business to get a greater understanding about the organization and develop and grow networks and connections across the company. In this purpose-driven leadership world we live in, the sell is becoming less arduous, as leaders want to give something back and see how they can add value to others in the organization.

HR also plays a key role in role-modelling what good 'coaching and mentoring' look like. HR directors or heads of L&D tend to do some form of coaching with senior leaders, whether this is a formal or informal role, and many are formally given an 'internal coach-mentor' role with their business partners.

Things HR/L&D should consider when implementing coaching and/or mentoring

As described in Chapter 13, it's critical that HR and L&D are clear on the overall purpose of the CAM implementation and how it will help deliver the organization's strategic objectives. If the aspiration is to create a 'coaching culture', HR need to be able to articulate a clear vision of what this will look like and to 'sell' the benefits to the line, who may take some convincing that it is either achievable or desirable. To reiterate a key point from Chapter 13, it's crucial that HR and L&D are clear on who the recipients of CAM will be, what CAM will look like and what the benefits will be. This is best summarized in a clearly articulated strategy for the CAM programme.

Once the strategy is in place, HR and/or L&D are responsible for designing a relevant framework that sits around it including setting expectations and standards and most importantly ensuring that those they are expecting to coach and/or mentor have the necessary tools and training to be able to execute it properly. This investment in coaching and/or mentoring training varies greatly, usually depending on the value placed on it by the business.

Last but not least, the often overlooked or most difficult responsibility of HR is measuring and evaluating the impact of coaching and/or mentoring. HR has become much more metrified over the past few years and as budgets tighten and organizations are looking for the return on investment, HR must be able to measure and prove the impact development activities such as coaching and/or mentoring are having on the business.

Summary

The roles and responsibilities of HR/L&D/coaching and mentoring lead in an organization are as follows:

- Ability to clearly articulate to the business 'why' there is a need to invest in coaching and/or mentoring and how they will address business issues and challenges.

- Alignment between the business and people strategies – to ensure that any coaching and mentoring activities are rooted in the organizational goals and objectives and executed through the people strategy.

- To design and create coaching and mentoring frameworks, tools and training to equip people in the business to be coaches and/or mentors.

- To be the gatekeeper for all internal and external coaching and mentoring activities, ensuring consistent quality of all coaching and mentoring activities.

- Sufficient expertise in coaching and mentoring to be the internal champion of any coaching and mentoring activities.

- To be a good role model for coaching and mentoring within their organization, setting the standard of what 'good' coaching and/or mentoring look like by being a coach-mentor to their business partner and key stakeholders.

- To foster and encourage a culture of coaching and/or mentoring within the organization, whether this be informal, formal or both.

For more information about how organizations are using coaching and mentoring please see Chapter 12.

HRBPs – the executors and champions of coaching and mentoring

I have termed the role and responsibility of HR Business Partners (HRBPs) as being the executors and champions of coaching and mentoring, because this really describes their role and responsibility – to execute and champion any coaching and mentoring activities within their part of the business aligned to the business and people strategy. Executing the strategy for coaching and/or mentoring in their part of the business may involve bringing in external coaches, or developing the internal mentoring capability by identifying and developing internal mentors and mentees. Just like the coaching and mentoring lead, they are responsible for being a champion/role model for any coaching and mentoring, to demonstrate to the business what good coaching and mentoring look like.

The HRBP as the internal coach

Like heads of HR or L&D, HRBPs often act as an internal coach to their business partners and in many organizations HRBPs are expected to coach. In a global confectionery company that we work with, the expectations of an HRBP are very clear: that they coach in their role as a line manager but also as HRBP to a management team, where their role is to be a coach to the leaders and the members of the team. The HR function invested in training itself, equipping HRBPs to offer internal coaching. HRBPs bought into their roles as internal coaches as it enabled them to have a seat at the table, influence their teams better using a coaching style and approach and ensure coaching was strategically aligned. The only caution they would share was that coaching can be a time-intensive activity, and whilst it was the HRBP's role to coach, they couldn't lose sight of their other responsibilities.

HRBPs have a role and responsibility to endorse and act as guardians of any coaching and/or mentoring frameworks that are in place, making sure that they are using them as well as encouraging the business to use them. Consistent use of those frameworks is important to ensure that any coaching and/or mentoring are being used effectively across the business.

HRBPs have a good insight and understanding of the people in their business area along with line managers, so their involvement in advising and putting names forward for internal coaching opportunities, building internal coaching and/or mentoring pools and matching coaches/mentors and clients is crucial.

HRBPs who act as internal coaches need to be careful that less competent managers and leaders don't delegate coaching to them (or to external coaches). And they need to identify when the best solution is coaching their partners to find their own solutions. When I speak to HRBPs, whilst there is a real desire to coach and they understand the benefits, there can often be this overwhelming urge to be of value by 'fixing the problems' for their business partners, rather than using a facilitative approach.

Summary

The roles and responsibilities of the HR Business Partner in an organization are as follows:

- Act as an executor and champion for all coaching and mentoring activities.
- Be an internal coach to their business partner(s) and team(s).
- Act as a role model for how to do good coaching and mentoring.
- Act as the gatekeeper for all coaching and mentoring activities, particularly the use of external coaches.
- Identify any training needs and support managers and leaders to develop their coaching and mentoring capabilities.
- Continue to develop their own coaching and/or mentoring skills by completing relevant professional development.

Line managers – coaching as part of the day job

The roles and responsibilities of the line manager with regards to coaching in particular have shifted over the past few years within organizations. This shift is driven by a recognition that coaching styles are effective – for example as organizations review their approach to performance management we are seeing a shift away from ratings to a much more 'conversational' approach. Line managers need to be equipped to have powerful conversations with their teams. As a result, organizations are investing in upskilling their line managers in coaching, with a particular focus on them being able to give better feedback and have better performance review and development conversations with their teams.

In order for line managers to be able to coach they need to be equipped with the right tools and training, therefore coaching training for line managers is imperative, whether this is built into traditional management development programmes or by providing coaching skills training. If line managers are properly trained in coaching, the delegation of coaching to external coaches tends to be reduced. However, as already discussed, there might be scenarios where it's appropriate and necessary to bring in an external coach. If managers are going to outsource coaching externally, it is really important that there is a clear justification for doing so and that there is clarity around what the line manager expectations are from the external coaching.

Line managers play a very different role when it comes to mentoring. Their role is simply to help their direct report (mentee) identify their goals for the mentoring relationship and to support their direct report in achieving these goals.

Whilst a line manager can coach, best practice advises that a line manager shouldn't be a mentor and that any mentoring should be conducted outside the mentee's reporting line. This is to allow the mentee to have honest and open conversations with someone outside their management structure but also to hear different perspectives and experiences from someone else within the business.

This shift in expectation is supported by The CIPD Annual Learning and Development Survey 2015, which found that whilst coaching is one of the top three development activities most likely to be used by organizations, the use of external coaches is decreasing as the role of the line manager as coach grows in importance. However, there will always be scenarios where the use of an external coach is the most effective choice. Line managers will ideally work closely with HR to identify those occasions.

This focus on the 'line manager as coach' is particularly evident in people-heavy industries such as fast-moving consumer goods (FMCGs), professional services and the NHS. However, it is not just these organizations who are focusing on upskilling their line managers to be able to coach; it's becoming much more widespread.

At the same global confectionery company, they have a philosophy that every associate (their term for employees) deserves a great line manager; line managers need to coach their associates as part of being a great line manager. Therefore, the primary owner of coaching is the line manager; the cornerstone for coaching throughout the business sits firmly with line managers. Coaching and mentoring are deeply rooted in the company's culture, with the founders holding the belief that you have to help people to make them better.

Summary

The roles and responsibilities of the line manager in an organization are as follows:

- Be a coach to their team collectively and individually.
- Encourage a coaching environment and peer coaching within their teams.
- Have and show a passion for people development.
- Use HR or external coaches selectively and effectively as resources.
- Be a role model for their teams so that when they become a line manager they adopt the same coaching approach with their team.
- Continue to develop their own coaching skills by completing relevant professional development.

For more information about the manager as a coach-mentor, see Chapter 12.

Strategic leaders – sponsors

Whilst HR might be responsible for executing coaching and mentoring and line managers for doing coaching, strategic leaders play a critical role in sponsoring, championing and supporting coaching and mentoring activities within an organization, making it a business imperative rather than a 'nice to have'.

When a global FMCG business created a global mentoring programme for high-potential women, the secret to its success was unequivocally down to the senior involvement and sponsorship of the programme right at the top – the CEO, as well as the chief HR officer and senior leaders. The need for a global mentoring programme was driven by the business strategy and translated into the people strategy, where it was clear there was a distinct lack of gender diversity within senior leadership positions. There was a shared consensus right at the top that the only way to reach the growth goals was greater gender diversity, and clear messaging to the business that this was a business imperative. This was backed up by clear expectations of leadership throughout the business – involvement in and support of the mentoring programme was not optional.

In the global confectionery organization mentioned above, coaching and mentoring are grounded in their business strategy and values. This company provides a great example of where the people strategy is part of the business strategy; coaching and mentoring are used widely and create an environment in which people want to stay and grow with the company.

When a global accounting and consulting organization wanted to create a coaching culture, they started building coaching capability at the very top, whereby senior partners were trained to become accredited coaches. They felt that if they invested in developing their senior partners to have the skills to coach, this would filter down the organization and be an effective way of creating a much-needed coaching culture, as well as senior leaders role-modelling the right behaviours.

Most larger organizations will run leadership development programmes which include coaching and/or mentoring as a key aspect, whether it's building coaching skills or pairing delegates with a coach or mentor to help with their development. Just as with line managers, there is an expectation that leaders will use coaching styles. However, in global and complex organizations, very senior leaders may struggle to invest time in coaching their direct reports and organizations frequently supply external or specialist internal coaches at this level.

I observe that leaders tend to play the role of a mentor, offering their knowledge, experiences and learnings to people who don't work for them. When organizations set up mentoring programmes to address gaps in their talent pipeline, leaders are called upon to offer mentoring to these identified groups. It is a win–win, as the majority of leaders want to give something back and are passionate about helping others, plus it enables them to work with people in different parts of the organization that they wouldn't normally work with. For the mentee, it gives them access to someone with expertise, experience and knowledge as well as insight into their part of the organization.

Summary

The roles and responsibilities of the strategic leader in an organization are as follows:

- Act as a sponsor for coaching and mentoring within the organization.
- Lead from the front and communicate how CAM fits into the business strategy.
- Act as an internal mentor who is willing to share their knowledge, experiences and learnings.

- Be open minded and willing to be coached by their HR business partner.
- Encourage their direct reports to access coaching and to coach their teams.

Client

When we look at the role and responsibility of the client in any coaching and/or mentoring activities we are talking about the client in two ways: 1) the organization as the client of any coaching and/or mentoring services, and 2) the individual coachee or mentee receiving coaching and/or mentoring.

Whether it's the organization or the individual, one fact remains consistent: it's really important to manage expectations of both carefully from the outset.

As an external provider of coaching and mentoring, we contract with the organizational client to understand what their expectations are of any coach-mentoring assignment as well as understanding the individual's needs.

We seek to ensure that the organization and the individual share clarity around the purpose and goals of the investment in coach-mentoring and wherever it is not unrealistic we engage in a three-way contracting process to ensure that all parties – the organization, the individual and coach-mentor – have shared expectations.

The role of the organizational client (usually a line manager) is not only to communicate clearly the organization's purpose in investing in the coach-mentoring assignment but also to provide support and encouragement to the individual.

The role of the individual client is to come to their coach-mentoring sessions with an open mind and a clear understanding of what it is they want to focus their coach-mentoring sessions on. They have the responsibility for making and keeping appropriate commitments to work on changes and to reflect on their experiences between meetings. They also need to give their coach-mentor clear feedback about what is and isn't working for them in coach-mentoring meetings.

Supervisor

As organizations build their internal coaching and mentoring capabilities there is need to ensure continued development and safe practice. Coaches and mentors need to be supported and to have a safe place to go/someone to talk to about their experiences and responses – a supervisor.

Supervision is certainly more commonplace in coaching than it is in mentoring and is actively encouraged for those doing a lot of coaching. However, we are starting to see an increase in organizations wanting to identify a mentoring supervisor for internal mentors who are part of an internal mentoring programme. This can either be someone internal, usually someone in HR/L&D who is responsible for setting up internal coaching and/or mentoring, or an external supervisor.

The role of the supervisor is explored by Angela in Chapter 15, but I see it at heart as being a sounding board, someone who has experience in CAM and is able to coach-mentor those involved in coaching and/or mentoring about what they are experiencing, whether this be positive or negative. Supervision is reflective, allowing the internal coach or mentor to review their learning and to explore how they can develop different coaching and/or mentoring skills and approaches to enable them to become better coach-mentors.

The supervisor plays a crucial role in ensuring ethics and standards are adhered to, whether they are external or internal. Supervision has tended to be managed externally but we are now starting to see the rise of internal supervision for both coaching and mentoring.

The role of the coach-mentor

Many organizations have invested in bringing specialist coaching and mentoring capability into the organization by identifying and building a pool of internal trained coaches or mentors. These internal resources are then able to provide specialist coaching to employees, reducing the reliance (and expenditure) on external coaches. As we saw in Chapter 12, this reflects the usual pattern of the evolution of a coaching programme over time, with increased use of internal resources and less reliance on external specialists. Over the past few years, many of our client organizations have invested in building their internal coaching capability by offering nominated internal coaches the opportunity to become accredited coaches and supervisors.

Unlike many coaching and mentoring organizations, at The OCM we advocate no single theoretical coaching or mentoring model but encourage the serious development of a wide range of approaches. This means that practitioners can work in a way that is skilful, authentic and most effective in the context of any particular client engagement. Our approach is essentially holistic and has been labelled as 'Situational Coach-Mentoring'.

At The OCM, we believe firmly in the term 'coach-mentor' as representative of a situational approach that gives the best outcome. A coach-mentor can adopt a more 'coaching-oriented' or a more 'mentoring-oriented' approach, depending on the needs of the client and the coach-mentor's own knowledge and experience. This means that the client is getting the best of the coach-mentor's broad experience. Interestingly, at the BLD Foundation* they also illustrated this in their mentoring guidelines, which clearly stated: 'At BLD Foundation, we believe that the role of the mentor is to advise, guide, support, and coach the mentee to explore options, focus thoughts, make better rounded decisions and take a proactive approach to his/her career.' Furthermore, two of our clients who have been building their internal coaching capability over the past few years are now calling their internal coaches 'coach-mentors' as they are providing individuals with advice, guidance and support as well as coaching them.

The concept of being seen as a coach-mentor gives the coach permission, when they have relevant knowledge and experience, to be more directive when the time is right. Kline (1999) summarizes this perfectly, describing coaching as 'helping others find the answers themselves, whereas mentoring is the same as well as providing guidance and advice where necessary'. Equally, it releases mentors from always feeling obliged to offer their advice, instead using good facilitative questions to surface greater insight. We often find exploring the different styles illustrated in Figure 14.1 below is helpful to ensure internal coaches and mentors appreciate the different stances they can adopt depending on the situation.

Figure 14.1 Six styles of coaching

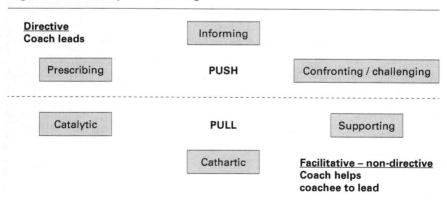

Being directive is not the same as telling someone what to do. But it does move away from a more rigidly 'non-directive' frame of coaching. Most of our clients value the flexibility of coach-mentors; we have heard time and time again from clients who have previously been coached about how frustrating it was if their coaches stayed in a completely non-directive space when it was not the appropriate position.

Often a coachee or mentee is keen to get some direction and input – perhaps challenging them to act on a commitment they have previously failed to keep or to consider other perspectives. Indeed, challenge by its very nature is often quite directive even if it is in the form of a question. A question I quite regularly use to directly test commitment is 'How are you going to convince me that you are going to do this now, when you never have before?'

Another perspective to consider is when you are working with a coachee who leading executive coach Michael Carroll describes as being in 'survival mode' – just trying to keep it all together when the pressure is really on. Often in those situations their capacity for thought and decision making is negatively impacted, so the coach-mentor can provide real help by helping them to see and face up to decisions that may need to be made. When working with someone who is in this situation, it is apparent within a minute of coaching them that they are on the edge. A great directive question to use could be: 'It sounds to me as if you need to decide what you need to focus on at this time' – putting the decision with them to make, but challenging them to make a choice.

Adding value to your client, whether you are labelled as a coach or a mentor, needs to be a balance between support and challenge – directive and non-directive. As long as the ownership stays with the client and the style is 'ask, not tell', the outcome should be a positive one.

* The BLD (Black Lawyers Directory) set up the BLD Foundation to support young people from ethnic minority and/or socio-economically underprivileged backgrounds towards achieving their fullest potential. Their work provides young people with knowledge and information about the opportunities available in the legal profession, equipping them with the skills to take advantage of these opportunities, and providing them with access to work placements and recruitment opportunities in leading legal firms and chambers nationally.

Conclusion

In this chapter I have explored who is responsible for coaching and mentoring within organizations, the different roles involved in making coaching and mentoring a success and the role of the coach-mentor.

What is apparent is that whilst the main role and responsibility for implementing any coaching and mentoring lie firmly with HR or L&D, there are others in an organization who have a key role to play in embedding coaching and mentoring. It is no longer something that HR or someone external does to the business, as coaching and mentoring are being internalized and internal capability developed.

Coaching and mentoring will have a key role to play in the development of people within any organization. The greater the connection and link to the business strategy the greater the engagement in CAM will be within the business. HR play a key role in ensuring the 'why', 'how' and 'what' questions are answered, involving key stakeholders in any coaching and/or mentoring and building a culture where great conversations take place.

Endnotes

CIPD (2015) Learning and Development Survey, CIPD [online] http://www.cipd.co.uk/hr-resources/survey-reports/learning-development-2015.aspx

Holley, N (2014) What CEOs want from HR, Henley Business School, Henley-on-Thames

Kline, N (1999) *Time to Think*, Ward Lock, London

Supervision in practice

15

ANGELA HILL

And what is it to work with love?
It is to charge all things you fashion with a breath of your own spirit.

KAHLIL GIBRAN

An evaluative review of supervision in the context of personal, professional and organizational development. This chapter will help you evaluate:

- the role of supervision in developing coaching capacity in the organization;
- the fundamentals for effective supervision;
- the concept of 'good enough' and 'fit for purpose' supervision;
- how you will assess supervision in relation to personal and the organization's needs.

Mel has spoken in Chapter 9 about the need for supervision to be situational, appropriate to the individual and context. He has pointed out that for a manager using coach-mentoring approaches as part of their role, supervision is less important, although supported ongoing learning and reflection on outcomes is. In this chapter we are looking at the vital role that supervision plays in supporting the internal and external coach-mentor and the role that supervision can play in embedding and sustaining the effectiveness of your coach-mentoring investment.

Perhaps due to the roots of supervision practice being found in other disciplines, the value and rationale for coaching and mentoring supervision in organizations are still being questioned. Sample comments include: a self-serving money-making exercise for the professional membership bodies; an unwelcome distraction from income-generating delivery of coaching services; a non-essential practice driven by the influx into coaching of psychotherapists and psychologists.

However, if we are genuine in our belief that all people have untapped potential and are committed to supporting individual and organizational learning, we cannot underestimate the value of a process that expressly deals with the qualitative, developmental and resourcing aspects of coach-mentoring in support of the organization's purpose.

At The OCM we believe that supervision and CPD are integral to sustaining effective coaching and mentoring for the benefit of individuals, teams and organizations. This is true for internal coaches who support transition, leadership and talent development, as well as external practitioners. Support, challenge and reflective practice provided in the supervision space enable the individual to review and fine-tune skills. With increased recognition globally that good-quality standards and ethical practice in the delivery of organizational coaching, mentoring and supervision are essential, all the professional coaching and mentoring bodies have developed standards or guidance for supervision.

The role of supervision in developing coaching capacity in the organization

If you agree that having good supervision is important to ensure ethical practice and ongoing development of coach-mentors, it seems self-evident that you would check that your external coach-mentors are both investing in and learning from it, and that you offer time out for supervision for internal coach-mentors. But what is 'supervision' in an organizational context?

What kinds of supervision are appropriate and sufficient?

There are many different definitions of supervision more or less relevant depending on context, with some of the most powerful or nuanced expressed metaphorically:

A beacon of reflection in a sea of complexity. (De Haan, 2012)

Treasure hunting. (Waskett, 2006, in Henderson, 2009)

A Zen garden. (Hill, 2011)

However evocative, none of these is particularly useful in assessing the appropriateness of a supervisor, the quality of the supervision offering or in shaping your investment in internal supervision.

The EMCC (European Mentoring and Coaching Council) is the first to have developed an ESQA – European Standards Quality Award – to accredit development programmes in coaching and mentoring supervision and we find their definition a practical description.

EMCC definition of supervision

> Supervision is the interaction that occurs when a mentor or coach brings their coaching or mentoring work experiences to a supervisor in order to be supported and to engage in reflective dialogue and collaborative learning for the development and benefit of the mentor or coach, their clients and their organizations. (EMCC International Vice President Quality, 2015)

The professional standards bodies are evolving their thinking about coaching supervision. The 'expert' model of supervision that gained ground initially has begun to make way for a more inclusive, emergent model. Asking what or whose purpose supervision serves can help differentiate and integrate what is relevant to help coaching in organizations deliver on priority outcomes now and going forward.

The core functions or tasks of supervision are common across many disciplines but have various names: supportive, normative, formative, educational, resourcing, qualitative, etc (Proctor, 2008; Hawkins and Smith, 2006).

In essence, supervision offers to the **individual coach-mentor**:

- safe space for collaborative dialogue;
- reflective practice;
- professional challenge;
- opportunity to share experiences and celebrate success;
- timely support with ethical dilemmas, from boundary issues to the more complex with potential for serious consequences.

In our experience, coach-mentors at all stages of development, from novice to highly experienced, will make time for ongoing improvement of inter- and intrapersonal skills. Supervision offers strategic thinking space and scrutiny to challenge their practice, work on recurring habits or patterns which undermine effectiveness, surface what works and why, share learning, maintain boundaries and continuously refresh and innovate. Proactive participation in supervision is a tangible measure of a coach-mentor's ongoing professional commitment to individual and organizational clients.

One result of supervision is that the coach-mentor develops greater understanding, skill and adaptability. This is clearly of value to the individual coach-mentor and, where offered to internal coach-mentors, can be seen as an investment in building organizational capacity. Coaching and mentoring done well are immensely satisfying and can be intense. Supervision supports and rejuvenates coaches, helping underpin their wellbeing. Planned for and sustained by the organization, supervision can ensure that the practice of coach-mentoring remains rooted in the organization's purpose and needs as well as integrating the needs of individual clients.

In addition, regular supervision within the organization offers the opportunity to gather organizational learning in a forum that preserves the confidentiality of the individual contract. This learning can:

- inform sponsors of coaching and mentoring of its effectiveness against organizational goals;
- allow planners of coaching and mentoring to focus investment in areas that will deliver greatest organizational return;
- alert leaders in the organizations to barriers and enablers to desired organizational development and talent; or
- inform performance growth.

Where organizations have both internal and external coach-mentors working in their organization, there is a great potential advantage in bringing both together in supervision to share learning and perspectives. This can give external coach-mentors a better understanding of organizational reality and internal coach-mentors the opportunity to challenge untested, shared 'assumptions'.

Supervision is key to optimize the benefits of coaching at EY. It's vital to ensure that we maximize the effectiveness of our 20 internal coaches, not only in terms of what they deliver but also to provide a safety mechanism for both clients and coaches. Supervision has embedded a strong quality control which makes sure that a high standard of coaching, providing real value to partners and directors, is delivered consistently across the firm.

We currently operate a model offering both internal and external supervision. Coaches really value the supervision they receive, as it gives them the reassurance and confidence that they are doing the right things, particularly in tricky situations, and provides another lens on the coaching relationship. The external perspective can be very valuable to ensuring that coaches are not taking an insular view, as well as supporting their learning with new approaches and ideas.

Nicki Hickson, Director of Coaching UK and Ireland, EY

Effective supervision of this kind provides additional quality assurance and governance of standards. Despite statistics suggesting that up to 92 per cent of those surveyed are in receipt of supervision (see Chapter 9), the proportion of coaches participating in regular sessions with a qualified supervisor is a lot less. Many coaches have relied on informal peer-to-peer supervision, as and when required for reasons of cost, difficulty finding suitably trained and experienced coach-mentor supervisors, ease of access or lack of choice with supervision formats. This is a reality which may contribute to the membership bodies' more recent emphasis on accreditation as another indicator of quality, professionalism and currency of practice.

> All coaches no matter how experienced have issues they do not see, communication not heard and challenges they are not communicating.
> **Arney and Schwenk (2006)**

The fundamentals for implementing supervision

What are the basics that you need to pay attention to in order to implement and sustain effective supervision in coaching and mentoring?

The following 'givens' are based on our combined experience from delivering coach mentor supervisor training, coaching services and coach mentoring consultancy, as well as learning from our alumni and sponsors.

Be clear on the purpose(s) of any investment in supervision:

Which of the three functions of supervision highlighted below would assist you most right now in ensuring that your organization's investment in coaching and mentoring fulfils its intended purpose?

Development	Quality Assurance	Resourcing
ability, understanding,	standards and	objectivity,
skills, capacity,	ethical practice	systemic awareness
multiple and diverse	effective outcomes	wellbeing
perspectives, creativity	relevant to purpose	support

Be clear on the difference

A starting point for effective supervision is to have a better understanding of the difference between coaching, mentoring and supervision. It is important to develop a shared definition that captures the purpose of these roles within your own organizational context. As with the situational approach in coaching or mentoring, the supervisor may adopt a coaching approach or act as a mentor at different times in order to deliver 'the transformational purpose of coaching and mentoring for individuals and organizations' (Gilpin, 2016). The perspective or 'gaze' in supervision is fundamentally different, deeper, broader, more oblique, as is the pace, which is often slower than you might expect in coaching assignments. Within supervision, more focus and space are given to what is uncertain or as yet unknown.

> We know a great deal more than we are aware.
> **Bolton (2014)**

Start at the beginning

Without consistent senior leadership backing, integration of supervision in the overall delivery of coaching and mentoring as part of the way you do business or realize the full value of investing in coaching and mentoring can be difficult to add in to existing plans and strategies, but this is not insurmountable. As with any investment in the organization's talent capabilities, it can be a challenge to gain resources for it at times of critical threat, uncertainty and change. So wherever possible we recommend building supervision in as part of the investment in coaching and mentoring from the start. At The OCM we have integrated supervision and reflective practice into all our coaching and mentoring development and bespoke services since their inception in 1998 and it has given us a highly effective and practical way to improve learning. Clients who have integrated supervision into their internal coaching resource report similar benefits. For example, in a review of RWE npower's internal coaching in 2014 (OCM Journal, 2014) the training of two internal coach-mentor supervisors was seen as key to the investment's success – together with the presence of senior leadership sponsors who could ensure that organizational learning gathered from supervision could be well integrated into leadership decisions.

Be strategic

Safe harvesting of themes and issues that emerge in supervision helps to re-orientate all coaching activity to individual and organizational purpose and need. Through supervision of internal coach-mentors, a lead coach-mentor (as described in Chapter 14), can read the degree of match or mismatch between coaching activity and organizational climate and strategy (Long, 2011), making timely adjustments to keep coaching and mentoring closely aligned to business purpose. Systematically taking into account this learning helps organizational strategy and planning remain in close contact with front-line realities and the needs of the key talent and future leadership pool.

Plan ahead, eyes wide open

Supervision is intentionally a 'safe space' for honest review, to offload and recalibrate coaching and mentoring practice.

To be effective in an organization, this requires the shared ability to manage factors likely to put at risk ethical and confidential boundaries. Examples would include: tensions arising from dual-role conflict, access to privileged information, management and sponsors seeking information, (St John-Brooks, 2014) and potential crossover in coaching and mentoring with other organizational policy, eg mental ill-health, bullying or sexual harassment, where confidentiality of the individual may of necessity be less secure.

Upfront clarity on and contingency planning for all these potential risks and others linked to business governance or ethical codes (EMCC/AC, 2016) through multiple layered organizational, group and individual contracting for supervision will go part way to laying the foundations. Vigilance, especially when new coaches and mentors join the community of practice, is also vital.

Be creative and innovate

As more supervision by trained and qualified internal supervisors takes place, there has been an increase in the variety of different formats for delivery of supervision. Blending supervision, be it internal and external, one-to-one and group, on-site and virtual, seems to be valued by our large organizational clients. The additional objectivity and detachment of an external supervisor are a valuable addition to but not a replacement for internally led supervision, which is more cost effective.

Figure 15.1 Blended mix of supervision options (OCM Supervision and CPD Conference 2012, Building Internal Coaching Supervision Capability, Long and Hill)

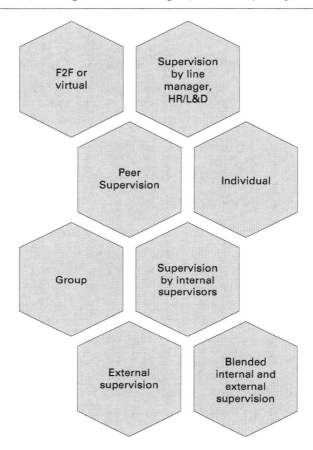

One internal organizational supervisor who participated in the OCM pilot awarded an ESQA in 2012, captures below the advantages of building internal capacity (OCM Conference, 2012):

'Knowledge of the challenges that the business faces means that we can contextualize the support provided. The biggest benefit to me has been the response from the individuals who are facing challenging issues and who are really appreciative of the time and support provided; in a changing business enviorment it is validation of the effort that is put in.'

'Commercially it makes sense for us, as it is far more cost effective to train two of our senior coaches to supervise members of our internal coaching team, than to purchase this service externally.'

Supervision practice developed in other disciplines is a wisdom pool for coaching and mentoring to draw from. However, models and approaches that work best in coaching and mentoring supervision are likely to be more situational, creative and systemic than the 'expert, teacher' one-to-one or authoritative model established for other disciplines (Chapter 9). Indeed, norms in pre-established formats may lead to getting 'hooked in' to a particular approach in supervision, coaching or mentoring, which constricts innovation. For example, a preoccupation with a 'purist' approach or with an exclusive individual focus, influenced by a construct of 'dysfunction in the oppressive organization' can block line of sight to systems, role, team, or wider stakeholder needs.

Recognize the risks of not having supervision

What would be the fallout from a breach of confidentiality, or from a coach continuing to work when they are temporarily incapacitated and not at their best? Supervision cannot eliminate this risk but can go some way to mitigating it.

Safety and trust in supervision are built on equality in relationship, respect for difference and joint responsibility. Peer supervision, if purposeful and carefully contracted for, can support this process but may fall short.

What steps have you taken to establish that external coaches are genuinely in receipt of regular, qualified supervision and have applied their learning or insights into their ongoing practice?

Evaluate and close the feedback loops

> Supervision is the forum par excellence to learn from practice. It is a reflective practitioner's oasis.
> **Carroll (2014)**

What make supervision so valuable are the new strategies and insight from examining different perspectives. Open and honest reflection on our coaching and mentoring practice before, during and after supervision, however, is incomplete without changes in self-awareness, approach or capacity leading to more effective coaching and mentoring. It is important to evaluate the impact supervision makes to ensure continued organizational support for the minimal but regular time out needed for it to be effective.

Implementing several different ways to capture information on the outcomes of supervision, including self-assessment, stakeholder feedback and tracking tangible outcomes from channelling organizational themes and trends, will inform the ongoing business case.

How we evaluate and close loops

The OCM 180 feedback benchmarking online questionnaire is a simple tool to produce quantitative and qualitative evidence to assess the impact of supervision on coaches in training and their practice across a range of relevant criteria linked to EMCC ESQA competences.

The OCM 180 benchmarking feedback tool

After candidates have held at least four coach-mentoring sessions with their coachees, The OCM 180 feedback benchmarking instrument produces quantitative and qualitative evidence to evaluate their progress in meeting the standards required for the award. The instrument uses an online questionnaire to collect data from the coachees on their perception of the candidate's process and personal skills and attributes as well as the benefits they and their organizations have gained from working with them.

The responses are consolidated into a single score and given to the candidate with a comparison of the average scores from the hundreds of other responses collected by The OCM. This comprehensive national average, unique to The OCM, provides a simple but effective benchmark for a developmental discussion with the candidate's coach mentor supervisor (CMS).

This qualitative and quantitative evidencing is also used for our professional coach-mentor team.

When we recruit members of our coach-mentor team, we look carefully not just at their qualifications, experience and references but also at the tone, flexibility and potential of their practice. We want to know what areas they have not yet fully developed, where they could extend and deepen their impact – whether it is in dealing with particular personality types or contexts or accessing a wider or more creative range of coach-mentoring stances.

The supervision of our team is vital to our capacity to meet client needs at both the organizational and individual levels. At the individual level, it provides a support in ensuring best practice, particularly when coach-mentors encounter difficult ethical or boundary-related issues in their work. And the ongoing learning that it provides enables practice that is resilient and effective across a range of situations and needs, because no matter how carefully we match client needs and members of our teams we have always to 'expect the unexpected'. At the organizational level, where groups of coaches are engaged across an organization, group supervision deepens the team's understanding of the organizational context and provides a framework within which we can gather organizational learning for our clients without endangering the confidentiality of individual assignments.

In order to assess not only the quality of the service provided to the clients at individual and organizational levels but also to monitor and provide feedback on the coach's development of practice for supervision we use a 180 feedback which enables us to track and report both to individual members of our team and across organizational assignments to our partners in HR and lead coach-mentors.

Diane Newell, MD Coaching Services, The OCM

Sharing our experience in building what works

As one of the first providers in the UK to be awarded an ESQA for a coach-mentoring supervision qualification, and with a continuing role evolving EMCC standards for supervision in coaching and mentoring, we believe in supervision that inspires and influences across diverse sectors. In developing our own innovative approaches to supervision, we drew from the CIPD 2006 review of good practice and responded to the needs of organizations wishing to realize the full potential of their investment in a coaching culture.

Part of this process was to evolve two concepts which we felt resonated with collaborative dialogue and participation in modern organizations.

'**Good enough'** *supervision in coach mentoring takes place regularly, pays equal attention to the needs of the client, the organization and the coach mentor, delivers the three functions of supervision and generates organizational learning.*

'**Fit for purpose'** *is supervision that regularly takes stock of tangible, beneficial outcomes in coaching and mentoring in ever-changing contexts.*

Our starting point was supervision that was 'good enough' to meet the growing demand for quality assurance, ongoing development and support for internal coach pools. Incorporating 'Lean' principles of continuous improvement, the supervision emphasizes bringing coaching and mentoring into alignment with current business strategy and harvesting themes and trends to support strategic planning. OCM supervisor alumni lead the integration of supervision in their client organizations either as internal senior practitioners or as external OD consultants.

'Fit for purpose' encourages flexibility in approach, content and format, enabling situational learning needs to be met (Chapter 9) as well as capturing the diverse insight that can arise from mixing novice and experienced coaches. Learning and the overall purpose of the organization are the drivers of the supervision process, not the display of knowledge or the current interests of the 'expert'.

Supervision which is intentionally more systemic broadens organizational perspectives or lenses in existing supervision models, recognizing how everything is connected, inside and outside. Figure 15.2 below illustrates the connections that are central to the effectiveness of our work in coaching, mentoring and supervision.

Figure 15.2 Supervision built in

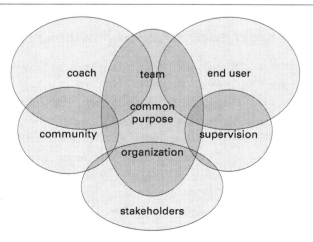

SOURCE: Hill (2013), EMCC Coaching in Education Conference, London

Outcomes of a 'built in' approach to supervision

Integration of supervision into organizational coach-mentoring has had benefits both expected and unexpected for clients. In the Figure 15.3 below we have shared some comments illustrating these from lead coaches who trained as part of our ESQA accredited programme's pilot group.

Figure 15.3 Comments from lead coaches – OCM Journal, 2012

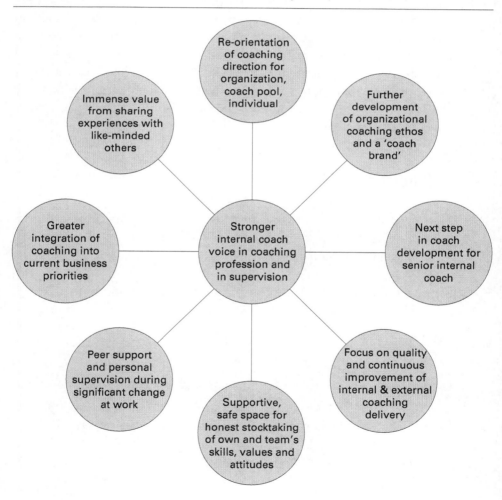

Summary

In this chapter we have considered in practical terms the role and purpose of supervision in organizational coaching and mentoring, the fundamental basics, two approaches that have resonated well with large organizations, and begun to consider ways to capture supervision impact and value.

The OCM approach to supervision has evolved as more coaches and mentors integrate supervision into their organizational culture, beginning with a framework that was 'good enough' supervision and now as a 'built in' essential to safeguard the organization's investment in coaching and mentoring; a framework that is 'fit for purpose'.

We have summarized our experiences on the core elements that are fundamental to making supervision a success in the organizational context and shared the experiences of many individuals and coach teams across different sectors. To finish, we have listed sample questions for you to reflect on for supervision in your context. These questions should broaden your thinking, evaluate your needs and prepare you for the active part you will play in your own effective supervision.

Checklist

Example of factors to consider in designing and implementing organizational supervision (extract from OCM Certificate in Organizational Coaching and Mentoring Supervision).

Role of supervision in developing coaching capacity in the organization

Strategy

- Why internal supervision and why now?
- Where does supervision sit within the organizational system, values and business objectives?
- How and when will you know these benefits have been delivered?

Fundamental basics of supervision

Boundaries and process

- What exactly is meant by confidentiality? When, why and how will it be deliberately breached?
- How will you manage any tension arising from multiple roles?

- What does 'safety' in the supervision space mean? How far can doubt, uncertainty, mistakes, performance issues and the emotional impact of coaching or organizational change be shared?
- Is supervision going to be mandatory or voluntary?
- What formats will be available: 1:1, group (different structures), telephone, peer, other?
- Will there be more or less supervision depending on experience and coaching hours?

Working Agreement

- What is included in the supervision contract?
- What supervisory support will be offered in between sessions and how?
- What is the optimum group size? How will you integrate new group members?

Concepts of 'good enough' 'fit for purpose' and 'built in'

Focus

- What supervision models or approaches will you use initially and with supervisees at different development stages?
- What ground rules exist for group formats?
- What methods will you use to evaluate the impact of supervision on the coach's work?

Becoming supervision 'savvy'

Preparation

- What do you want from your supervision session?
- Reflect on and own your shared responsibility to make it happen.
- Carve out time and mental space to tune into who you are and what wants to be heard.

During

- Sense-check regularly and notice any insight or subtle shifts in the moment.
- Offer and seek feedback.
- Remain open to difference in style and experience.

After

- Notice what came up as well as any new or different insights following the session.

- Prioritize, note and take action on what needs attention in your work or in yourself.
- Celebrate and take credit for connecting with your practice, client progress and highlights.

How will you assess supervision in relation to the organization's needs?

Learning

- How will you safely facilitate the transfer of learning to other organizational programmes, eg leadership and talent, performance management?
- How will you celebrate and share success?
- Have you a balance of approaches taking into account different stakeholders?
- What procedures exist to handle concerns about mental health issues, business risk and referral for therapy?

Endnotes

Arney, E and Schwenk, G (2006) Best practice survey of coaching supervision, Bath Consultancy, Bath

Bolton, G (2014) *Reflective Practice: Writing and professional development*, 4th Edn, Sage, London

Carroll, M (2014) *Effective Supervision: For the helping professions*, Sage, London

De Haan, E (2012) *Supervision in Action: A relational approach to coaching and consulting supervision*, Open University Press/McGraw Hill

EMCC/AC (2016) Global code of ethics [online] http://www.emccouncil.org/webimages/EMCC/Global_Code_of_Ethics.pdf

Gibran, K (1996) *The Prophet*, Penguin Classics, London

Hawkins, P and Smith, N (2006) *Coaching, Mentoring and Organizational Consultancy: Supervision and development*, Open University Press, Maidenhead

Henderson, P (2009) *A Different Wisdom: Reflections on supervision practice*, Karnac Books, London

OCM Journals (2011–2016) Long, De Haan and Duckworth, Hill, Gilpin, Keane and Cooper

Proctor, B (2008) *Group Supervision: A guide to creative practice*, 2nd Edn, Sage, London

St John-Brooks, K (2014) *Internal Coaching*, Karnac Books, London

Coaching the team

16

JACKIE ELLIOTT

In organizations the team is often the key to determining performance. We all know teams full of bright, talented individuals that just don't deliver, and we may have been lucky enough to experience teams that really do deliver more than the potential of the separate individuals alone. In this chapter, I will explore what it means to coach the team, the role of the external team coach, and that of the leader in coaching their team.

Introduction to team coaching

While the bookshelves are full of books dedicated to teams, team building and team development, the term 'team coaching' only started to appear in articles and in coaching practices around 2002. These early publications and studies focused mainly on building great teams and the dynamics of team structure. One of the first texts to focus solely on team coaching was *Coaching the Team at Work* (2007) by David Clutterbuck. Here Clutterbuck looked at bridging the gap between academic theory and the practical learning of managers and coaches in working with teams.

While Clutterbuck's work provided the foundations for team coaching, it would be true to say that most of us practising coaching at this time were not delivering team coaching as he described, but much more as:

- one-off enhanced team facilitation events such as using coaching-style conversations to transform the approach of a team strategy meeting (often off site);
- consultancy and assistance in the structure and running of regular team meetings;
- individual coaching or 'interviews' with team members providing high-level organizational themes back to the team leader.

Through all of these approaches, little was done to embed the learning over time and create self-directed learning of the team to transform performance.

These embryonic concepts of team coaching were galvanized by Peter Hawkins in his book *Leadership Team Coaching*, published in 2011, where he argued that '... teams need to be high-performing learning systems that can transform the wider system they serve'. It has been from here that the transformational impact of team coaching has started to become regarded as an effective tool in team development and releasing team performance. However, it would be true to say that at the time of writing this chapter, team coaching is still very much in early adoption across organizations, with few regularly using this approach with their teams. Much like the early days of coaching and mentoring, it is most often 'called upon' when a team is deemed to be broken or not performing.

Being part of a great team can be a magical experience where the sum of the many deliver and overachieve on a regular basis. The goal of team coaching is not just to 'fix problems' but to release the potential, building on the inherent strengths of the team and creating a self-reliant and resilient unit that delivers the desired results again and again.

Why team coaching now?

Today, successful leadership teams have to manage the expectations of all stakeholders, run and transform their business, at the same time as increasing capacity and working through systemic conflict driven by complex and interconnected global drivers. The major leadership challenges lie not in the parts but in the interconnections, interfaces and relationships. Leaders have to be 'team leaders' first in order to manage cross-functional, diverse teams effectively, and this requires a dramatically different approach to the traditional hierarchy of executive management.

In their 2015 book *Digital to the Core*, Raskino and Waller state that 'winning digital business will be a team sport'. With the digital revolution impacting every business function in every business, leaders are turning their attention to how to 'fast-track' the performance of their teams. The speed of performance of the team, across all sectors, has become critically important; leaders need the 'magic' to happen sooner and are looking for ways to achieve this.

Highly agile teams of experts brought together to achieve a specific goal are the new currency in organizations. Faced with increasing levels of uncertainty and ambiguity these team members need to be able to draw on each other quickly and confidently, clear and committed to a common goal. For many organizations dealing with rapidly changing ambiguous environments, getting the maximum potential out of these fluid teams is a key differentiator and competitive advantage.

Teams transcend every area of endeavour from sport to politics, from science to the arts, but little is done past more traditional team development activities to focus on the team itself as a unit of production that requires investment and attention to function effectively.

What do we mean by coaching a team?

As outlined in the introduction, over the years we have been working with teams the emphasis has moved away from the one-off team development or team-building intervention to a systemic approach encompassing the full remit of the team, their stakeholders and the environment in which they function.

Early, one-off interventions often proved hugely successful in addressing one or two key elements of a team's development and were generally focused on addressing the perceived dysfunctions of a team. The frustrations of this targeted one-off approach were experienced as a lack of 'learning how to learn as a team'. This meant that as the situation, or the team, changed, the team was not able to adapt its behaviour, and so benefits were often not sustained much past the high-energy, feel-good intentions of the intervention.

As the speed of change and the complexity of technology and the workplace have increased, it has become clear that a more holistic approach is required. Today we believe in a multidisciplined approach, tailored to the specific and unique needs of each team. For coaching to be considered team coaching, as opposed to group coaching or coaching in a 'one to many' situation, the team must have a purpose or learning goal that is common to and shared by all members of the team.

A definition of team coaching could therefore be said to be coaching a team to achieve a common goal through reflection and learning. Indeed, the identification, clarification and agreement of what the goal is, how it is measured and how the team and its stakeholders will know when it has been achieved, are often one of the first roles of a team coach.

By coaching a team to work together effectively and collaboratively, the team coach provides the space to cultivate high performance and release the strengths from within. A typical team coaching agreement could contain elements of any or all of the following as depicted in our Team Coach-Mentor Model:

Figure 16.1 Team coach-mentor model

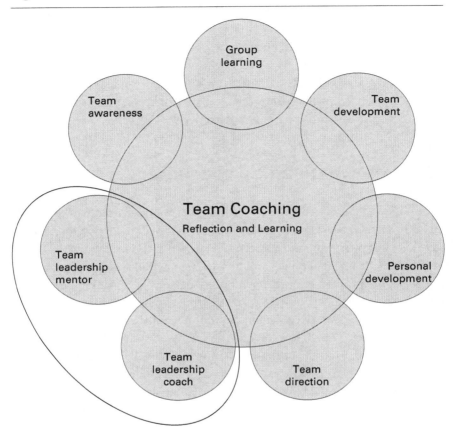

Team Direction – provide clarity, focus and commitment to the goals and objectives of the team.

Team Awareness – increase understanding of the team dynamics and individual team members, how they perform and behave together within the wider system/organization.

Group Learning – develop problem-solving, interpersonal and communication skills facilitated to include feedback and interaction with all team members.

Team Development – learn how to make decisions and take actions that will lead to better efficiency, productivity and quality of work life.

Personal Development – expand self-awareness, knowledge and improve individual personal skills.*

Team Leadership Coach-Mentoring – provide perspective, insight, expertise and experience to challenge and support the team leader.

*May include individual coaching.

The performance of a team is not just related to the interrelations of the team members or to the extent to which they share a common goal but to how well the team understands, manages and delivers both internally to each other and externally to its stakeholders. Team coaching has to pay attention to and enhance the team's performance in all areas that the team touches.

In the Newell Grix model you can see the elements both internal and external to the team that emphasize the complexity of this undertaking.

Figure 16.2 Newell Grix Model

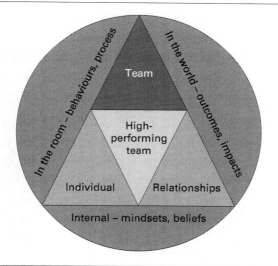

Team	• Develop collective capacity and learning • Increase productivity of the group
Individual	• Hold self accountable for personal growth (has required skills, knowledge and experience) • Ownership of personal performance (delivers on commitments)
Relationships	• Raise interpersonal effectiveness • Hold each other accountable (through increased awareness and understanding)
In the room	• Deliver process improvement • Enhance collective behaviour
In the world	• Engage stakeholders (colleagues, clients, suppliers, official bodies, etc) • Transform the business (through role-modelling and raising the bar)
Internal	• Create awareness and maintain collective values and behaviours • Enhance self-reflection and learning

The team coach must hold, on behalf of the team, the systemic view of the team and its position within the wider organization in which it works. Just as in individual work, the role of the coach is not to create a dependence on their skills but rather to build the team's capacity to 'self-coach'. Over time, the role of holding a systemic view is transferred to the team leader and the team as part of the team learning so that the team is self-learning, self-reliant and self-sustaining.

Learning teams: the link between high-performing teams and teams that can reflect on their own process

How do you recognise a resiliently high-performing team?

When the learning of the team goes beyond the learning of the individual and the team, out into the organization – when how the team performs and behaves influences those teams around them – this is when you know your team is high performing. It is the responsibility of each team member to hold themselves and their fellow team members accountable for this learning over time.

In his HBR article, 'When teams can't decide', Bob Frisch lays out that the real problem behind teams failing to make decisions is not a failure of the leader or communication but rather of the process. For years, people have looked to blame the team leader for many of the failures of a team but inherent in the act of arriving at a collective decision, on the basis of individual preferences, is the process. If the process by which the team will work to achieve any given task is not considered or that process is then not adhered to, the team will continue to procrastinate, delay and waste valuable time and resources.

For too long, leaders have ignored the team as a unit of productivity that requires attention in its own right, expecting teams to just form and function. The assumption appears to be that given enough time the team will simply evolve through the life cycle of team formation into a high-performing unit! We have all worked in enough low-performing teams to know this isn't automatically the case. To overcome this, teams must first learn how to learn together, and then how to apply this learning to their everyday decisions and transactions.

Teams learn best through an iterative process of trial and error, as shown in the Learning Cycle diagram in Figure 16.3.

Figure 16.3 The Learning Cycle

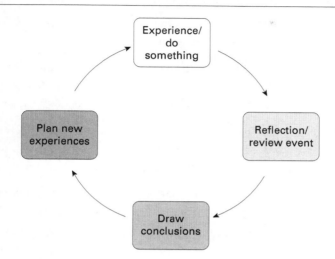

It is supporting this iterative and reflective process, and developing the team's capacity to undertake it for itself, which is the team coach's key purpose. Following an iterative approach to the work a team undertakes can help uncover hidden assumptions and unconscious preferences, speeding up the delivery of their goals but also leading to greater self- and collective awareness, meaning group learning is enhanced and expedited.

To support this level of learning, the team coach has to be open and transparent about the frameworks, process and techniques they are accessing as they work, enabling the individual team members to reflect and learn in their preferred learning style.

Role of the leader in coaching the team

In today's rapid workplace, many team leaders find themselves having to balance the role of team leader alongside a full-time operational role, putting pressure on the leader to create a fully functioning and effective team quickly and efficiently.

Regardless of any other responsibilities a team leader might have, be they as CEO/MD or first-level line manager, as leader of a team they are accountable for:

- the performance of the team;
- defining the direction and success of the team;
- interpreting these in all aspects of the team's influence and performance whether they are internal to the team or external.

It is incumbent on the team leader to have the right links, influence, connections at all levels – individual, team, organization and market/societal – and drawing on these a team leader must demonstrate leadership through:

- providing guidance and instruction to the team based on strategic management direction;
- monitoring the quantitative and qualitative result that is to be achieved;
- motivating the team to actively participate using their knowledge and skills to achieve the shared goals;
- leading by setting a good example, coaching and developing team members;
- maintaining healthy group dynamics by facilitating problem solving and collaboration;
- assuring the personal development of the team members through blended learning skills, training and knowledge acquisition;
- creating a learning environment that encourages creativity and risk-taking;
- recognizing and celebrating team and individual accomplishments and achievements.

Given the changing dynamics of the workplace, no one team remains the same for any significant period of time. For resilient high performance in the team its leader must create a team that can work without them and is able to respond successfully to shifts of goals and resources at short notice.

In a high-functioning, self-supporting team, no one person holds the sole responsibility for team leadership, with team members each taking responsibility for performance improvement at the team level and for achieving the end result. So the team leader must be able to relinquish control of certain aspects of authority and power where and when it is more appropriate for another team member to lead but be ready, willing and able to step back in as required.

Team leaders will need to access many of the skills and approaches of the coach-mentor as they:

- identify the strengths of the individuals and the team;
- expand the team's sphere of influence;
- maintain an atmosphere of learning through supportive challenge;
- implement an effective feedback mechanism.

Accessing this 'coaching' style does not mean that a team leader abandons their authority, responsibility for performance or capacity to be directive. Just as we expect skilful coach-mentors to move gracefully across the directive to non-directive spectrum in response to the needs of the client, so too must the team leader be prepared to be both authentic and adaptive. As Jones and Goffee say in their book *Why should Anyone Be Led by You?*, leadership is all about being yourself, with skill.

It is in this area that we see the most growth in demand for team coach-mentors. Leaders are increasingly aware of the benefits of coaching as a leader; it's a natural development from having coaching conversations as part of a leadership role into using coaching as a way to lead a team to enhance performance. As a result, more and more managers are looking to team coach-mentors to guide and direct them to be able to effectively use an authentic and skilful management coaching style.

Role and relationships of the team coach-mentor

As discussed earlier on in this chapter, the role of the team coach is to build self-sustaining capacity for learning in a team, and to catalyse their performance in line with goals.

With the enormous pressure on leaders to deliver more with less, faster and more collaboratively than ever before, leaders are increasingly drawing on the expertise of the team coach, expecting guidance and direction in managing a team and demanding that more of the coach's personal experience in working with teams is brought to bear in delivering against the coaching contract. In short, coaches are expected to be mentors to the team leader in all matters pertaining to leading and developing a team. It is for this reason that we believe the best, most comprehensive, definition to accurately describe this relationship is team coach-mentor.

A team coach-mentor will:

- Mentor and guide the team leader, acting as an adviser, counsellor and trainer at various stages in team's development, transferring their knowledge and skills in how to nurture a team's development to provoke long-term transformational change.

- Coach and support the team members in a wide range of situations, where the individual may be outside of their comfort zone and in an actual or potentially distressing position.

- Provide a mirror and challenge to the team, raising awareness and ambition.

- Be a consultant and educator as needed – bringing expertise and understanding of what makes a resiliently high-performing team.

In a typical coaching engagement, a team coach-mentor will work with a team over time (typically six months) within the changing context of the wider environment/organization to improve performance. A good team coach-mentor will provide and hold the space for reflection and learning, developing these skills within the team itself: in short, building the confidence within the team to function at the highest level.

In our experience there are four key relationships in effective team coach-mentoring, each of which must be in place for team coaching to be at its best. It is the role of the team coach-mentor to openly establish these relationships, making clear to everyone involved in the team coaching engagement the expectations of each role.

For each of these four relationships the teach coach-mentor will undertake the following:

1 **Team leader.** Work closely with the team leader to initially commission coaching then mentor the leader through perspective and insight to challenge and support personal and team growth.

2 **Trusted teammate.** Nurture and guide the team's early adopters (those people who are evangelists of team coaching within the team), encouraging their advocacy, active involvement and two-way feedback; build a sustainable capability.

3 **Team members.** Build rapport and trust with individual team members through one-on-one interviews and team meeting activities/events.

4 **Team (as a whole).** Provide the space to cultivate high performance through reflection and specifically selected learning tools/techniques to meet the situational needs of the team to achieve their goal.

It is the relationship between the team coach-mentor and the trusted teammate that we believe is a key differentiator for the success of a team coaching contract. The trusted teammate is a valuable insider who is able to hear conversations outside the 'coach to leader' and 'coach to team member' relationships, providing access to the evolving and multiple perspectives within the team.

The trusted teammate should be someone who embraces the team coaching outcome and goals, and believes that for the team to achieve their goal they will need to behave, think and act differently. They will be a catalyst and role model for change and most importantly a trusted individual throughout the team, someone able to build open and transparent relationships with a desire to ask the challenging questions and provide support to other team members.

Establishing a psychologically safe place is critical to the success of any coach-mentoring relationship, and a key part of the coach-mentor's role and practice. Amy Edmondson, Novartis Professor of Leadership and Management, Harvard Business School, has the following description of psychological safety: 'Psychological safety is a belief that one will not be punished or humiliated for speaking up with ideas, questions, concerns or mistakes.' In the context of team coaching, this 'safe space' will extend to all touch points between the team coach-mentor and the team, whether they are face-to-face, over the telephone, using messaging apps or e-mail.

Promoting that safe space within the team and between team members is also vital. In the recent research by Charles Duhigg (2016), a study of 180 teams from all over Google could find no significant patterns in the data on the success of a team and 'who' the team was made up of regardless of personality types, skills or background. Instead they noticed two behaviours that stood out: first, good teams had members who spoke out roughly in the same proportion and second, they had high 'average social sensitivity' – a fancy way of saying they were skilled at intuiting how others felt based on their tone of voice, their expressions and other non-verbal cues.

Providing psychological safety is a difficult and often perilous thing to achieve. It is here that all the skills and knowledge of an experienced coach-mentor must be brought to bear.

Areas of special attention for the team coach-mentor are:

- Ensuring equality in shared thinking and speaking time across the team members, including the team leader.

- Establishing an agreed way to work across the team to free people up from the pressures and distractions of operational urgency (exceptions of business-critical nature will always happen but it is important that the coach-mentor challenges the norm as to what constitutes 'critical').

- Encouraging appreciation and acknowledgment of successes and innovation.
- Managing conflict, allowing slow emotional release to maintain a safe environment.

Team coach-mentoring contract

If psychological safety is to be established, it is important that from the very first touch points the relationship, expectations and processes of a team coach-mentor engagement are open, transparent and known to all involved. The simplest way in which to enable this is via the team coach-mentoring contract.

A team coach-mentoring contract has to capture the accountability for change in performance and/or behaviour of the team, with the focus being on the team as a unit of production. When working with teams we often ask team members the following types of questions to help establish and share both where the team is now and what needs to change and improve:

- What are the conversations the team should be having and with whom?
  - What does the team avoid talking about?
  - What phrases and language does the team use the most?
- How will you know when the team has achieved its goal?
- How do you explain your team and team goal to your employees/ stakeholders?
- What distracts the team from its objective?
- In what ways does the team undermine its own performance?
- What do you value most from being part of this team and why?
- What does the team not see in you where you can bring value to the team?

One of the most effective ways to ask these questions is in one-to-one interviews with each team member as part of the commissioning and contracting process. The team coach-mentor can start to build rapport with the individual team members while assembling a comprehensive picture of the current reality for the team. It is here that the team coach-mentor first identifies the gaps in what 'the team' perceives against the desired state, paying attention to the three levels of insight:

- self (team member);
- inter-team relations;
- team in the world.

Team coaching objective

All coaching and mentoring, to be successful, must be rooted in the imperatives of the business and integrated into the people strategy of an organization; this is equally true for team coaching. It is not enough to describe the goal of team coach-mentoring as being 'to develop a high-performing team'. The team coach must support the team to define what high performance means for them and how that performance will support the organization's needs. Successful team coaching will work on how the team can be highly productive, using its resources effectively to meet those goals.

There are three coaching focus areas to achieve a highly productive team:

Engagement

- All the team focused on the common meaningful purpose (informs decisions and drives actions).
- Dedicated to the success of all team members (all success and failures a shared responsibility).

Commitment

- Build shared commitment against common goals and performance targets.
- Autonomy to deliver against agreed targets and goals.

Potential

- Testing assumptions, striving for better (new thinking for greater performance).
- Collective contribution to development and growth (support personal growth and stretch beyond comfortable boundaries).

Summary

To be successful, a team coach-mentor must work with a team over time to identify, develop and release the inherent capability in the team. They must enable the team to identify common purpose and deliver against clear and compelling goals. Goals will shift more or less rapidly over time, but stability of purpose is a key factor in the success of the team's development, not least in the team's ability to create a self-sufficient unit that is strong enough to withstand the loss and changeover of team members. If the purpose is in a state of flux or not sufficiently robust, the ability of the team to weather the storms of change is hugely reduced.

The coach-mentor must pay attention to both the relationships and the individuals of the team. They need to create and maintain safe space, and key to that is managing their own relationships with the team and the health of the coach-mentoring contract with it. They will often need to be agents of change – raising awareness of team members to the possibilities of the team and its current position in order to create motivation, nurturing those most engaged to become trusted teammates and catalysts for change and providing support for the team leader to grow their capacity to lead change.

The team coach-mentor must be a highly skilled coach-mentor, able to make the complex understandable; to do the simple things well, building capability and creating the time and space for the magic to happen and the team to learn how to deliver great results consistently.

CASE STUDY   T-Systems case study and learning

The early stages of any piece of coach-mentoring are vital to its success. And where team coach-mentoring is new to an organization the early stages of the first engagements are critical. This brief outline describes my early work acting as a team coach-mentor within T-Systems, working with a delivery team and the first impacts of that work.

Commissioning and contracting involved interviewing every member of the team, asking what they thought a team coach would bring them. They were clear on what was needed, if not entirely clear on how a team coach might work. The overriding response was, 'We are a team who need to work better together to achieve our stretching goals and meet customer expectations.'

It is no mistake that team coaching is described as so much more complex than 1:1 coaching. This complexity in this case extended beyond the dynamics of the interrelations of the individual team members, to the team's position within the wider organization and further again to the external stakeholders, whether customers, suppliers or sponsors.

Having initially built on the team's purpose to develop a meaningful common goal that made sense in the context of the wider organization and could be easily understood to gain employee buy-in, much of our early work together focused on the development of the team's understanding and awareness of each other's roles in achieving that purpose and goal.

As we opened up that discussion it created an awareness of pressure points across the team that had previously been unspoken and this exposure of vulnerability was at first challenging and alarming for many. At this point the maintenance of psychological safety was key but over time and with my support, the team were able to open up to and embrace this new level of consciousness.

This process inevitably meant that focus was taken away from the day-to-day business operations in our work together and this at times proved frustrating to some, while others felt that more in-depth work was needed to build on and embed the learning before moving on. I was consciously working hard to listen to and transparently balance the needs of individual team members while keeping us all true to the objectives of the contract.

The early areas of improvement that the team noted were the establishment and successful implementation of an organization-wide purpose and goal, and greater awareness of team strengths and weaknesses. Ultimately, I believe that the most valuable success of this early team coaching experience in T-Systems was to establish the real benefit of 'learning together as a team' which opened the door to further learning and more opportunities for teams to benefit from team coach-mentoring.

Endnotes

Clutterbuck, D (2007) *Coaching the Team at Work*, Nicholas Brealey, London

Duhigg, C (2016) What Google learned from its quest to build the perfect team, *The New York Times* [online] http://www.nytimes.com/2016/02/28/magazine/what-google-learned-from-its-quest-to-build-the-perfect-team.html

Frisch, B (2008) When teams can't decide, *Harvard Business Review*, November

Goffee, R and Jones, G (2015) *Why Should Anyone Be Led by You? What it takes to be an authentic leader*, Harvard Business Review Press, Boston, MA

Hawkins, P (2011) *Leadership Team Coaching*, Kogan Page, London

Raskino, M and Waller, G (2015) *Digital to the Core: Remastering leadership for your industry, your enterprise and yourself*, Routledge, Abingdon

Coach-mentoring in the system and the impact of culture

17

ANGELA KEANE

We've already seen in this book that coach-mentoring takes many forms. It is also about reflection and deeper understanding of 'the stories that explain ourselves to ourselves' (Sacks, 2002). Understanding how and why we react as we do – and we all react in different ways – can be helpful in making a transition to a new way of doing, seeing or behaving. It is with this in mind that I believe taking systemic and cultural perspectives into account can enrich and greatly assist the coaching and mentoring process. In this chapter, I outline what exactly it means to take a systemic perspective when coaching within an organization.

I make a link too between systemic elements and the corporate culture, showing how taking account of both is important if not essential.

Many organizations are increasingly complex and globalized. Others are working to meet the needs of complex and globalized customers and partners. Either way, there is an increased need to work smarter in and with complex systems. Many multinationals are finding a coaching and mentoring approach supports their workforces to work more effectively in this environment, in pursuit of increased innovation, profitability and growth.

Coach-mentors work 'systemically' with individuals and teams, increasing their ability to manage their impact in the complex interwoven relationships of the organizations and teams in the system. Where there are people from a variety of national, organizational or professional cultures in those teams (which is pretty much always) coach-mentors will also be working to increase their clients' awareness of others' cultural perspectives, and the impact of the cultural lenses through which their clients view the world.

Exciting and great work is being done in this area by coaches who are courageous enough to continuously experiment and broaden their offerings in an effort to inform and enlighten individual coachees' and teams' perspectives in the face of the multilayered differences of their colleagues from around the world. I have seen one multinational technology giant support their local managers in China to adapt their overly deferential engagement with US board members through deeper understanding and appreciation of the board members' mindsets. Additional work could be done in reverse, enabling the US board members to appreciate their local managers' world views so they too can adapt their communication style appropriately.

Working and living in systems

A useful way of thinking about systems is to think of a white fluffy cloud on a spring day. It's an attractive image, but hidden in that cloud are all kinds of movements, interactions and interdependencies. Its very existence hangs in the balance, vulnerable to change caused by air temperature, air movement and human intervention. (Whittington, 2012)

Coaching with a systems mindset has justifiably become more popular, enabling coachees and teams to see the bigger picture and the impacts resulting from the interconnections that make up their worlds of work and life.

In an effort to find fresh ways of explaining and describing this, I often use the analogy of the inside of a Swiss watch, where there are many 'wheels' of varying sizes, all interconnected in some way although many do not directly touch each other. The movement of one wheel provokes the movement of another, and so on. The result is that there are constant motion and reaction, with the movement of one and all parts dependent on the movement of others. Attention needs to be paid to the cyclical nature of the system (as opposed to a linear view) and to take account of the overall system as well as its parts.

We are all influenced by and have impact on the systems around us

The point of this illustration and indeed of the systemic perspective is to help raise awareness and understanding of the complex interconnected environments in which we all live and work. It is all too common for us to be totally absorbed by what's happening within our immediate environment. And let's face it, managing what's immediate and now can take up all our attention and energy.

But there are real merit and benefit in developing the habit and capacity to 'zoom out' of the daily fray, and instead aim for what I call a 'Tim Peake' perspective! I was struck by the recent images of the earth Tim Peake was able to see from on board the International Space Station... he could see 'a plume of smoke rising from Mount Etna, forest fires over Canada, a mountain lake in the Himalayas glinting in the reflected light of the setting sun' (Cadwalladr, 2016). He could see the full length and breadth of our rivers, he could see where green fertile land ended and desert started. He could literally see the patterns and how they connect, which could never be seen from up close down here on Earth. As we await the scientific analysis and significance of these new observations, suffice to say that this outer-space perspective allows us to see things differently. From this vantage point, we are able to notice different characteristics and effects which in turn can inform us and help us understand in a new way.

Coming back to the business world, a typical example might be of a global executive, managing a team of individuals spread across several countries. Whether the organization is of a matrix structure or more hierarchical, the principle still applies to a greater or lesser extent. Any decisions and/or behaviours generated by this executive and his/her team will not only affect them directly, but will in turn impact other teams and the individuals with whom they engage. There will be a ripple effect up and down, across and beyond the organization.

Coach-mentoring can ensure executives pause in order to realize this. It can be very helpful to coachees to not only spend time contemplating the knock-on effect of their actions on the immediate and visible but also to reflect on the likely impact on more distant people, structures and processes.

A recent example of the consequences of not taking sufficient account of the systemic view occurred in Her Majesty's Revenue and Customs (HMRC). In a staff-reduction and cost-cutting exercise, it appears that assumptions were made that went unquestioned about the volume of people who would use a new online service rather than the telephone in communicating with

HMRC. This resulted in the system overloading and crashing, with much frustration experienced by the public. There were insufficient staff to answer telephone queries, not to mention conduct audits and deal with more complex and ongoing cases requiring the expertise of those who lost their jobs. The National Audit Office reported that for every £1 reduction in HMRC's annual telephone transaction costs there has been approximately a £4 increase in the time and money spent by customers – the taxpayer (Sayal, 2016).

The individual as a cultural system

We are all influenced by and have an impact on the systems around us, including the systems of unconscious assumptions, beliefs and biases that make up culture.

Having considered systems of 'tangible' interlocking cause and effect relationships, let us now consider the cultural systems that we live in and the more intangible elements and effects of those systems.

One element of a cultural system is 'identity'. None of us have just one 'identity' – we are and have a system of identities that define us relative to others. Coach-mentoring is a route to self-knowledge – a space in which we can develop and deepen our sense of self. It is a safe, non-judgemental place in which we can begin to know ourselves in an uncritical way. Depending on what resonates most strongly for an individual, the quest for greater appreciation and understanding can start anywhere – their nationality, their gender, their profession. Supportive and empathetic coaching allows us to start to see who we are – get a sense of our own identity – and as that takes shape for us, we also begin to get a better sense of others' identities. To take a systems perspective, we are all relative to each other.

When working with and around the topic of culture, I ask coachees to consider their own identities. Culture is a group phenomenon; it cannot exist without a group to exist within, and by considering all the various groups and subgroups to which they have belonged or engaged with throughout their lives, coachees begin to build up a much richer picture of who they are and how they define themselves – their own cultural identity or system if you will. The family we were born into, our gender, the year and even the month in which were born, the schools we attended, the groups in the playground in which we played, the faith group we may have belonged to, the sports we played, the musical instrument we played, the subjects we chose to study in secondary school… and so on – each and every one of these has contributed to our cultural make-up.

I am much drawn to the work of Salman Rushdie, not just for its literary power but also for the perspective he offers on how we react to the challenges of cultural 'mixing' and identity. Whether by flight from war or poverty, or just because it is now easier thanks to technology, in the last 100 years or so, unprecedented migration has meant that we are more likely to come face to face with people who have different cultural systems and identities to us. Even within the same country, people have left the country-side and villages to migrate to cities in numbers never before seen in this world. Think of China in the past 20 years, where literally hundreds of millions of peasants have moved to the cities. This 'mixing' brings us up against both differences and commonalities of identity.

Our identity is deeply rooted in place – where we come from, where we are known by others, where we know the language and communicate with others around us. When we leave that place – migrate to somewhere different – we step into a place where we are unknown, where we do not know anyone, we experience different belief systems, different language, different behaviours of daily life. We, and often those we come into contact with, are keenly aware of 'difference' and seek to construct a narrative based on the perspectives and identity of 'place'.

But we are complicated beings and often contradictory. Our identities cannot be described by place alone. Being able to consciously recognize how we define and describe ourselves is a way of understanding that complex identity. We might identify ourselves by our physical appearance as tall, short, fat, slim, bald, bearded and so on, and by describing our profession as musician, accountant, engineer, hairdresser. These complex, multifaceted identities can create apparent 'inconsistencies' in behaviour depending on which identity facet is 'on' at any time. Consider how we behave when we are with our parents, or with a group of old school/university friends, or how we are with our boss... these are all different ways of being you/me! And in truth, we are almost infinitely variable. This infinite variation should mean therefore that we are capable of finding commonality with others, no matter where we are all from.

Cultural gulfs are created when we narrow our identities – to female or Christian or French, for example. This one-dimensional approach highlights our differences in a stark and even frightening way, which can break down connections and empathy, increasing the possibility of fear and defensive-ness and possibly resulting in conflict. This is shown in stark relief in racial intolerance, but its echo can also be seen in organizations, for example in conflict between engineering and marketing departments, or regional and global elements of a matrix.

And we can experience those conflicts of identity within ourselves too, where our membership of one group leads us to resist cultural behaviours that are expected as part of our membership of another group. Two aspects of our identity 'clash' and the one that we choose to adhere to will be strengthened, whereas we may experience a sense of alienation from the other. Coaching to increase understanding of the contradictory elements of our own cultural system, and the impact our behaviour will have for others in the system, is an important part of growing a coachee's capacity to 'choose' their responses.

For example, your coachee might work in a fast-paced, high-paid but stressful role. Amongst his/her colleagues, there might be a strong cultural habit of going out together once a week in order to alleviate the pressure. This ritual is part of what defines membership of the group. If your coachee also defines themselves as 'fit and health conscious' they may be keen to focus on their health and fitness and might elect to avoid the weekly drinking habit. As a result, they might encounter a sense of not-belonging and alienation. The degree to which your coachee engages with the cultural mores of this group might well impact the degree to which he/she feels they belong and connect with the group, whether communications are all that they could be with the line manager and so on.

Less visible but no less important are unconscious biases, assumptions and beliefs which our cultural path gives us. They are the 'truths' about the world, about how it works and what is 'right' that we hold so deeply that we are no longer aware of them until they are confronted or challenged. Coaching can be hugely instrumental in surfacing these and enabling the coachee to see the role they play in their lives and behaviours. Awareness leads to choice. The coachee is then in a position to make informed choices about possible adjustments for future actions and behaviours.

Cultural identities can serve to unite or reinforce the differences between individuals. This can empower us or disable us. Coaching helps us disentangle and clarify our thoughts around the web of differences in which we operate. It can help us to see 'difference is the source of value' (Sacks, 2002) rather than a dividing force.

The organization as a cultural system

If an organization can be seen as a system, and departments, teams, employees, shareholders, management all as subsystems, then it follows that the system can have a cultural make-up and unique identity. In working with teams to help them become more efficient and productive, or imagine trying to bring about a shift in the culture of an organization, it could be useful to take account of the cultural and systemic perspectives.

Taking an even wider view, coaching with a systemic perspective can be used to change or adjust an organization's culture. This might start with the organization's current culture – its values, beliefs, behaviours and assumptions. Understanding how these all work together, feeding into and off each other, could lead to clarity around what needs to change in order to create the new preferred ideal culture. An example might be the shift to a more coaching style of management, away from a 'command and control' approach. Working out what values, beliefs and behaviours are associated with the latter will then enable employees to not only define what the new set of values and behaviours should look like, but also reinforce the understanding and commitment to help make them happen.

Just as we humans each have our own cultural IDs, the combination of a group of humans goes towards forming the cultural profile of an organization. We frequently hear mention of the 'corporate culture' prevailing in a company, and how significant this is in relation to how a company is perceived by the outside world as well as internally. Consider the cultural ID of the executive suite, the shareholders, the various departments, from communications/PR, to HR, to finance, sales, engineering, etc. Anyone working across these 'divides' will likely be aware (and certainly should be) of significant differences in style and approach to work and relationships. Being able to appreciate the drivers and motivations operating within the sales team would enable the finance team to adapt and flex for the sake of more harmonious and effective meetings.

One of the most interesting aspects to consider here is that of unconscious bias, and the way that it exists in individuals and organizations. 'Our unconscious biases define the boundaries we are unwilling to expand' (Life at Google, 2014). The unrecognized and unchallenged existence of unconscious bias in an organization can result in blind spots around behaviour and decreased diversity in hiring, leading to a loss of potential talent, reduced creativity and robustness in the face of global challenges.

It stands to reason that recruitment policies contribute enormously to reinforcing or dismantling certain cultural mores in an organization. There is increasing realization around the role unconscious bias plays in the choices and selections we make, with some companies beginning to experiment with new approaches to lessen the effects of the bias. We've become accustomed to omitting details such as age from our CVs. This principle is extended further by removing names and any details that might identify the gender and ethnicity in an effort to choose the best-qualified applicant. There are already success stories to prove the benefit of this approach. For example, since 'blind' auditions were introduced, there has been a sharp and significant increase in the number of women in orchestras, as any information or indicators relating to their gender are removed, and when they are invited to demonstrate their musical abilities, they do so hidden from view.

On-boarding and transition coaching

A significant niche has emerged in the coaching world around 'on-boarding' and 'transition', ie supporting executives to quickly adapt to new roles so that they are effective as quickly as possible.

The systemic and cultural lenses have an important role to play in this work. The coach can help the coachee to anticipate, see and feel the differences at play in their new organization and role by asking questions such as:

'What differences do you see existing between your previous and new situations?'

'In what way does it feel different in the new situation?'

Introducing and embedding a coaching culture

As developed in Chapters 11–13, the role of coaching and mentoring is increasingly understood in a wider context, that of supporting the organization to achieve its overall objectives. This is positive news for people and business alike as it implies a change in managerial style – less autocratic and directive – with more ownership and responsibility being taken by employees and less dependency on managers to have all the answers. It suggests a more dynamic, energized and engaged workforce constantly striving for progress and improvement in themselves and in how they do their work. This results in an organization that continues to evolve and adapt in an ever-changing world, and should help ensure financial strength and survival.

It takes time to assess and devise appropriate interventions to start the shift towards a more coaching culture, but it is not as difficult as it may seem. The OCM, more recently with their ELECTRIC™ model (see Appendix), has already worked with several organizations to introduce a shift in managerial style, focusing on the critical coaching skills of listening, questioning and feedback. There is sufficient positive and immediate feedback to be heartened by the results and to encourage more organizations to take the leap.

What impact can coaching and mentoring have on the capacity of individuals and teams to consciously work with and on the systems and cultures that impact on them?

All this complexity can be paralysing for us. It can be tempting to just focus on what we can immediately see and touch, whilst ignoring the bigger, more distant aspects of a situation.

Coaching and mentoring can play a precious and powerful role here. They can provide the time and space in which to begin to map in a meaningful way what that bigger picture looks like for a coachee and/or a team. They can begin to populate their own personal system and culture map, and in so doing, begin to understand at a much deeper level how varied and rich their lives are. They can also feel simultaneously how powerful and powerless they can be as part of this map of interconnectedness and difference.

Conclusion

Coaching is a way of getting to know ourselves at a deeper level, helping us appreciate the complexity and often contradictory nature of our make-up, striving for a balance between appreciating the richness and benefits of our differences whilst ensuring we are not separated or diminished by them. By adopting systemic and cultural perspectives in our coaching approach, we can enable coachees to start to make sense of their complexity and that of others, and understand the impact they have on others. In so doing, they can begin to develop ways in which to harmonize relationships through finding common ground whilst also being enriched by the differences. Through this, better and more effective communication can be harnessed at individual and team levels, leading to more collaborative, productive and expansive working relationships. It is suggested that by opening and broadening our world view, rather than simplifying and narrowing it, we can embody diversity in ourselves and others for ultimate unbounded possibility.

Through this deeper understanding and acceptance, coach-mentoring can help us be strengthened and more confident as individuals, which in turn enables us to strengthen our teams and organizations.

Endnotes

Cadwalladr, C (29 May, 2016) Major Tim Peaks answers schoolchildrens' questions from space, *Guardian* [online] https://www.theguardian.com/science/2016/may/29/tim-peake-ground-control-revive-science-interest-schools-space

Sacks, J (2002) *The Dignity of Difference*, Continuum, London

Sayal, R (25 May, 2016) Customer service 'collapsed' at HMRC tax advice line after cuts, *Guardian* [online] http://www.theguardian.com/politics/2016/may/25/hmrc-tax-advice-line-customer-service-collapse-cost-staff-cuts

Whittington, J (2012) *Systemic Coaching and Constellations: An introduction to the principles, practices and application*, Kogan Page, London, p 33

What's next?   18

DIANE NEWELL

The world of organizations is changing fast and the ways in which coaching and mentoring support the learning, performance and potential of individuals and teams will need to respond to meet those changing needs.

In this section I have gathered up some of the major themes of change that I perceive and I have explored what they might imply for our implementations of coach-mentoring in future. I do this with some trepidation, conscious that my readers are sitting in the future I am writing about and possibly chuckling over my misapprehensions! However, the broad and overlapping themes of 'Change' will doubtless remain and I hope that this section will help the reader to challenge their own assumptions as well as affording a retrospective look at mine. In particular I want to focus on:

- Changes in people – how we think, our beliefs and assumptions.
- Changes in technology – in particular the technology of communication.
- Changes in organization – how we organize and shape work in response to the needs and opportunities we face.

The idea that we face unprecedented levels and speed of change today has been mooted and challenged (The Economist, 2016). Whether it is unique or not it is certainly true that people working in organizations in very different locations and sectors currently report a sense of being driven to hyperactivity by the range and volume of inputs they are dealing with. That in turn is driving a lack of opportunity to reflect individually and collectively in organizations and a constant sense of ambiguity and uncertainty in what we need to achieve and how. That environment (currently labelled VUCA for Volatile, Uncertain, Complex and Ambiguous) demands better conversations, better learning, better collaboration and at the same time makes them more difficult to achieve. If you have read this far you will already be clear that coach-mentoring as a philosophy and as an activity can help individuals and organizations to be successful and resilient in that world. In effect, the great conversations that happen in a CAM culture help individuals, teams and the organization as a whole to constantly learn, support each other's learning and share learning; it creates a habit of individual and organizational reflection which keeps the organization resilient.

The ways in which we implement coaching and mentoring need to take account of the changes we face in our world, the opportunities they may give us to do things differently and the risks and derailers they might present. For ease of discussion I've pulled out my three main themes of People, Technology and Organization – even though they clearly intertwine and interrelate.

Changes in people

Who we are is important, and in the first section of Chapter 5 Mel and Eric explored the importance of individual differences in the practice of coach-mentoring. Each of us is a unique and precious mixture of our genes and experiences. We are both responsible for our history and created by it. As CJ never quite said (*The Fall and Rise of Reginald Perrin*), I didn't get where I am today without being me and I wouldn't be me if I hadn't got where I am today. The importance and impact of experiences in shaping us drive a difference between the 'culture' of different nations, professions and generations. In the previous chapter, Angela has looked at both the way in which the systems we experience shape us and how we ourselves are complex systems of interacting and sometimes competing cultures.

As you consider how your organization might best invest in coach-mentoring in future you will need to consider whether the cultural mix and range of the population will change. In particular, consideration must be given to the changes in need driven by the arrival in your organization of new generations – the so-called 'Millennials'.

The Millennials – what you need to consider

- Millennial attitudes and values aren't exclusively a matter of age. There are 'Millennials by nature' in every age group and lots of 20-somethings who share the approaches of their Gen X forebears.

- The 'stereotype' of this generation as lacking social skills, being needy and undisciplined or feeling 'entitled' to great jobs without putting in the spade work tells us more about the misunderstandings and frustrations of their baby boomer leaders than it does about what is actually a remarkably articulate and creative generation.

- What Millennial values represent is a shift in attitude to work (and life) that is likely to grow and pervade society in future and has particular relevance to how people want to be developed and led.
- Five key differences are:

  1 More individually driven – clearer about what they want out of work and life, less likely to be willing to sacrifice their needs. And that seems to remain true with promotion; they are less willing to adopt the work-filled lifestyles of their Gen X leaders.

  2 Digitally savvy – more comfortable than previous generations, using communication over a wide variety of media, but with a real need for personal access to and input from those whose expertise they need and value.

  3 Schedule intolerant – this is the Internet generation. They want information when they want it how they want it. And if they can't access it swiftly they'll move on to find it elsewhere.

  4 Higher value for 'purpose' – both seeking to develop and pursue their own purpose and showing a greater desire to be part of organizations with a purpose that they identify with.

  5 Greater cynicism about 'brand messages' – this generation mistrusts messages from organizations of all kinds and will test what they are told against the reality of their experience and that of others.

(Deloitte, 2016)

Potential implications for coach-mentoring implementations

- A Millennial isn't going to want to wait for the next scheduled training course to get the skill or knowledge they are seeking. What they want is to be able to access and talk with the person that can help them. Those conversations present a valuable opportunity to go from 'information exchange' to true learning (see description in Chapter 4). If you are to meet their need and access the opportunity, your senior professionals, leaders and managers need to be able to have authentic and effective conversations. This may mean developing the skills and confidence to use coach-mentoring approaches in a much wider population as part of your investment in the leaders of today and tomorrow.

- Defining the purpose of any coach-mentoring relationships will need to take account of these shifting needs, whether between manager and direct report, or a specific internal or external coaching or mentoring relationship. Millennials may be less interested in coaching and mentoring as a way to increase their 'success' and more motivated by opportunities to grow and work in ways they find satisfying.

- Millennials will rapidly become disengaged in an organization that promises development if they can't see evidence that their development is invested in. Internal coaches and mentors may be key therefore to meeting this need. What's more, if it meets with their personal purpose and needs, Millennials themselves may be enthusiastic about developing and offering coaching and mentoring to others.

- Your implementation should take into account opportunities for and benefit from reverse mentoring – Millennials are better adapted to the digital world, are more tech- and communications-savvy than their bosses, and may both relish and benefit from an opportunity to reverse mentor.

- We will all need to be ready to challenge our assumptions about the most effective ways to deliver coaching and mentoring – will the Facebook experience drive less need for 'confidentiality' in coaching and mentoring? This generation may have a different sense of where the boundaries should be and be more willing to participate in group coaching openly. And technology will offer wider options about how we coach and mentor.

- In particular we will need more flexible 'client driven' access to coaching and mentoring – this generation both values more 'personal' time with their coach-mentors and expects 'instant access' to information and connection via the web, twitter, WhatsApp, etc. So traditional 90- to 120-minute one-on-one face-to-face meetings with a coach-mentor every month alone may not suffice. They are more likely to see asynchronous communication (e-mail, text, etc) as an integrated part of the coach-mentoring relationship and to want to reach out to coach-mentors as and when they want them rather than to predetermined schedules.

- Build for fun? There's a recognized need to make learning generally more engaging and your coaching and mentoring implementation is no exception. Particularly for more goal-driven, performance coaching interventions, gaming approaches offer a great support to maintaining momentum on goals.

Changes in technology

We are all aware of the extraordinary changes communications technology is creating and of the opportunities it offers to communicate in a variety of ways. Organizations need to think about how they use communications technologies in all areas of work – in coaching and mentoring, which rely on communication and relationship at their heart, this is particularly important.

Our investment in coaching and mentoring needs to consider potential new opportunities to bring coaching and mentoring to the organization more effectively and efficiently. Many clients already access coaching remotely via telephone/video calling and we recognize the need to train coach-mentors as well as their clients to have effective conversations in those media. In future we may need to make similar investments in our abilities to use text, e-mail, messaging apps, social media and simulated realities. But as you think about how you are using coach-mentoring in your organization, I would encourage you to go beyond 'efficiency'. Coach-mentors (internal or external) should be role models in your organizations in how to communicate – and that includes how they make use of the full range of communications technologies to meet particular clients' needs.

Implications for coach-mentoring implementations

- There are clear implications for the training and development of coach-mentors, particularly for older generations who may be less comfortable in some media.

- There may also be an impact on how we contract and manage coach-mentoring relationships, to allow for a true mutuality of responsibility in determining how to communicate between coach and client.

- Taken together with Millennials' need for 'access', the new communications technologies may change how we measure and define any coaching or mentoring contract. It may be more appropriate to contract external coach-mentoring as a relationship with purpose over time rather than a 'number of hours', for example.

- I hope that there may be exciting opportunities for using 'virtual realities' as part of coaching. There seems to be an obvious application in creating 'meeting space' but I hope we might look to go beyond that in our future coach-mentoring implementations to developing tools and approaches that allow clients to model and gain insight into their world and themselves, and to experiment with and develop different options of behaviour.

Changes in organization

The speed of change and the complexity and global nature of organizations and projects create a need for adaptability and agility that is driving a change in how we organize. Many of us already work in a number of fluid, impermanent and often virtual teams where roles and responsibilities have to be regularly renegotiated and clarified. The implications for how individuals manage their time, their priorities and their development or career are complex, making it more important than ever (particularly for those Millennials) that they have strong mentoring relationships. Added to this, the 'boundaries' of our organizations are becoming more porous – we are increasingly seeing teams encompassing members from more than one organization and a greater tendency to be open to collaborations across boundaries rather than trying to replicate resources and expertise that others already have. This increasingly networked nature of our organizations creates a shift in the skills we need. For example influence, or the ability to 'get things done' without direct line authority, is becoming a key skill at every level of seniority and responsibility, where a generation ago it was the preserve of the senior leader. The capacities that are needed for success in the new organizational world are largely interpersonal and behavioural. They are about 'who we are' and how we impact on others and so they are difficult to 'train' effectively; coaching is a much more effective intervention.

Some possible implications for coach-mentoring implementations

- Coaching and mentoring have always been particularly valuable in developing these 'soft' leadership skills and in supporting successful promotions and transitions. In the Sherpa 2016 Executive Coaching Survey, 'people who need leadership development' and 'people in transition' represented 61 per cent and 21 per cent respectively in answer to the question 'Who needs executive coaching most?' There will continue to be a real need for leadership development – and a lot of transitions to manage! By investing in the leadership agility and resilience of individuals through coach-mentoring, we invest in the agility and resilience of our teams and organization. Linking coach-mentoring investment to the leadership capacity of individuals and to preparing for and managing through transitions is likely to be an important part of your strategy.

- There is no point in building coach-mentoring implementations that wait for a 'stable' situation in which to improve a team or an individual's performance. Change, and so the need to develop in response to change, will be with us constantly. This means that coach-mentoring needs to be part of our everyday conversations as well as a specific developmental intervention and that the purpose of any coach-mentoring investment is likely to include developing a capacity to self-coach. This is particularly relevant to your investment in team coaching where part of the team coach-mentor's role must become developing both the team and its leader(s) to challenge their current performance and to support each other to make the changes needed.

- The combination of unclear organizational career pathways and the millennial need for seeing opportunities to develop in line with their own purpose will create a greater need for mentoring around 'career' development. Developing organizational mentors may be a key investment both in retention and in making yours the organization key talent wants to join.

- Teams and organizations will be less homogeneous and much more likely to contain people from different national cultures and backgrounds. This, combined with the fluid nature of teams in the future, may well drive a much greater need for cross-cultural intelligence, especially on the part of team leaders and coach-mentors. This will have implications for your development of leadership and internal coach-mentors, as well as your selection of external coach-mentors.

Coach-mentoring is an investment in future as well as current performance and resilience for your organization. The seeds you plant today will need to bear appropriate fruit in the future as well as meeting today's agendas and so your plans must take into account the particular changes that you face. I have selected a few broad themes but I encourage you to have some great conversations of your own – test and explore with others in your organization as well as outside it to identify the key changes in people, technology and organization that will impact on you. Ask your young recruits and those quitting your organization. Involve yourself in conversations across your organization and with your suppliers, customers and competitors. Ask your R&D department about disruptive technologies and your strategic planners about likely scenarios. Read widely and ask a lot of 'what ifs'. But above all build for adaptability and flexibility – because no matter how much planning we do the future will always (I am glad to say) be a surprise!

Endnotes

Deloitte (2016) Deloitte Millennial Survey 2016 [online] http://www2.deloitte.com/global/en/pages/about-deloitte/articles/millennialsurvey.html

The Economist (2016) The Creed of Speed, *The Economist* [online] http://www.economist.com/news/briefing/21679448-pace-business-really-getting-quicker-creed-speed

Life at Google (2014) Google video on unconscious bias – making the unconscious conscious [online] https://www.youtube.com/watch?v=NW5s_-Nl3JE [accessed 10 October 2016]

Sherpa Coaching (2016) Executive Coaching Survey, public report, Sherpa Coaching LLC, Cincinnati

APPENDIX
The OCM ELECTRIC Coaching™ and ELECTRIC Mentoring™ framework

The ELECTRIC Coaching™ and ELECTRIC Mentoring ™ framework provides a practical guide to help structure impactful conversations in the workplace.

ELECTRIC stands for:

- **Engage** – This is all about putting the person first with the work focus second, you coach the person not the issue. Build rapport and demonstrate equality.

- **Listen** – This is all about actively demonstrating your full attention to the person throughout the conversation. Seek to understand, clarify meaning and do not judge.

- **Explore** – This is all about using insightful questions to encourage exploration of the subject. The questions should be clear and effective, avoid long and complicated questions.

- **Challenge** – This is all about challenging and testing motivations before any firm plans and targets are agreed. High performance comes about when the right balance of support and challenge is provided.

- **Target** – This is all about ensuring that at the end of the conversation the other person (or people if it's a group) leaves with a clear target to work towards. Clarity on actions and timescales is important.

The 'RIC' part of the framework should be used for any conversations that are not 'one-off' interventions; for example, with your direct reports or team.

- **Review** – Consider progress. How did they get on? What's been happening?

- **Insights** – Enquire what the other person is discovering or realizing about themselves, others and/or their context. What insights have they surfaced?

- **Conclude** – Encourage the other person to speak about their 'new present' and consider any new opportunities being explored.

INDEX

Note: page numbers in **bold** indicate figures; numbers in *italic* indicate tables.